CHANGING DESTINIES

United Kingdom Council for Psychotherapy Series

Recent titles in the UKCP Series
(for a full listing, please visit www.karnacbooks.com)

The Role of Brief Therapies in Attachment Disorders
Lisa Wake

Therapy with Children: An Existentialist Perspective
Chris Scalzo

Why Therapists Choose to Become Therapists: A Practice-Based Enquiry
Edited by Sofie Bager-Charleson

The Use of Psychoanalytic Concepts in Therapy with Families: For All Professionals Working with Families
Hilary A. Davies

How Money Talks
Lesley Murdin

What Will You Do With My Story?
Elizabeth Meakins

Psychotherapy and Spiritual Direction: Two Languages, One Voice?
Lynette Harborne

Addictive Personalities and Why People Take Drugs: The Spike and the Moon
Gary Winship

Why Can't I Help This Child to Learn? Understanding Emotional Barriers to Learning
Edited by Helen High

LoveSex: An Integrative Model for Sexual Education
Cabby Laffy

Psychotherapy 2.0: Where Psychotherapy and Technology Meet (Volume One)
Edited by Philippa Weitz

Awakening Through Dreams: The Journey Through the Inner Landscape
Nigel Hamilton

Managing Difficult Endings in Psychotherapy: It's Time
Lesley Murdin

Handbook of Working with Children, Trauma, and Resilience: An Intercultural View
by Aida Alayarian

Love and Therapy: In Relationship
Edited by Divine Charura and Stephen Paul

CHANGING DESTINIES

The Re-Start Infant Family Programme for Early Autistic Behaviours

Stella Acquarone and
Isabel Jimenez Acquarone

KARNAC

First published in 2016 by
Karnac Books Ltd
118 Finchley Road, London NW3 5HT

British Library Cataloguing in Publication Data

A C.I.P. for this book is available from the British Library

ISBN 978 1 78220 223 3

Edited, designed and produced by The Studio Publishing Services Ltd
www.publishingservicesuk.co.uk
e-mail: studio@publishingservicesuk.co.uk

Printed in Great Britain by TJ International Ltd, Padstow, Cornwall

www.karnacbooks.com

CONTENTS

To my husband, Don Hughston, and his mother, Lib
for their love and support.

ACKNOWLEDGEMENTS

My thanks to the families that trust us and work so hard to change their path for a happier and more integrated life with their child with autistic behaviours. I am grateful to my colleagues in the team for their willingness to dare to defy misconceptions and enter into this fascinating work with curiosity and enthusiasm, and to the nurseries and institutions who help us manage our cases, who allow us to enter their environments, give guidance to their staff, and give us feedback. To Caroline Hunt, a big thank you for the editing, proofreading, compilation, and all that you do to turn manuscripts into a book. A heartfelt appreciation to Gary Hixson and the staff at Hixson Design (USA) for the many-layered strategy of the front and back cover design. And my thanks to Don, for the scales and graphics and general support and patience.

Disclaimer

In the pursuit of confidentiality, the case studies presented in this book are a composite of characteristics, behaviours and family set-ups that are common to many children. Any resemblance to a particular child, family or case is purely coincidental.

ABOUT THE AUTHORS AND CONTRIBUTORS

Stella Acquarone, PhD, is an adult and child psychoanalytic psychotherapist and founder of the Parent Infant Clinic and School of Infant Mental Health in 1990 and the International Pre-Autistic Network (an international charity registered in the UK). Based in London, she has worked with parents and infants for thirty-two years in the National Health Service (NHS) and privately, pioneering and laying the foundations of parent–infant psychotherapy. Academic, clinician, teacher, lecturer, conference organiser, researcher, and author, she has presented, led workshops, and trained professionals all over the world and has published many papers and several books, including *Infant Parent Psychotherapy: A Handbook for Professionals* and *Signs of Autism in Infants: Recognition and Early Intervention* (Karnac), and *Upalala, Helping the Helpers,* containing anxieties in the professionals working with under fives and their families. She has been researching and working with infants with autistic tendencies since 1980 and her Re:Start programme offers an intensive early intervention treatment approach administered by a multi-disciplinary therapy team and based on psychoanalytic thinking.

Denise Challis, MA, MB, BChir, MSc, DCH, FRCPCH, is a consultant paediatrician specialising in neurodevelopment and neurodisability. She is the immediate Past President of the Association for Research in Infant and Child Development, a member of the British Paediatric Neurology Association, and the British and European Academies of Childhood Disability. Dr Challis has specialised in paediatrics over the past forty-three years. She currently consults at The Portland Hospital, London, specialising in the assessment and treatment of children from all over the world with neurological conditions, including autism, cerebral palsy, epilepsy, neurodegenerative diseases, and a wide range of congenital disorders. Her special interests include the holistic management of the care of children with complex, chronic disorders from initial assessment, particularly using the Griffiths mental development scales. She lectures regularly in the UK and abroad, particularly in China, partly to facilitate the growing use of assessment in diagnosis and provision of therapy for children with disabilities in the population there.

Geoff Ferguson is an adult psychoanalytic psychotherapist who trained at the London Centre for Psychotherapy and has worked as a psychoanalytic psychotherapist for nearly thirty years. He has been the Chair of the Forum for Independent Psychotherapists and has served as their Chair of Ethics. As well as seeing individuals, he is also involved in training and supervision, including for the Refugee Therapy Centre. He is currently the Director of the Parent Infant Clinic, London.

Dominique Hawksley is an integrative child psychotherapist and social worker who has experience in working therapeutically with children and their families in a range of settings, including voluntary sector organisations, schools, CAMHS, and the Parent Infant Clinic, London.

Isabel Jimenez Acquarone, PhD, scientific psychologist, received her doctorate from Imperial College, London for developing a biological marker for temperament using heart rate variability, trademarked as TQ™ (temperament quotient). She is the founder of ARE, Ltd, a temperament consultancy, research and treatment centre based on three axes of temperament: adaptability, reactivity and equanimity. She is also a UKCP-accredited parent–infant psychotherapist, an international graduate member of the British Psychological Society and professional member of the Institute of Clinical Research.

Valerie Sinason, PhD, MACP, M Inst Psychoanal, FIPD, is an adult psychoanalyst and adult and child psychotherapist specialising in disability, trauma, and abuse. She is currently President of the Institute for Psychotherapy and Disability and Director of the Clinic for Dissociative Studies.

UKCP SERIES PREFACE

Alexandra Chalfont
Chair, UKCP Book Editorial Board

Philippa Weitz
Commissioning Editor, UKCP Book Editorial Board

The UK Council for Psychotherapy (UKCP) holds the national register of psychotherapists qualified to work with children and young people and of psychotherapeutic counsellors, listing those practitioner members who meet exacting standards and training requirements.

As part of its commitment to the protection of the public, UKCP works to improve access to psychological therapies, to support and disseminate research and to improve standards, and also deals with complaints against organisational, as well as individual, members.

Founded in the 1980s, the UKCP produces publications and runs meetings and conferences to inform and consult on issues of concern to practitioners and to support continuing professional development.

Within this context, the UKCP book series was conceived to provide a resource for practitioners, with research, theory, and practice issues of the psychotherapy profession at the heart of its aims. As we develop the series, we aim to publish more books addressing issues of interest to allied professionals and the public, alongside more specialist themes.

We are both extremely proud to be associated with this series, working with the UKCP Book Editorial Board to provide publications that reflect the aims of the UKCP and the interests of its members.

FOREWORD

Valerie Sinason

Whether we are in a crowded shopping centre or on a busy street, the piercing cry of a baby can be deeply unsettling. Whether our wish is to silence the baby, be angry with the adult, support the adult, or hold the baby (choices that can hint at the kind of resources or attachment we experienced when little), we are all affected by the sound. Evolution depends on the tiny helpless baby having tools that will have an impact on adults. The baby who does not smile, who sleeps all the time, who does not make eye contact—these babies change the smaller universe of those closest to them in the same way the cry or scream disrupts the larger universe.

However, early clinical interventions to aid the family (usually the mother) and the baby or small child are open to more external conflict than later ones. Why is this?

Child psychotherapists and adult psychoanalysts use infant observation as a foundation stone of their training. The trainee observes a baby for an hour a week for one to two years and goes to weekly seminars to discuss and reflect on their findings. Those who have not yet begun their own therapy or psychoanalysis find they need to after this experience! Without words, a baby's powerful preverbal communications lodge inside us. The task of the parent or carer is to receive these powerful communications while remaining loving and calm, so that the baby can develop emotionally through a remarkable relational transformation. The baby pours into the receiving part of the carer's mind and heart everything that is unbearable, and the good-enough parent/carer is able to hand back something filtered and helpful: a little like a dry-cleaning service. This gives the baby the wonderful experience of trusting that their painful, messy, and indigestible feelings will be received and returned in a filtered, digestible way.

Obviously, some babies are an easier match for their families than others. For example, a mother who longed for a quiet baby might get a noisy, vibrant child; a father who expected his baby to sleep for hours might get one who is wide awake most of the day. Some babies make the most depressed, disorganised parent look like a Madonna, while others make the most resourceful parent look fragile and volatile.

This delicate balance between baby and parent or attachment figures and the wider social container, which either supports or burdens the new parent/s, is one that is prone to powerful feelings of splitting, blame, and projection. John Bowlby's seminal work on attachment theory, describing how a baby needs a consistent one-to-one attachment figure (whether mother, father, grandparent, or nanny), was immediately misheard and misquoted, and sparked an enormous backlash from those who feared mothers were being blamed for their child's disorder. Societally, a mother's place is in the wrong, and the vulnerability of a baby is something so hard to consider that there are enormous societal pressures to scapegoat either a parent (usually the mother) for not responding the right way—with the right food, the right stimulation—or a professional for pointing out the baby or small child's need.

A newborn baby might be new to the world, but has already had three-quarters of a year sensing and responding, seeing and smelling. We know that if a mother experiences stress and violence during pregnancy, this can have a great impact on the foetus. The more we become aware of the richness and complexity of the foetus's experience, the more concerned we should be about just how much can affect a newborn. This puts the professional in this field in a complex position, too.

In 1943, when the American psychiatrist Leo Kanner came up with the diagnosis of autism, he observed a lack of maternal (and paternal) warmth, and the concept of a "refrigerator mother" soon became a standard attack for parents of children with autism. In 1969, Kanner emphasised that he had always said that autism was an innate condition but had been misquoted as blaming the parents. The child psychotherapist Frances Tustin condemned blaming parents, and dedicated her first book "To the parents who have entrusted their children to my care". She stressed that "psychogenic autism" meant only that no organic damage could be detected by the means available.

In continuing to campaign for support for parents and their babies, Dr Stella Acquarone, a pioneering child psychotherapist and psychologist, steps into a minefield. However, as a professional with a mission, it is one she is well prepared for.

Over the past thirty years, and including the time when the word "autism" was not so readily used, Stella Acquarone has been working tirelessly to show us that conditions that have already become rigidified in early childhood can be changed by offering psychoanalytic therapy to infants and their families.

In 2004, she published her long-awaited *Infant–Parent Psychotherapy: A Handbook* (Karnac). In it, Acquarone details her understanding of the parent–child dynamic, based on her observations of over 3,000 children. Indeed, in the 1990s, a significant group of us considered that she had personal profound experience of more babies with problems than any other UK psychotherapist or clinician. In 2006, she set up the International Pre-Autistic Network (ipAn), a charity dedicated to helping parents who have early concerns about the development of their child.

With the excellent clinical and research work currently being done in the Tavistock Clinic Under-5 Workshop and the Anna Freud Centre, it is hard now to recall that Acquarone's work preceded these. Furthermore, now that every child psychotherapist has been made aware of the neurological advances in child mental health, it must not be forgotten that Acquarone helped to put these issues on the map in the first place.

What we see in *Changing Destinies* are her typical combinations of qualitative and quantitative clinical research, the voice of the baby and the child, the voice of the parents, the neurological findings, attachment findings, and clear descriptions of treatment outcome.

Alongside all of this is Acquarone's deep belief in the use of psychoanalytic understanding and observation, as well as an unwavering respect for the parents' awareness that something "is not quite right".

> We consciously leave the conventional tools, practices, and theories behind to enter a space regulated by the novelty of the unknown. We retain our capacity to reflect on our experience, reactions, and feelings, and travel guided by psychoanalytic and biological concepts to investigate this new world with a humble, explorative attitude.
>
> We experience the new land from the perspective of its inhabitants, and we try to understand how it feels to be able to escape excitement or overwhelming situations by looking in the air or at the movement of the trees; to calm oneself with different manoeuvres such as rocking, looking, or flapping hands; to avoid touching or being touched; holding or being held.

The structure of this book, with its excellent diagrams and photographs, is also part of the containment. Part I is about understanding why we (both professionals and parents) know something is wrong, Part II provides a detailed description of the Re:Start treatment model, and Part III outlines the family support, both during and after the treatment programme.

Acquarone includes her own infant–parent chart (Acquarone Scale), developed to aid a full assessment of both the mother and child, and, in the following pages, shares with the reader the Re:Start three-phase treatment programme of assessment and formulation, therapeutic intervention, and integration.

The work is intensive and demands heavy staffing ratios, which means that, outside of National Health Service (NHS) investment and involvement, Acquarone's pioneering Parent–Infant Clinic, charity, and training can only disseminate to a small number of families. *Changing Destinies* is, therefore, crucial in offering to a far wider audience the chance to note the way pre-autistic vulnerabilities in babies and young children can be transformed. It is not just an essential textbook documenting a successful treatment model to aid researchers and clinicians, but a precious tool for concerned parents, allowing them to recognise the signs of pre-autistic behaviours and to request the necessary help for themselves.

Introduction

> "Walking silence, like a phantom in the midst of his family. Rolled up in a corner moving gently from side to side. Sometimes under a table or chair. Trying to catch the light through the curtains. Fixated on a frail, gentle movement in the air, or on the lines in the fabric. It seems so interesting to him: the motes of dust suspended in the beam of light; all the lines of the textile interweaving. Or perhaps it's the blankness of it all, or simply the consistency of colour and structure—something that provides calm and safe feelings. He hides himself in an invisible space, one that nobody knows about and where no one can reach him."
>
> (Stella Acquarone, clinical notes)

Joseph was a boy who stood, or crouched, on the periphery of his family, seemingly more interested in catching the light, alone, than joining in with his family. He has two loving parents shocked by the diagnosis of autism, and a lively sister who wonders about her brother's delicate "non-existence". He was like a teddy bear, either cuddled up in himself or not looking at his family. He had no expression on his face and would run away rather than join in with them. Joseph's family wanted to find him, to look at him, to have him look at them. At times, his sibling tried to "make" him join in, wanting to do things to him, things she would not dare do to other children, only to objects. His parents sought opinions and advice to understand how to reach their son.

This book is about how Joseph was helped to move from being on the periphery to wanting to join in with his family. To move from catching the light, alone, to touching his mother's face and saying "I love you mummy".

My idea is to contribute to the thinking, understanding, and working with young children (aged six months to three years) with autistic behaviours. For this purpose, I use the psychoanalytic technique, as I believe that, alongside all the sensibilities and fragilities that these children present, there is an emotional evolution that becomes more and more entrenched and difficult to reach the older they get. From the beginning, the physical and the emotional interact with each other, and it is important to acknowledge and study both.

As well as Joseph, this book looks at three other children: Geronimo, Nicola, and Filippo. Some of their behaviours are similar but their experiences are unique and their internal conflicts different, and so the paths to resolution are individual to each child and their family.

This book is for those families who feel confused by their child, who feel as if their "baby" does not know them, or wishes to. It is for those families who are stuck—who have tried so hard to reach their child and yet who feel as if the child has retreated further. This book is for families and about families. For, as the child has his (or her) own individual sensitivities, so the family has its own way of responding to these. For the child to change, the whole family must be involved, and must change also.

This book is also for those professionals who work with infants presenting autistic behaviours. It will outline how to identify early signs of autism and, most importantly, offer a model of treatment that helps reach those children who have become cut off from themselves.

In the following chapters, we will present our intensive infant–family treatment programme—Re:Start, so called because one of the premises is to help the child and the parents to start again. We show how we help them return to the scene of newness and curiosity that the newborn brings and find out how the experiences are lived, and we aim to pinpoint the characteristic present in the child and in the parents (and siblings) that allows, or hinders, joyful family interaction.

The Re:Start programme is designed for very young children and their families. Its aim is to enable children to control their autistic behaviours or help them disappear altogether, if treated at under two years of age. Distilled from over thirty years of clinical practice in the field of parent–infant psychotherapy and informed by our ever-increasing understanding of autism and brain development, this programme offers a comprehensive approach to identifying concerns, treating families, and training professionals.

"Something is wrong"

Driven by a deep concern for their infant's behaviour, a large number of parents contact London's Parent Infant Centre (formerly the Parent Infant Clinic). Many have specific concerns about their child's eating or sleeping patterns. However, an increasing percentage has less concrete worries. "Something's wrong," they say. "My baby doesn't seem to know who I am", or, more specifically, "My baby wouldn't recognise me from a stranger". We hear phrases such as "My baby doesn't look at me", "I just can't get through to him/her", and "I feel something is not right". We listen closely to their concerns, since parents know their child better than anyone. We observe and assess the infant's interactions, paying special attention to the concerns raised by the parents. From our clinical work, it is clear that parents often know when something is not as it should be; they are the first "radar" for pre-autistic behaviours and other future disorders in childhood. In this book, we focus specifically on the early treatment of young children with pre-autistic behaviours—from pregnancy to three years of age.

Pre-autistic babies are sensitive souls. They seem to retreat from stimulating emotional interactions and cocoon themselves in their own world. Such behaviours are not far removed from normal child development. A visit to a fairground can be, for some, exhilarating, fun, and stimulating; for others, it can feel overwhelming, invasive, and frightening. For the overwhelmed, the best way to find peace and quiet is to remove themselves from that environment of multiple stimuli and seek a calmer place where personal space can be controlled. This fairground analogy shows how people ordinarily intentionally retreat into their own self when the external world is experienced as being "too much". Everyone has a desire to protect themselves from a fear of being overwhelmed, and everyone has a different capacity to bear potentially overwhelming stimuli. However, what is "too much" for one person can seem trivial or even imperceptible to another. For the infant with a low capacity to bear overwhelming stimuli, there are fewer options of retreat. Eyes can be closed and the head turned away, but the infant cannot physically seek out a calmer place; instead, sensitive babies retreat from perceived excessive stimuli to an internal space rather than an external one.

The autistic space can be defined by the space in which a person, a child, or a baby hangs as if suspended from the reality surrounding them. It is apparent in the blank gaze on a child's face while he looks into the air, maybe at the movement of trees and clouds, or maybe into space, or at the spinning wheels of passing vehicles. In this state, the child is openly unrelated, not communicating with those objects that occupy his attention and, at the same time, not interacting with other human beings present. This lack of human interaction, due either to a difficulty of understanding it or a sensitive reaction to what feels too overwhelming, is what leads parents to ask, "What is wrong?" Unable to hold their child's gaze in a meaningful way, they seek help in finding alternative methods of reaching out and engaging their child.

This autistic space can be confused with normal resting spaces in development but has a different quality, since it is a "cut-offness" rather different from withdrawing and pausing. In normal resting spaces, the baby is still connected to the person from whom he needs to retreat, becoming almost passive while knowing the person is out there waiting and attentive. In the cut-off state, there is no emotional connection. The infant is instead active in controlling the distance between him and others, an avoidance of interaction, and a rejection of meaningful relationship. This behaviour of inner flight seems to be caused by an incapacity to put the different aspects of an experience together, or a fear generated by an experience that cannot be processed, managed, understood, and contained.

Understanding and containment is provided by all parents who engage with their infants as they struggle to process and retain the many new experiences of the world into which they have been born. Some babies, however, are harder to engage making it more difficult for their parents to reassure and comfort, to understand and contain. Families of very sensitive babies can find themselves bending over backwards to engage their baby and to receive from them an indication that the infant acknowledges their presence, working hard to overcome the infant's resistance to communicate. While some infants respond to their parents' efforts to engage them, others do not, and some retreat further. Without successful engagement, the infant's retreat to the autistic space can become a way of living in later development and then a style of life.

Our aim at the Parent Infant Centre, and one that we propose in this book, is to assist parents in finding and engaging with their child: to develop the child's capacities to tolerate and enjoy the world around them and to develop the parents' capacities at understanding their infant's behaviours. To do this, we need to understand why the infant retreats to the autistic space, identify the barriers to their re-engaging with those who love them, and what motivation is needed to draw them out of themselves.

The infant's internal world is a complex one. We need to pay heed to the many differing biological and psychological aspects underlying the individual's make-up, and the possible barriers within and between them. These aspects include:

- sensory capacities—how the external world is perceived;
- motor capacities—reacting to others by presenting a positive posture towards them or leaning back in rejection;
- emotional capacities—including both the feelings involved in being in a relationship with others and the ability to accept co-regulation and develop self-regulation of one's own inner states;
- social and communicative capacities—the ability to interact with others.

Through careful observation and sensitive intervention, we are able to begin to create an understanding of how the child perceives the world, which aspects are unusually frightening or overwhelming, and to hypothesise about how we can work alongside the family to bring about meaningful change.

Exploring and discovering

Exploring and discovering the unique personality and sensitivity of an infant is akin to discovering a new land. We tentatively set foot in a land where we do not speak the language or have the same parameters, and yet, while there, we manage to create sense and understanding, not because we are better or know more about what is good, but because we want to build bridges for mutual enrichment. To gain as full an experience as possible, we start by respecting the uniqueness of each infant and family, and lose our prejudices or rules for treating other kinds of personality disorders. We consciously leave the conventional tools, practices, and theories behind to enter a space regulated by the novelty of the unknown. We retain our capacity to reflect on our experience, reactions, and feelings, and travel guided by psychoanalytic and biological concepts to investigate this new world with a humble explorative attitude.

We experience the new land from the perspective of its inhabitants, and we try to understand how it feels to be able to escape excitement or overwhelming situations by looking in the air or at the movement of the trees; to calm oneself with different manoeuvres such as rocking, looking, or flapping hands; to avoid touching or being touched; holding or being held. We use observation, art, and our own emotional radar to extract and explore the infant's experience of their world. We then reflect on what we have learnt, informed by neurological, biological, and psychoanalytic knowledge, in order then to make sense of both our and the infant's experience. Finally, we use this new sense to inform our intervention methods, and begin to initiate and enhance interactions with the infant. At the same time, we explore the individual worlds of the parents and the siblings, in order to fully understand the dynamics of how the family interrelates. We also journey with different family members into the emotional and sensory world of the infant to enhance each individual's understanding of this unique child and to develop new ways of being with one another. Our exploration of the inner emotional world of every family member enables us to fully map the emotional and cognitive field surrounding the infant and to draw up a new landscape that meets the needs and sensitivities of all.

Maybe what is written in this book will encourage therapists to explore further the uncharted lands of the pre-autistic infant and their individuality. I say "uncharted" because, in this book, we are going to move beyond the behaviour that we see and try to understand what has caused it. Instead of changing the behaviour from the outside with rewards, we stimulate changes from within the child as he becomes more comfortable being in a family and social setting.

An outline of the different sections of the book

This book is divided into three parts. Part I considers how we know that something is wrong, and what we think can be done about it: the careful assessment, knowledge, and tools needed before we set off on our "voyage of discovery". We consider the early warning signs: the behaviours that suggest a child might well develop autism. We look at the theoretical underpinnings, questioning how it is that psychoanalysis can assist us in understanding and treating early autistic behaviours. We examine the neuro-relational basis of our approach, confirming the validity of early intervention. Finally, we emphasise the need for a robust independent assessment by a paediatrician in order to ensure that this land does need mapping (are there red flags, or is this just a "hiccup" in normal development?), and to refer back to and evaluate our progress.

In Part II, we show our treatment model: the Re:Start intensive infant–family programme. We outline its three phases: assessment and formulation, therapeutic intervention, and integration. In the assessment and formulation phase, we illustrate how observation and psychoanalytic understanding of the non-verbal communications in the pre-autistic baby or very young child, his/her parents, and siblings can assist us in understanding the function of their autistic behaviours—what it is they retreat from. Knowing this, we can then help bring about the necessary change in their environment and relationships to reduce the overwhelming, fear-provoking stimuli. In the therapeutic intervention phase, we explain how we create the environment in which change can come about. We discuss the interventions undertaken with the family: with the whole family, the infant, the infant and parents together, and the siblings individually and as a group. We describe how, in working with the infant, we sit on the floor with the child and parents and help the parents to understand their baby using the following principles: observe, explore, pursue, try, and enlarge. We examine our use of psychoanalytic concepts and of the creative arts (art, storytelling, dramatisation, sand tray, etc.) to help the family express their feelings, their hopes, and their fears, to think creatively and consider new possibilities. Essential to this process is the development of the "team mind" created by twice-daily supervision, reflective practice, and an awareness of the transference–countertransference that serves as the backbone for the treatment. In phase three, integration, we consider the support offered to the family to consolidate the progress made during treatment.

We illustrate all of this with four case studies. Having explained in Part I "why" we offer the Re:Start treatment, these case studies aim to illustrate "how" it works. In each one, we go step by step through the journey of discovery: how we explore the infant's sensibilities and emotional transmission, the impact of parental "ghosts" and the impact of siblings, and how we bring about change through interventions with the family, the individual, and as a group. First, Joseph, an in-depth case study looking at the process of the treatment. Geronimo highlights the particular complexity in working with the older child whose behaviours have become more entrenched. Nicola, by contrast, is an example of working with a much younger infant and highlights the specific techniques used. Finally, with Filippo, we illustrate how we work with the siblings. Throughout these case studies, we share the practical experiences, the theoretical understanding, and how the emotional relationships develop, conveying the intense, fascinating, and dramatic process as it unfolds.

The final section of Part II considers how we work with the child in their context, looking beyond the walls of the clinic to the child's wider environment. We describe the role of family observations during home visits to see for ourselves "the family way of living and coping" in their natural environment. We discuss the importance of follow-on work to both consolidate change within the family and enable change within the wider network, which includes the school or nursery, as well as those who spend a lot of time with the child, such as grandparents or nannies.

Finally, in Part III, we share the views of the families who have been through this treatment and hear their experiences: the obstacles they faced, and the achievements they made. It was their faith in their concerns and convictions that enabled their child to receive an intervention that helped to change the course of their emotional development and, thereby, their destiny.

PART I

UNDERPINNINGS OF OUR APPROACH

CHAPTER ONE

Understanding early signs of autism in babies

Stella Acquarone

How can we tell if a baby is retreating to an autistic space? In this chapter, we consider the early warning signs of autism. In order to see what is wrong, it is first important to do a brief review of what is right, and so we look at the typical traits and behaviours that are characteristic of newborns. It is at this stage in the early emotional development of the child that it is possible to detect if there is a difficulty in the development of communication. We also discuss the role of "significant others", before concluding with the five areas to consider when looking for specific signs of autism and a scale to measure them against.

Signs

A sign is a representation of an object that implies a connection between itself and its object. A natural sign bears a causal relation to its object—for instance, thunder is a sign of a storm. However, a conventional sign is by agreement and can be varied. Usually, the goal is to elicit a response or simply information, as with medical symptoms. It is not the illness or a disorder. In our work in preventing autism, we have coined the term "pre-autism". Pre-autism is not a state or a normal phase in development. It is a process in which development is being arrested and includes the period when parents realise that something is wrong but do not know what. The early signs can sometimes be detected from birth, but are usually more clearly manifested from three to four months of age.

Characteristics of the newborn

Following infant research studies and observation of newborns, we can say that the typical baby presents the following characteristics at birth.

Contact signals

The senses. Babies use their eyes (Brazelton et al., 1974; Muratori & Maestro, 2007; Murray & Andrews, 2005; Murray & Trevarthen, 1985, 2007; Trevarthen, 1979; Trevarthen & Hubley, 1978), voice (Bullowa, 1979; Danon-Boileau, 2007), body movements, touch (Delafield-Butt & Trevarthen, 2013), and sense of smell (MacFarlane, 1977) to communicate. The baby actively seeks contact, wanting and exercising social interaction (Murray & Andrews, 2005; Trevarthen & Delafield-Butt, 2013; Trevarthen et al., 1981). Stern believed that when mothers and babies interact face to face, this might even reproduce in another sensory mode a shared understanding of the other's emotions, their senses, their movements, their intentions, their "vitality contours", to use Stern's phrase (1985). It is almost as if they are able to communicate beyond the behavioural act itself.

Looking is a subtle instrument of contact and exchange. It implies alternating attention, or reciprocal investment. It is the window to other people's experiences, and it mutually reinforces the dynamics of the mother-infant relationship. With their eyes, babies can follow the people that they love. Babies find meaning in the faces of these people by looking at them (Photo 1). They can also "go away" by looking elsewhere or closing their eyes (and going to sleep).

By gazing at their mothers, babies internalise the image of themselves in their mothers' eyes. This helps newborns to form the first positive image of themselves. According to Winnicott (1971), the baby

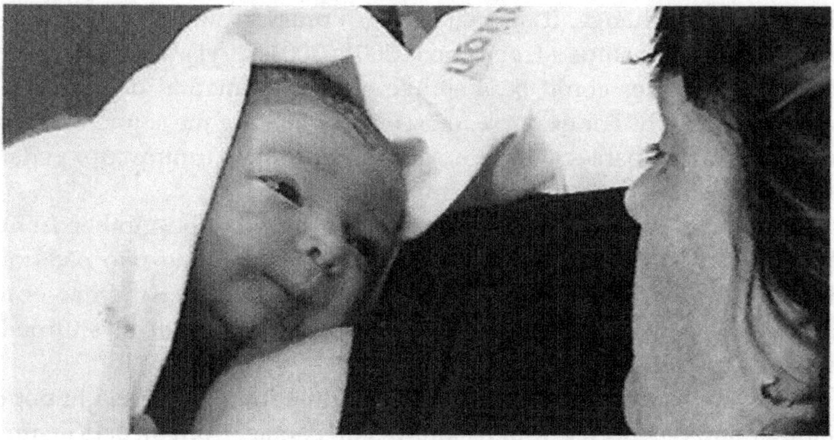

Photo 1. Newborn holding mother's gaze.

derives its fundamental sense of existence and goodness from what it sees reflected in its mother's face: on that most basic of levels, we are what we see. However, we should be aware that if the mother's own preoccupations intrude on the mother–baby relationship, it can transform the experience into a negative one and undermine the baby's sense of self (Klein, 1961).

The baby can *hear* voices inside the womb from four months, and so the mother's voice, in all its expressive varieties and emotional tones, becomes the "psychic life" of the infant. Babies can also discriminate other sounds and voices around them, such as those of the father and siblings. Hearing the mother's voice (and the father's) could ease the pain of separation after delivery. The baby's calling impulse (instinct as far as it exists from birth) is represented in the cry. It is a social sound, an innate call for attention and entertainment, and not just a demand for his needs to be satisfied. Pines (1984) observes that the mother provides another source of information for the "self of the neonate" to be actively mirrored by another responding self. "It is the contrast between similarity and difference. It is difference that carries information, and difference is only understandable in a context. Without difference there is no change and no development" (p. 33).

It is important to note that "motherese"—the slow and repetitive child-directed speech typically used by carers—or the use of a pleasant tone and attitude when communicating with the baby stimulates the psychic exchange. It also encourages brain growth and development of relationships (Trevarthen, 2001, 2004, 2011). Deafness and hypersensitivities could be a source of developmental delay if not attended to early. For example, on seeing or hearing the sound of their mother, typical babies will look, gurgle, pull their tummy up, pedal their feet, or wish to be picked up.

Likewise, the baby will recognize the *smell* of the mother from birth. MacFarlane (1977) demonstrated this by placing two pads of breast milk—one of the mother's and one of another mother—on either side of the baby's face and seeing how the baby always turned towards the mother's.

Touch, meanwhile, is linked to the stimulation of oxytocin in both mother and newborn through skin-to-skin contact from birth (Kerstin, 2011). The skin covers the whole body providing an overall "container for the body and the mind" (Bick, 1968).

> . . . in its most primitive form the parts of the personality are felt to have no binding force amongst themselves and must therefore be held together in a way that is experienced by them passively, by the skin functioning as a boundary . . . But this internal function of containing the parts of the self is dependent initially on the introjection of an external object, experienced as capable of fulfilling this function. Later, identification with this function of the object supersedes the unintegrated state and gives rise to the fantasy of internal and external space. (Bick, 1968, p. 484)

Just as the sense of touch for the blind person is like a second pair of eyes, so, too, for the baby, who, with hands and mouth, allows proximity, exploration, distance, or protection as needed. At the beginning everything is mouthed and grasped.

Touch and the feeling of containment resulting from skin-to-skin contact provide a firm grounding for the personality to develop. An example could be of the baby at the breast who caresses the finger of the mother, feeling protected in her arms, and connected through their skin and mutual touches.

Signs of satisfaction

Observation shows that when babies have their needs satisfied, they acknowledge this by relaxing and smiling.

The feeling of satisfaction comes from the capacity to feel a need, which is then linked with the object of desire. This creates gratitude towards the source of the satisfaction, which in most cases is mother's care, attention, and love. It is then that the baby gratifies the mother by looking at her and smiling. The baby is able to feel the separation between them, and experiences a sense of pleasure and trust. Recognition of the mother generates in turn feelings of gratitude and concern.

The new sensations experienced immediately after birth can be intense for the baby, and while some babies are able to regulate their emotions, others have to go slower, sleeping a lot. If the mother, in her reverie, wants to protect the baby from this confusion and prefers to continue the illusion of being together, she provides care on demand.

The baby has to learn to be separate from mother, and cope with sensations that are satisfied by an external person. If not, babies might feel as if their mothers belong to them, which could be experienced either as wonderful or overwhelming.

Signs of emotional regulation, and creating rhythms

From even before birth, babies will suck their thumb or hand if they feel hungry. Babies like the feel of being in control of themselves with their eyes, sounds, and being held by their parents.

Signs of passion

Trevarthen (1998b) wants us to know that babies are passionate communicators. They demonstrate their excitement when they are the focus of a patient, caring, and talkative parent. They do this by moving their body in different ways: pushing their tummy forward, pedalling their feet, and moving their arms, offering a foot for their parent to "eat", and sucking on and caressing the mother's breast, face, or whatever is available from her, while making contented noises.

Babies' innate capacity to imitate (Trevarthen, 1979, 1998a) helps them to provoke parents into interacting with them (Nadel & Decety, 2003; Nadel et al., 1999) and become the focus of attention (Photo 2).

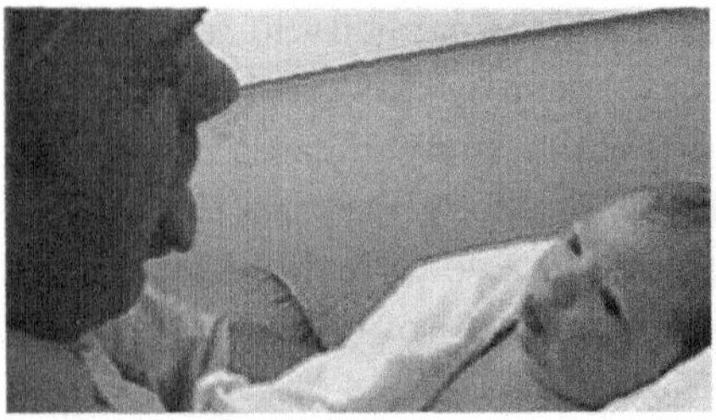

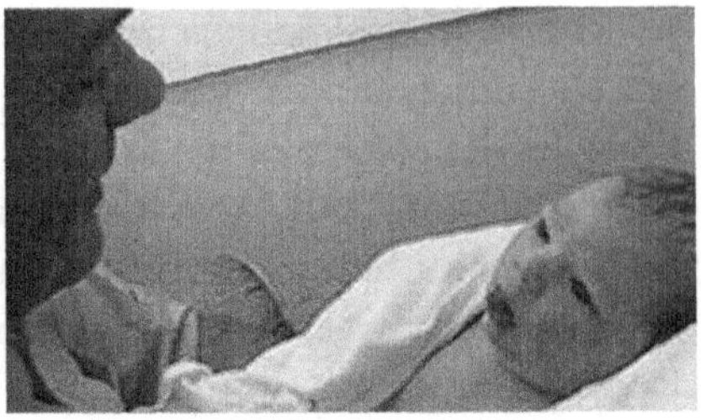

Photos 2 and 3. The father makes a face at the baby. Four seconds later, the baby imitates.

Signs of intimacy and attachment

In our observations, we also incorporate research carried out by Panksepp (1998) and Brazelton and colleagues (Brazelton & Nugent, 2011; Brazelton et al., 1974) into the capacities of the newborn and the presence and importance of joy and play, joy and passion (Trevarthen, 1998b), and the feelings of intimacy experienced from the start and which act as an organiser for healthy emotional development.

We consider the integrating force of intimacy (Figure 1.1) and we look at the concepts of attachment, attunement, and positive feelings, because these

- facilitate the production of neurones and neural links: the basis for cognitive and emotional intelligence;
- release the bonding hormones oxytocin and vasopressin (linked to the feeling of love) (Kerstin, 2011);
- activate the baby's vagus nerve, which regulates the function of the major organs, rebalancing disruptions to heart rate, digestion, breathing, and the immune system caused by stress.

Expectations and experiences in the family relationships before birth

Our hypothesis is that the wireless network of emotions is activated during pregnancy. The foetus experiences emotions that might be felt as calming and pleasant, or uncomfortable and unpleasant (O'Connor et al., 2003, 2005; Glover, 2014, 2015; Glover & O'Connor, 2002). At this stage, attachment starts forming: either in a positive way or, as Glover

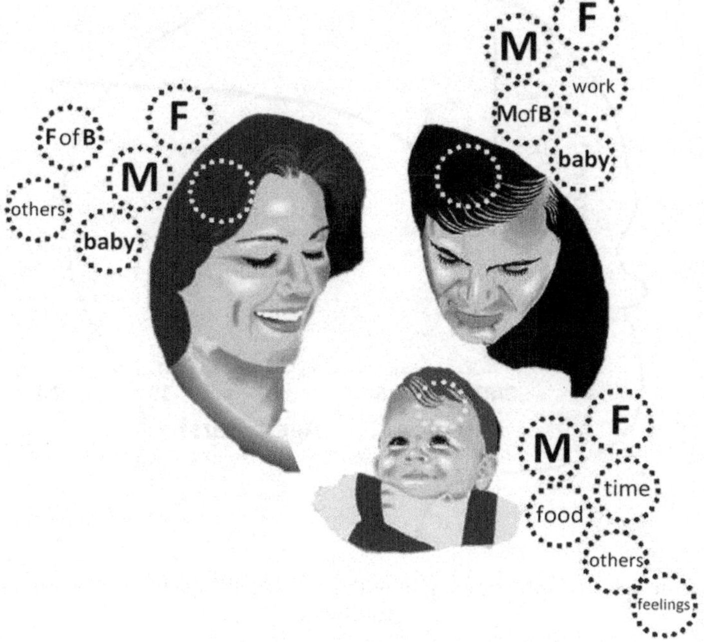

Figures 1.1. Intimacy and the eternal triangle.

describes in her published works, it can become problematic and lead to anxiety and feelings of insecurity in the unborn child (Glover, 2014, 2015; Reissland et al., 2013; Talge et al., 2007; Van den Bergh et al., 2005; Wainstock et al., 2013).

During pregnancy, mothers may experience a mixture of feelings: some might have a healthy ambivalence, some could be completely absorbed in the process of pregnancy, taking care of what they eat, what they breathe, what they do, while other mothers might be in complete denial of the process (Mancia, 1981; Masakowski & Fifer, 1994).

Neonatal research confirms that even genetic endowment may be modified or inhibited by the specific emotional climate of the family environment. MRI scans have revealed specifications in brain malfunctioning and the interpersonal nature of brain development at this stage of life (Raphael-Leff, 2007) (Figure 1.2). Neuroscience research has shown the interactive nature of the baby's brain and early neuroplasticity; therefore finding out if developmental processes have been derailed should be encouraged as early as possible (Schore, 1994).

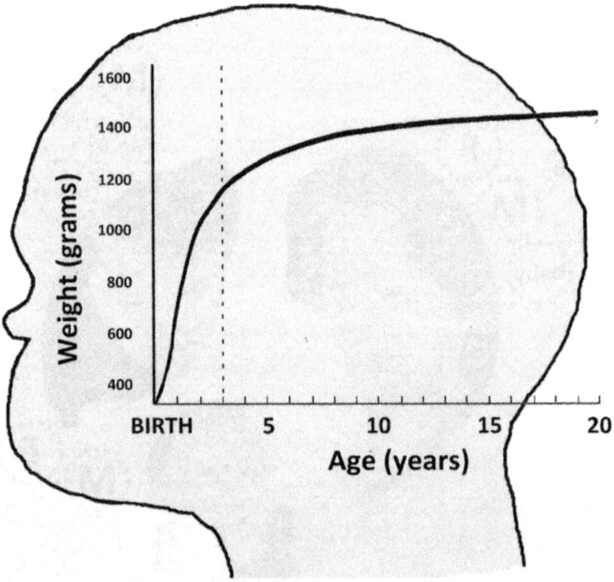

Figure 1.2. Graph showing how the brain develops from conception to adulthood.

Normal development or impaired?

Psychiatrists Kanner (1943), Bettelheim (1967) and various others indirectly blamed the attitude of the parents for their child's autism. However, research has shown that some infants are simply unable to adequately process their parents' or their own senses and emotions. In order to discuss what is not right, we first look at what is expected or required for happy and healthy development to occur (Schore, 2001; Panksepp, 2001).

The baby's environment

The mother's womb is the baby's first physical environment. Some argue that the space between the parents' wish for a baby and conception is the first "psychic environment". While experience in the womb can affect the developing baby, birth can be seen as the first life "event": the moment when both baby and mother must come to terms with being separated.

The work of separation from the mother is usually initiated by her through a gentle process of disillusion. This is assisted by the role of the father (or other), creating a triangle: a third position in the mother–child constellation from which the father helps the infant form a different relationship with him and allows the mother to separate herself safely from the infant.

Both parents are keen to claim ownership of what their child has inherited from them (his nose, his smile), while also beginning to recognise their child's own unique personality. Both parents are also affected, often unconsciously, by the "ghosts" of their own childhoods: memories and emotions that are often exacerbated by the fears and frustrations of becoming a parent.

The baby seeks to communicate with the parents, and they with their baby. Calling for attention by crying, kicking, babbling, or grimacing, the baby expresses himself. Parents learn to identify their baby's needs, voice them, and meet them in a calm and patient way. Joy appears in anticipation of satisfaction, in the recognition of the different ways of fulfilling their baby's needs, whether by entertaining, feeding, or changing. This reciprocal relationship is fun and exciting, and so the baby continues to seek attention.

It is when the mother cannot offer a stable frame of reference and feels depressed or physically exhausted that a worrying space appears in which the baby feels it is dangerous to seek attention. When this is the case, and the mother cannot hold, soothe, or make sense of her baby's experiences or emotions, due to her own inner turmoil, the baby might seek to retreat from all that seems overwhelming.

Early signs of autistic behaviours

The baby with autistic behaviours is unco-operative and does not seek, in meaningful ways, the company of other people.

There are five areas to consider: interpersonal–social; sensorial; motor–posture; emotions (affect); impact on the carer. These are outlined in more detail below.

Interpersonal

From birth, babies are naturally inclined to be social. With pre-autism, however, the baby will appear as lacking immediate response and/or have no interest in the adults' attention, showing no attraction for the mother's face and no curiosity. These signs will appear as

- gaze avoidance, lack of imitation (Nadel & Butterworth, 1999), disengagement of visual attention, atypical forms of eye contact, visual tracking (Massie & Rosenthal, 1984; Zwaigenbaum et al., 2005; Elsabbagh et al., 2009);
- eye tracking decreases at two to six months old (Boraston & Blakemore, 2007; Jones & Klin, 2013);
- lack of calling/enticing adults or children into interacting (Nadel et al., 1999; Trevarthen & Delafield-Butt, 2013);
- more interest in objects (object-relatedness) than people (Maestro et al., 2005);
- lack of babbling (Massie & Rosenthal, 1984); delayed expressive and receptive language (Zwaigenbaum et al., 2005);
- lack of joint attention (at around one year);
- no smiling by four months;
- disjointed affects: that is, the baby's reactions do not relate to the other's emotions. For example, he may smile when the mother is upset, or be frightened when she smiles (Massie & Rosenthal, 1984; Zwaigenbaum et al., 2005) (Photos 4 and 5).

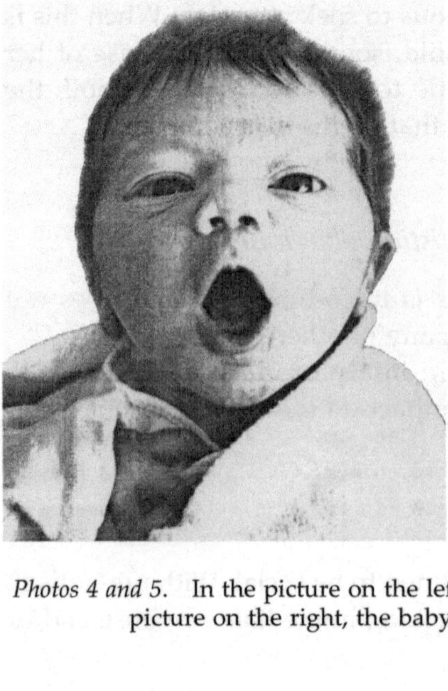
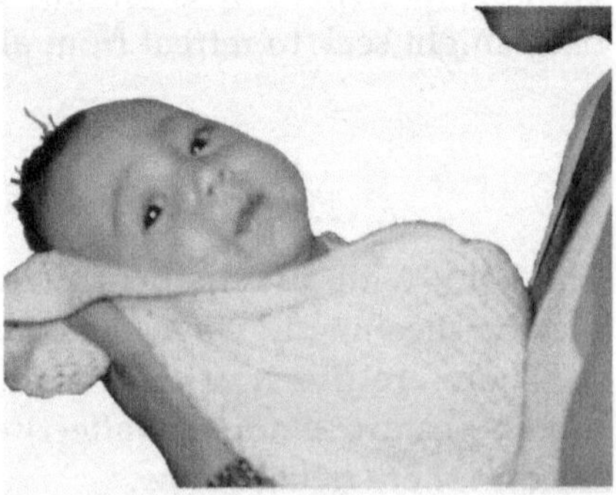

Photos 4 and 5. In the picture on the left, the baby is interacting, whereas in the picture on the right, the baby is exhibiting gaze avoidance.

Sensorial

Regarding the specific relationship with the mother or carer, here we explore the baby's use of his senses and determine any deficits in the sensorial spectrum. Signs include:

- lack of recognition of the mother's smell (MacFarlane, 1977);
- dislike of the tone and/or volume of the mother's voice; prefers whispers (auditory hypersensitivity) (Acquarone, 2007);
- prefers to look in the air or is focused on bubbles or floating dust: that is, objects rather than the mother or other people (Baranek et al., 2005; Maestro et al., 2005; Zwaigenbaum et al., 2005);
- hypersensitivity to touch or ways of being touched, indicating early sensory over-responsivity (Ben-Sasson et al., 2008);
- not turning towards the mother's voice (Blasi et al., 2011);
- self-erotic sensual relationship over one sense (Massie & Rosenthal, 1984), and sensory-orientated behaviours (Zwaigenbaum et al., 2005);
- no orientation towards the direction from which their name is called (Zwaigenbaum et al., 2005).

Motor–posture

Here, we explore the infant's posture and movement in relation to the mother or carer. Poor muscle tone (psychomotor) skills may manifest themselves in the following ways:

- the baby may be hypo- or hypertonic when in the arms of the mother. Displays a lack of "moulding" within the mother or carer's arms or body (Baranek, 1999; Baranek et al., 1997, 2008);
- head lag: signifying weak head or neck control (Landa et al., 2012);
- lack of grasping (David et al., 2012; Massie & Rosenthal, 1984);
- repetitive hand movements or gestures; making strange noises (Massie & Rosenthal, 1984);
- grimacing (Massie & Rosenthal, 1984);
- movement disorders revealed in the shape of the mouth, not meeting some or all the developmental milestones, including lying, righting, sitting, crawling, and walking (Teitelbaum et al., 1998);

- dislike of being picked up or held (Baranek, 1999; Baranek et al., 1997, 2008);
- lack of curiosity (Acquarone, 2007);
- excessive or odd interest in tongue movement within the mouth (Negri, 1994);
- general difficulties in showing a desire to communicate through their movements: that is, arms forward, pedalling with their legs, pushing the tummy forward, etc. (Baranek, 1999; Baranek et al., 1997, 2008).

Emotions (affect)

Here we look at how the mother's emotions are received/felt and how these might be interwoven and/or integrated within the infant's mind. Signs that the child is having difficulty in this area include:

- deficits in the transmission of emotions (Acquarone, 2007);
- extreme defences, such as denial, rejection, dissociation, and isolation (Fraiberg, 1982; Massie & Rosenthal, 1984);
- decreased expression of positive affect by twelve months (Zwaigenbaum et al., 2005);
- delayed expressive and receptive language (Zwaigenbaum et al., 2005);
- displays of extreme anxiety or distress, or a complete lack of either (Massie & Rosenthal, 1984);
- easily fearful (Massie & Rosenthal, 1984; Negri 1994);
- irritability (Negri, 1994);
- lack of fun, enjoyment, and passion in the infant's relationship with "significant others" (Trevarthen & Delafield-Butt, 2013);
- pattern of early temperament, with marked passivity and decreased activity level at six months, followed by extreme distress reactions, and decreased expression of positive affect by twelve months (Zwaigenbaum et al., 2005).

Impact on the carer

In addition to observable "signs" in the child, it is as important to consider the parents. Imagine how difficult it must be for the parents to relate to their child (with their disinterested, slower, unaffectionate manner) and who desperately try to find some measure of pleasure and satisfaction in joint experiences (Trevarthen, 2001; Danon-Boileau, 2007). In fact, when I first started attending to babies with avoidance behaviour and communication difficulties, I based my interventions on the parents' concerns. I soon realized that the "something wrong" intuition of the parents corresponded to what we would nowadays describe as dysregulation and autistic behaviours (Goldberg et al., 2008). Parents are the best mental health "radar" for realising, from their baby's behaviour or lack of communication, the need for help and skilled attention.

The Acquarone infant–parent chart and scale

The Acquarone scale is an observation checklist that assists clinicians in identifying pre-autistic behaviours in infants from zero to three, an age group not included within the scope of traditional autism screening tools. I initially devised the scales (modified from Massie & Rosenthal, 1984) to assist in my own casework, and have revised them over time to become a tool used by all practitioners at the Parent Infant Clinic, London. Its accessible format ensures that it will be of value to a wide range of practitioners who have contact with infants in their early months and years, from health visitors to paediatricians to psychotherapists. Screening can be done in person during an hour-long observation, or remotely through the observation of video footage.

In our approach, it is important to use a scale and to put down on paper any initial behavioural difficulties that are observable. These are measured against normal infant development characteristics to help us highlight any areas of concern. Our simple observational scale measures the mother and child's behaviours separately to find out where the main focus of the intervention should be.

Key areas focused upon include:

- primary intersubjectivity—the infant's motivation of relating to others;
- deficits in the sensorial process;
- poor motor (psychomotor) skills;
- deficits in the transmission of affect and the impact of behaviours on the other.

Should four or more areas of concern be highlighted during a screening assessment, early intervention is deemed imperative.

There are two scales (assessment and follow-up for both babies and mothers/carers) (see Figures 1.3 and 1.4) and three charts (a case summary for both babies and mothers/carers). The scales and charts provide a detailed snapshot of the "before" and "after" of an intensive early intervention, and support conclusions about the underlying effectiveness of the intensive treatment in both the baby/child and the mother/carer.

This scale requires having good observation skills, usually developed by having studied Bick's method of infant observation (visiting a newborn from birth to two years for an hour in their home and then writing down, after the visit, the details, including their emotional reactions; this is then discussed in a small group to understand what lies behind the behaviours observed). Thorough training in how to fill in the scale correctly is essential to ensure reliability and accuracy.

There are two kinds of marking in the observable behaviours: one is the frequency of behaviour seen; the other is assessing the emotional climate of the relationship. If we have been allowed to video the assessment, we fill in the scale after watching the video; if not, then from detailed memory of the clinical consultation.

There are two steps to filling in the scale.

Step 1: We note the frequency of the behaviours that appear in the infant, and mark them as follows: Never (value 1), Rarely (value 2), Frequently (value 3), or Always (value 1). Behaviours that Never appear or Always appear are both extremes that are considered signs of alarm, as they do not offer much capacity for change and therefore hold a degree of difficulty. In the follow-up session, we repeat our observations and fill in the scale again.

Since our work aims to help relationships, build communication, and improve the child's sensorial, motor, emotional, and cognitive capacities, we hope to see from the scale a move from the outside (extreme behaviour) columns towards the middle two, Frequent and Rarely. Therefore, if a certain behaviour that was originally observed as happening Always starts to become Frequent or Rarely, we consider this progress in development.

Step 2: We then assess the quality of the emotional interaction observed between the parents and child. To this effect, we describe the behaviour in the scale in blue (in this book, the blue marks and lines

ACQUARONE DETECTION SCALES FOR EARLY RELATIONSHIPS®

EARLY SIGNS OF ALARM – pre-Autism

ASSESSMENT – INFANT/CHILD

name: **NAME**

age: DD MMM YYYY *date of this observation:* DD MMM YYYY

	NEVER	RARELY	FREQUENT	ALWAYS	OBSERVER REACTIONS
1. GAZING *Eye-to-eye contact within a relationship and the maintenance of this contact*					
2. BABBLING *Making sounds for the benefit of the partner in the parent-infant relationship*					
3. CALLING *– The facial expressions – Noises or gestures that seek to produce an affectionate response from the partner*					
4. IMITATING *– Moving mouth, tongue, etc., in imitation of mother's (or another) – The repetition of a sound or a movement heard or seen by the child*					
5. PROVOKING *Inciting the person into interacting, not just to use as an instrument to do something for him/her*					
6. POINTING *Indicating with index finger to a person about an object of interest*					
7. FEEDING *Child's attitude during the intake of food, including anticipatory behaviour (e.g. head-turning, moving arms the food/breast)*					
8. JOINT ATTENTION *Looking in the same direction*					
9. PLAY *– Capacity to play the same game for more than 5 minutes, and share with another person – Take turns and stay with a person – Children* 10. ALONE					
11. RELATING *Behaviours indicating the capacity to relate & accept emotional warmth.* *– Mother, Father* *– Other caregivers* *– Other unfamiliar adults* *– Siblings* *– Other unfamiliar children*					
12. REACTIVE BEHAVIOURS *tolerance to frustrations, including:* *– a) Capacity to accept emotional warmth – b) Capacity to bounce back after stressful event – c) Capacity to adapt to changes...please indicate*					
TOUCHING 13. *Skin-to-skin contact initiated by infant for play or affection* 14. *Does the child touch paint, foam, sand, water, playdoh, plasticine and other messy substances*					
RESPONSE 15. *Response to sounds* 16. *Response to noise* 17. *Response to name* 18. *Response to light & patterns* 19. *Response to smells*					
20. COMFORTING *Child's ability to find relief from distress by themselves (e.g. thumb sucking, touching hands, playing with one car, others)...specify*					
HOLDING 21. *The posturing of the child when he is supported in the arms of the mother (e.g. floppy, rigid, restless) – General muscle tone when sitting or standing* 22. *Stereotypic movement of arms, eyes, etc.* *– Walking: on tiptoes or sluggish* 23. *Use of hands: for grasping, for helping himself* *– Use of body: to reach, to climb, to hide, other...*					
24. EXPRESSIVENESS *The body or facial expression of emotional states (e.g., sad, worried, anxious, bland, happy, or others)...specify*					
25. SELF HELP DEVELOPMENT *– Ability to cope independently with the environment, (e.g., dress) – Eating* *– Being careful with him/herself or others*					

ANY OTHER OBSERVATIONS NOT LISTED ABOVE:

Figure 1.3. The Acquarone assessment scale for an infant or child.

appear in grey) if there does not appear to be much emotional warmth or real happiness, joy, and fun evident in their relationship. In the follow-up session, we measure any change in the emotional climate between the parents and the child, such as having developed a capacity to feel joy, fun, and become passionate communicators. If there is a change of this kind, we mark this in red (in this book, the red marks and lines appear in black), to indicate good emotional connection.

ACQUARONE DETECTION SCALES FOR EARLY RELATIONSHIPS®

EARLY SIGNS OF ALARM – pre-Autism

...affecting the baby or being affected by the baby...

ASSESSMENT – MOTHER/caregiver

name: **NAME**
child: **NAME** *age:* **DD MMM YYYY**

		NEVER	RARELY	FREQUENT	ALWAYS	OBSERVER REACTIONS
INTERPERSONAL	**1. GAZING** *Eye-to-eye contact with the baby and the maintenance of this contact*					
	2. BABBLING *– Making sounds for the benefit of the parent-infant relationship – Talking*					
	3. CALLING *Facial expressions, noises or gestures seeking to produce an affectionate response from the infant*					
	4. FEEDING *Mother's attitude towards infant's hunger and need to feed: – Does she anticipate behaviour and have meal or breast easily available? – Does she pay attention, talk with the baby and enjoy feeding? – Does she interrupt with any excuse (e.g., talks to others and looks away)? – Is she fearful, full of anguish or has she any delusions? – Is she apathetic?*					
	5. GAMES / PLAY *– Playful encounters, including songs and teasing*					
	6. RELATING *Behaviours indicating the capacity to relate & accept emotional warmth towards the baby*					
	7. REACTIVE BEHAVIOURS *including: – Tolerance to frustrations – Capacity to accept emotional warmth – Capacity to bounce back after stressful event – Capacity to adapt to changes*					
SENSORIAL	**8. TOUCHING** *– Skin-to-skin contact initiated by infant for play or affection*					
	9. COMFORTING *– Mother's ability to find relief for the baby's distress*					
MOTOR	**10. POSTURE** *The posturing of the mother when the infant is supported in her arms or any other way (e.g., other, rough, balanced precariously)*					
AFFECT	**11. EXPRESSIVENESS** *– Expression of emotional state (e.g., sad, worried, anxious, bland, happy, others)...specify*					
	12. UNDERSTANDING OF EMOTIONS *– in themselves – in the baby*					
	13. PAST *– Psychiatric illness – Other difficulties*					

ANY OTHER OBSERVATIONS NOT LISTED ABOVE:

Figure 1.4. Acquarone scale for assessing the relationship between mother or primary carer and infant or child.

Reviewing the scales for follow-up

Filling in the charts for both infant and mother (or primary carer) enables us to:

- know whether the main difficulty lies with the baby or the mother. For example, whether the baby does not wish to communicate or if the mother is unable to pick up on the baby's relational cues. Therefore, the scale helps us to differentiate between pre-autistic behaviours in the child or signs of depression in the mother;
- obtain a "history" of each carer;
- monitor the quality of the attachments;
- share our understanding of the parent–infant relationship;
- share our understanding of the relationship in question with colleagues;
- evaluate any change over the period of treatment, and in the longer term;
- pass on the information we have gathered to other professionals as necessary;
- monitor progress for research. For each case study included in this book, we show the scale before and after treatment, and in Appendix I we include the average number of children treated under one year of age, as well as for those under two and three years.

It is important to stress that the Acquarone Scale not only allows us to identify early signs of alarm but, more importantly, enables us to offer interventions to the infant and their family. We do not wish to simply "diagnose", leaving the family stuck with a "label" of behaviour, but to identify concerns in order to act upon them. We believe that pre-autistic behaviours can, if treated early enough, be addressed and altered, and that, alongside the parents and family, we can create a change in the environment to enable the child to find ways to relate rather than retreat. We illustrate our methods in the following chapters.

Summary

While the majority of babies thrive and are able to form healthy emotional relationships, it is clear that there are many babies who do not. Early signs of alarm and pre-autistic behaviours can be detected from as young as three months of age. We believe that with psychoanalytic and neuropsychological intervention, these behaviours can be brought under control. We are also convinced that by identifying concerns early and undertaking treatment we can give children the opportunity to live a life without autism.

CHAPTER TWO

A psychoanalytic approach to treating early signs of autism

Stella Acquarone

The general approach of the Parent Infant Centre is to understand and work with early emotional difficulties between parents and their babies in a psychoanalytic manner.

Why psychoanalysis? Because it works with parents and with babies, and because it works where there are no words. The aim of psychoanalysis is to understand the ideas, conflicts, and emotions (sometimes unconscious) that lie behind the behaviour shown. It equips us with the skills necessary to reach the unstructured minds of children who find the world and relationships confusing and overwhelming. It provides the knowledge with which to understand their confusions and reluctance to relate to others, and the method through which to bring about change and create the basic conditions necessary to construct a mind motivated and able to relate and communicate. The essence of the analytic work is based on the quality of the relationships viewed and studied by the psychotherapist. All the nuances of this delicate atmosphere are noted with as little interference as possible from devices and/or personal theories and opinions.

We have in front of us a baby or toddler showing signs of autistic behaviour and their worried parents who do not understand what is happening. The baby is not relating, or was relating but has suddenly stopped, losing language skills and interest in other people. The parents feel overwhelmed by feelings of guilt and worry. They want to know how to help their child but are helpless. If the child is not relating to the mother, father, and other people around him, his capacity to create neural connections is in jeopardy, since what is not used is lost. Synaptic pruning, when the unused, unconnected nerve cells are eliminated, naturally occurs in normal brain development. If this process is affected, it can lead to sensory overload in the child.

We counter this by setting up ways in which the infant allows their parents to reach him, thereby unlocking the potential of new sensory experiences that were previously too overwhelming. We provide the basic sources of motivation and co-operation that might allow for interaction, attention, concentration, and tolerance.

Psychoanalytic theories provide a framework to aid our understanding not only of child development and family relationships, but also of emerging pre-autistic behaviours. The psychoanalytic setting provides the space and time free from the interruptions of everyday life in which to observe and understand relationships. The psychoanalytic method provides non-verbal tools to help us understand the patient.

Psychoanalytic framework

The creation of the self or the state of unintegration

An understanding of the development of a sense of self, and of self in relation to others, is key. Our work is greatly informed by the ideas of Winnicott, Bick, Bion, and Tustin, among others.

Winnicott (1949) described a "holding phase in infancy", which is the creation of a psychosomatic existence, a primary integration, referred to as an "indwelling of the psyche in the soma".

> There comes into existence what might be called a limiting membrane, which to some extent (in health) is equated with the surface of the skin, and has a position between the infant "me" and his "not-me". So the infant comes to have an inside and an outside, and a body-scheme. In this way, meanings come to the function of intake and output, moreover, it gradually becomes meaningful to postulate a personal or inner psyche reality for the infant . . . the beginning of a mind as something distinct from the psyche. (Winnicott, 1960, p. 45)

Winnicott talked about his theory of mental development as being dependent on "good enough mothering", deficiencies in which leave the infant likely to be subjected to sudden or chronic states of disconnection, leading to unthinkable anxieties. However, we hypothesise that this concept also applies to cases of highly sensitive or fragile infants who, even with the presence of a "good-enough" mother, are unable to process all the aspects of the mother and cannot see her in her totality, which is frightening and can lead to feelings of confusion and disconnection. These are the babies that are born vulnerable because of their innate sensibilities and deficiencies.

Bion (1962) calls the fear and anxiety that a baby might experience at birth as a "nameless dread". He believed this to be a consequence of the failure of the environment to provide "realisations" to the preconceptions formed by the baby in the womb.

Followers of Melanie Klein's theories (Kleinians) and other researchers of early child development often take for granted that the baby is born with a rudimentary ego capable of integrating perceptions and experiences, or integrating the part objects from the paranoid–schizoid position. Through the case studies we present in the following chapters, it appears that some babies can feel lost or have difficulty finding comfort on the mother's breast. Most infants are born ready to deal with the world and are able to cope with the changes from prenatal to postnatal life, but there are some that are born more immature or fragile or with specific deficiencies.

Bick (1968) hypothesises that

> . . . in its most primitive form, the parts of the personality are felt to have no binding force amongst themselves and must therefore be held together in a way that is experienced by them passively, by the skin functioning as a boundary. But this internal function of containing the parts of the self is dependent initially on the introjection of an external object, experienced as capable of fulfilling this function. Later, identification with this function of the object supersedes the unintegrated state and gives rise to the fantasy of internal and external spaces. Only then the stage is set for the operation of primal splitting and idealization of self and object as described by Melanie Klein. Until the containing functions have been introjected, the concept of a space within the self cannot arise. Introjection, *i.e.* construction of an object in an internal space is therefore impaired. In its absence, the function of projective identification will necessarily continue unabated and all the confusions of identity attending it will be manifest. (p. 484)

Perhaps Freud (1923b) seemed to have been alluding to something similar when he said that "the ego is first and foremost a bodily ego, it is not merely a surface entity, but is itself the projection of a surface" (p. 26).

The conceptualisations from Bick have thrown light on the primitive states I have encountered in the psychotherapy of early autistic behaviours in infants and the distortions in the mother–infant relationship. These infants seem to lack the capacity of ordinary newborns to process experiences with the mother and family, or even to perceive in the ordinary way (as sometimes babies can hear, but are not able to feel the containing object and feel left in an unintegrated state, or see, but in a great deal more detail than normal).

> The need for a containing object would seem, in the infantile unintegrated state, to produce a frantic search for an object—a light, a voice, a smell, or other sensual object—which can hold the attention and thereby be experienced, momentarily at least, as holding the parts of the personality. (Bick, 1968, p. 484)

Bick goes on to explain that when babies are not able to experience the different aspects of the mother in the holding, talking, smelling, and feeding experience, they cannot experience their skin as a boundary between the internal and external world. This creates a disturbance that "can lead to development of a 'second skin' formation through which dependence on the object is replaced by a pseudo-independence" (p. 484).

Psychoanalytic thoughts on pre-autism

Although autism in children has long been studied and given rise to different treatment approaches, the identification of infants showing early signs of developing autistic behaviours is very new. "Infantile autism" was first used in 1943 by Kanner to describe young children with signs of extreme aloneness and lack of emotional and social relatedness. A year later, the term "Asperger's syndrome" was coined to describe a similar group of children, but who do not present with mutism or any serious delay in their language development. Autism is diagnosed in children who display impairments in socialisation, communication, and imagination (Wing & Gould, 1979). What is causing these difficulties is controversial: there are more than 150 different causes cited in scientific papers. What is certain, however, is that psychoanalysis can help us understand and treat the behaviours of autistic children.

I have coined the word "pre-autism" to refer to a state possibly conducive to autistic behaviours, which can be treated by giving special attention to the triggers to those specific defensive/protective ways of adapting to their experience.

Prenatal or postnatal trauma

Some psychoanalytic thinking asks if autism is a response to prenatal trauma (Maiello, 1995, 2001; Piontelli, 1992) or to postnatal and early infancy traumas. Babies might have suffered from an "infantile post-traumatic stress disorder" (Reid, 1999), which could manifest as "reactive autism". It could also be as a result of a traumatic event in the mother's life, which might have left her numb and unresponsive, and the baby, believing that he caused that damage, takes it on as his own (Acquarone, 2009).

I propose that trauma in a baby or young child can go entirely unnoticed. Trauma can be a minor event from an adult point of view, and so it might have to do with the way the child perceives or processes the information. Trauma can result from a series of small events around a child's birth and history. This probably accounts for the high proportion of autism in premature babies. Limperopoulos (2008) has discovered that approximately one in four premature babies will present early autistic behaviours.

Unintegration is also a theme with Mahler (1958). She focuses on the sensorial capacities of the infant, stating that babies seem to receive many sensations from the inside of the body and from the environment. The autistic child cannot integrate such sensory impressions into a meaningful whole or incorporate them into coherently perceived objects.

Bion approaches unintegration from another tack. He uses the term "transform", meaning that impressions are digested by the mind into something useful. He refers to the "process of transformations", which includes beta elements (sensory) into alpha elements (elaborated), as being crucial to the building of a child's mental apparatus.

Such processes allow mothers (and analysts) to attune themselves to the sensory and proto-thoughts of children (and patients), helping them to progress. But what happens if this process becomes complicated by over-exposure to overwhelming tensions or sensations that can be traumatic for the baby? The result is unintegration and difficulty in establishing a sense of self.

It is important to acknowledge that what is traumatic for the baby might be unseen or unknown to the mother/family, as the infant will be hypersensitive in one or a variety of senses or slow to process individual experiences. How do we help these children achieve an inner balance when they feel so easily overwhelmed by physical urges that need to be satisfied and, as a result, they become separated from the continuity of the experience?

Moreover, it is unclear whether the mother–child relationship is a pleasing or painful one. Further complications might follow when we wish to help integration, and so we need to consider the dangers posed to the parents or to the baby before intervening. In all cases, our overriding aim is to achieve a pleasurable and safe relationship between mother and baby.

Unintegration is also the subtext of Ratey's (2001) observation that "autistic children often shun many kinds of physical contact", which has led him to believe that sensory information from the outside world might come at autistic children too fast for their brain to process, and they are simply overwhelmed by surrounding stimuli. As a result, the child "shuts down", or attempts to escape from the stimuli, which is a primitive response and internal mechanism to regulate themselves in the face of a confusing external world. This is further compounded by their inability to pay attention because the sensory information they receive is processed in a fragmented and/or distorted manner due to their primitive information processing. Healthy babies, for example, shift their gaze from the eyes to the nose to the mouth of the mother within a fraction of a second. However, an autistic baby can take up to six seconds just to process the nose. Because of this delay, the baby cannot take in the whole face at once—only parts of it. Consequently, it is easy to miss social cues such as a smile or a frown. Such babies are unable to prioritise the multitude of sensory signals pouring into the brain and they shut down the stimuli in order to avoid further over-sensitisation. In these cases, the early experience imprints on the growing connections of the brain cells, which act as a buffer to generate object relations and thus compromise the mental and emotional capacities further. This might mean that if a mother (or psychotherapist) tries too hard to bring a child with autistic behaviours into a relationship, it could well antagonise them further rather than bring them closer.

Meltzer (1975) understood unintegration to be a passive defence against anxiety. He refers to the abnormally acute perceptual sensitivity and emotional sensibility of some infants. This sensibility could lead to "dismantling". He uses the word "dismantling" in relation to unintegration: a process in which the child focuses on one part of an object rather than on the whole, and so splits the sensory apparatus. Awareness is scattered and the self is "dismantled", and the child is left dominated by primitive emotions, some of which may be painful. Looking at unintegration in this light, it seems that Meltzer conceived a mind that pathological psychogenic autism is related to a passive type of destructive regression and the collapse of previously developed structures. While Meltzer talks about an active process of reversal acting as a passive defence against anxiety, other authors, such as Winnicott, Bick, and Tustin, see it as a natural state at the start of development, one that exists prior to the mother influencing the infant's natural capacities.

While I was working under the supervision of Tustin (1973–1979), we discussed an infant's natural capabilities. My own experience as a mother of two lively newborns and my observation of babies in the nursery of maternity wards, where they were put after birth (until 1975), had shown me that, from birth, infants are active in their calls for attention, communication, and social encounters; furthermore, they help guide their parents to their individual needs and ways. In her last paper presented to the Association of Child Psychotherapists, Tustin (1994) states,

> I should like to think about an error made by many psychoanalytic therapists (including myself), to which I drew attention in a paper published in *The International Journal of Psycho-Analysis* as recently as 1991. In that paper I pointed out that observational studies of babies by workers from many countries – such as Colwyn Trevarthen (1979) in Scotland; Daniel Stern (1983, 1985) in the United States; Miller, Rustin and Shuttleworth in England (1989); Piontelli (1992) in Italy; Perez-Sanchez (1990) in Spain – had shown conclusively that there is not a normal infantile stage of primary autism to which the pathology

> of childhood autism could be a regression. This has been the mainstream hypothesis concerning the aetiology of childhood autism to which many psychoanalytic therapists have subscribed, especially in the United States and in Europe. This flawed hypothesis, based on faulty premises, has been like an invasive virus in that it has permeated and distorted clinical and theoretical formulations. It has perpetuated these distortions and obstructed communication between psychodynamic workers with autistic children. It has also obstructed communication with our Jungian colleagues, for example with Dr Michael Fordham, whose model is of a "primary self" that innately unfolds (or not, as in autism) to reach out. (p. 3)

Tustin concludes the effect of knowing this information:

> Also, if we see autism as a serious developmental aberration it will mean that we will be firmer and less indulgent in our approach to them, than if we see it merely as a regression to a normal stage of infantile development. We will be more active to correct deviant tendencies.
>
> It also means that a sentimental and unduly romantic view of the early mother and child situation will be modified. We will take a more stark view that the craving for a superhuman mother can never be realized and that an important part of early learning is the gradual coming to terms with this frustration and all that this disillusionment implies. We will have a more compassionate attitude towards the mothers of these children. We will also know that we cannot achieve the perfectionism that these children seem to demand of us. (p. 20)

These statements highlight the struggle in the early treatment of this "developmental aberration" and suggest that there is a duty to help these children enter mainstream family life rather than constantly indulge in the two usual justifications: that the behaviour is "organic" and, therefore, incurable; or that the children simply "don't understand" and, therefore, can do what they like. Helping these children can effect change. In the words of the main protagonist in the biopic *Temple Grandin* (by Merritt Johnson and adapted from Grandin's memoirs, *Thinking in Pictures*: *My Life with Autism*):

> My mother refused to believe that I wouldn't speak. And when I learned to speak, she made me go to school. And in school and at home, manners and rules were really important. They were pounded

into me. I was lucky. All these things worked for me. Everyone worked hard to make sure that I was engaged. I mean, they knew I was different, but not less.

The autistic evolution

Bowlby (1969, 1988) formulated the concept of attachment which is the particular tie that infants have with their mother from birth, seen through particular behaviours that promote closeness and protection.

We can imagine that fragile infants (either because of mysterious sensibilities or with a make-up that is not conducive to being able to wait, to hear, or see properly, or process the perceptions in the right order, or integrate them into the same picture) might not allow a secure attachment to take place.

Furthermore, if babies consider the mother a part of themselves, when the mother is with the father or is busy, it might be felt as an abandonment or "tearing away" of a part of themselves and manifesting as trauma. In this case, the social drive seems not to appear as primary, and the nourishing drive becomes split, relinquishing the sense of pleasure in the need for self-preservation. In fact, the pleasure is transformed into panic as the child has lost the object that can give satisfaction. Relating to the mother becomes unpleasant, full of angst, and even persecutory.

We talk about stages of pre-object before object relations become established; however, certain children seem to pick up different characteristics that prelude a different evolution. The child needs to survive but cannot attach to the mother, and neither can he find rest, peace, or motivation in her care. On the contrary, filled with different and changing perceptions, the child feels increasingly terrified, as there is no external person that can hold the experience (as a protective adult) or a primitive ego in himself that is capable of maintaining a link with the external world or with a containing mother in an active effort to find sense. Perceptual fragments of all sorts appear—ever changing and ever present—and so the child seeks out a beam of light upon which to focus, as this feels more stable than the living mother or her breast.

If we follow this line of thought, we can understand the negative mirroring from the mother, and the baby not finding overall containment for his unbearable feelings. As Sartre says in *No Exit* (1955), "Hell is other people".

The internal occupants of the mother's mind are too many and mixed with the baby's own internal turmoil from which the infant cannot escape; unless they keep remembering, bringing back pleasurable experiences, their eyes can close or look into the air, perhaps at a simple object or at the shades of light, the effect of a breeze, or other things we cannot imagine but are only seen by the child who has a different perception of what is around us. They can become fixated on a simple pattern, perhaps because they see vibrations in the markings or modifications that are not visible to our simple eyes. Cushioned by their fantasies, they escape into these autistic spaces.

The capacity to be alone

It is important to see how babies in the autistic evolution prefer to be alone. This is not because they are internally in the presence of the mother (Winnicott, 1958) or have an internalised mother that accompanies them, but because they do not trust anyone; they are imagining being back in the womb or are taking themselves elsewhere so that they do not have to face the aggravation of dealing with people, or, more specifically, the mother. Children in the autistic evolution do not necessarily sleep all the time, but are entertained by their hands, or the material of their blanket, or the frills of the curtain.

All of this is very difficult to decipher when it comes to treatment, as treatment in the autistic evolution belongs to a world of different dimensions, space, and time.

Psychoanalytic setting

To decipher the world of the baby with pre-autism and to understand the impact of the interpersonal relationships within the family, we need a laboratory for studying these personal relationships. What better place than a consulting room specially designed for babies: a warm, calm, pale room; a white blanket on the carpet; simple toys to play with. Everyone is seated at the same level: often the floor, but sometimes on low tables and chairs. Here, there is a space and a time to observe. Here, we can listen to the young child and the parents, both together and individually.

We use toys to engage and assess the child's sensitivities, likes and dislikes, their sense of pleasure and delight. These include: feathers, colourful and plain teethers, wooden spoons and blocks, little figures, balls of different sizes and textures, fairies made out of gauze, pieces of fabric with different textures and patterns, a family of large cuddly teddy bears, and household items. The "infant" in each member of the family is explored, and we explain the dynamics occurring between them, in relation to each other, and in relation to us therapists.

Art materials and sand trays are also available. Art enables them to express and explore their inner world through metaphor. It gives them the opportunity to map their expectations and disappointments, to explore their dreams, develop their imaginations and to practise new behaviours. Creative work can present a new perspective from which to see oneself, learn about oneself, and bring about change.

Psychoanalytic method

During every consultation, the psychotherapist focuses on the interactions between all those present (for example, the parent, child, and psychotherapist), as habitual patterns of relating will be reproduced in order to understand their subtlety and strength. There could be dynamics that are loving, supportive, and healthy, or, conversely, contorted, vicious, and unhelpful. They are linked to each family member's history of experiences. Psychoanalysis has learnt to look into the present dynamics to see how feelings and experiences express themselves and to identify which patterns do not belong to the present or to the persons in question. This is called transference: in the psychotherapist, the patient's experiences from the past are relived and re-enacted. Through analysis and understanding, these experiences become transformed in a more digestible way, and the mother and baby are able to move on emotionally, step by step.

The consultant is a human being as well, and is always affected by the way the mother and baby expose their difficulties. The unravelling of what is happening is a delicate and sensitive skill that makes the consultant react, bringing back memories of similar experiences and feelings. The family learns new patterns of relating, and the psychotherapist learns new things about them. The reactions produced by the family in the psychotherapist is another instrument that is helpful in understanding their deeper, unknown conflicts. The psychotherapist's reactions, feelings, and thoughts are charged with the patient's own fantasies, experiences, desires, and needs. The technical term for this is "countertransference". Countertransference enables an understanding of the continuous influence of unconscious feelings, hopes, and worries within the family and of the resulting entrenched behaviours. Once there is knowledge and awareness, it is possible to bring about change. It is even more important when the subject is a baby or non-verbal child who cannot be understood by the family and is brought to us by parents in despair.

An illustration of transference and countertransference

Giacomo was two months old when he came to see us with his mother. She was concerned that he slept too much and that when he was awake, he appeared "cut off" and did not look at her. Her husband refused to come to the appointment, believing that help was not necessary. The mother had mentioned, when requesting the appointment, that she had had a complicated delivery and spent time in intensive care.

On arrival, the mother and baby were welcomed. The baby was sleeping with half-closed eyes and the mother told us about his continual sleep and the fact that he never looked at her. When she started telling me, in a very flat tone of voice, about the birth, of a terrible infection and thrombosis after an emergency C-section, of being terrified when wheeled from the theatre to intensive care, and of feeling "trapped between monitors", the baby moved and grunted.

While the mother talked, I was aware of experiencing extremely strong emotions. I felt, in the transference, a terror. It seemed as if the mother was overwhelmed by the events of the traumatic birth and her fear that she very nearly died. This fear seemed to be so powerful that the mother had shut down into a depressed state to avoid it. While very engaged in her story, I began to wonder if it was time for the session to end, even though it had barely started. I wondered if the wish to be elsewhere was a countertransference reaction: it was as if I wanted to escape the dread in the room. I wondered whether the desire to escape was projected to me by the baby or the mother. I wondered if the baby needed to escape, to shut down in order to avoid feeling suffocated by his mother's terror. Beneath the terror, I felt an immense sadness.

The mother picked up Giacomo, half sleeping and grimacing with his hand spread out in front of him. I started talking to the baby in a gentle voice, saying that he liked to go away and come back, and talking about the horrible things that had happened to him. He opened his eyes and looked directly at me; I smiled and he smiled back. The mother immediately said that he never did that with her. I suggested that from what she was telling me and from my observation of her baby waking to show me his discomfort, I thought that they were both emotionally traumatised by the events of the first fortnight after the birth. I mentioned, too, that they had not been able to find each other yet; that both of them were terrified of what the present holds.

The mother started crying and so did the baby. The mother dried her tears and said that the baby had never cried before either; she quickly stuffed his dummy in his mouth, not letting him cry. I mentioned that perhaps they both needed to cry together, to share a very frightening time. The mother stood up and cradled the baby, without looking at him. I felt an underlying feeling of anger, and wondered if it was fury that was stopping the mother being able to look at her son. I mentioned her hate and anger towards the baby, that she might be blaming her near-death experience on him. She admitted that although she knew it was not his fault, she felt angry because all her illusions about having a natural birth had been shattered. I talked a little about how, while she was sharing her agony with her husband and parents, the baby had been in the hands of the nurses and the new external world had not been held and explained to him. The noises from the monitors, the anguish around him, and all his new sensations had been left undigested and had led to a "blockage" in being able to relate to her. The mother said that it was true; that she did not realise he might have felt anything, that it could have affected him, too. The baby stopped crying and looked at her for a moment. Her shoulders dropped with relief. It was an extremely emotional moment.

This description from my first session with Giacomo shows the degree of dissociation already in place in the baby; how, not having had his overwhelmed feelings contained by his mother (due to her being overwhelmed herself), he had retreated into himself. Creating a space in which the mother could reflect on the childbirth experience that had been too traumatic to be held in the present allowed her to start experimenting with, and finding out about, the baby. In turn, Giacomo showed curiosity about this new container mother—the mother he recognised from pregnancy. Babies communicate their needs and desires from birth (Trevarthen, 1979) and from their prenatal life (Piontelli, 1992), and there is transference of experiences from birth. Giacomo's mother needed help containing her own trauma, grief, anger, and terror before she could be able to do the same for her son.

About identification and projective identification

Another important concept that we use from psychoanalysis is the process of identification: that is, feeling similar to someone else. This requires a sense of space between the child and other people. Children develop the ability to identify with others based on their understanding of empathy. Empathy is important in "knowing others", in the so-called "theory of mind", as discussed in Cathy Urwin's paper given at the 1993 ACP study weekend.

In "adhesive-at-oneness", the child feels the same as someone else and is "stuck" to them as to an inanimate object. This helps them to feel that they exist. It is about survival, or "going on being", as Winnicott so aptly describes it. It can, however, prevent the development of identification, as adhesive-at-oneness does not allow the space for awareness of the other to grow. In autistic children, we can say that the normal oscillation between the state of "at-oneness" (Mitrani, 2001) (which fosters empathy) and an awareness of separateness becomes frozen into an abnormal, perpetually rigid state of adhesive-at-oneness (which prevents empathy). The child is almost "frozen stiff" with terror. Empathy, identification, and, indeed, all psychological developments associated with the processes of introjection and projection, such as "bonding", and the experiences of "psychic birth" and "individuation", are prevented. The child does not feel, speak to, or respond to other people.

When mother and baby come to the consultations, even though they are two separate people, they are in a state of symbiosis and oneness. This difficulty is transferred to the present and to the psychotherapist: countertransference occurs. Their past and present difficulties are transferred in their body language, narratives, and memories.

We allow space for each one of them to communicate in whatever form it takes, and we react with our minds and bodies to their messages. We let mother and baby reveal in their body language and memories part of themselves. Unaware of many processes happening, the therapist will identify with either of these persons as a protection or as a disconnection, and, with hindsight, will be able to understand more deeply what they are going through.

Keeping in mind the individuality of the psychotherapist, the exploration of her ways of feeling will be through another mechanism of "projective identification", by which we can put ourselves in place of internal aspects of the person. What the psychotherapist often finds is a process of difficulty in differentiation between the infant and some internal parts of the mother; the separation implies pain, and the separateness is difficult to achieve. Self-soothing mechanisms appear through exacerbating their sensuality. The infant becomes identified in an adhesive way, to continue the "one-ness" with his mother and, thereby, avoiding the anxiety and all the terrors mentioned by Winnicott, Meltzer, Mahler, Bick, and Tustin.

Separation: the road to recognition and gratitude

From the state of "one-ness", the infant needs to be able to recognise the mother, which, in turn, comes from the capacity to separate from her. Recognition appears when the child sees the mother as fulfilling his needs. From this ability to separate, a transitional space will be created that will allow for the inclusion of a third person—the father—and relationships will become richer and serve as a model for future relationships. Recognition of the father makes the child take on board the language of the community as a cultural requirement, with repression as an inevitable cost (Lacan, 1966).

Eye contact and gestural communications will develop from the intentional imitation towards their identification. Rhode (2005) mentions that

> . . . it seems that the position of the child relative to the mother's internal object is an expression of the Oedipal constellation in relation to eye contact, on a very primitive level that concerns the child's experience of existing. I have argued that these Oedipal conditions must be

> in place for developmental imitation and introjection to go ahead. They must also be in place, I believe, to allow for the much more sophisticated shifts in identification and point of view which are implied by Britton's work on the third position (Britton, 1989, 1998) and by Hobson's Relatedness Triangle, which addresses the relationship between the infant's attitude towards the world, the other, and the other's attitude towards the world (Hobson, 2002: 107).

According to Tustin (1990), the failure of children with autism to develop empathy might be traced to an insufficiently robust sense of self: putting themselves in someone else's shoes might feel like losing any sense of who they are.

We consider further the implications of establishing a relationship between three people, not only for emotional development, but also for language development and the capacity to communicate between the parties. We consider how successful triangular relationships include the "loss" of the mother, as well as the "use" of the mother, and the father, in enabling emotional experience to become thought (Bion, 1962). Urwin (2002) emphasises the significance of the survival and development of the self in achieving separation. She believes that it is "the presence of a containing object which makes possible the survival and development of the child's sense of self and its verbal evolution" (p. 76).

Summary: linking our experience

The "autistic evolution" develops in fragile infants who feel traumatised by their experience of the world. This trauma may have many roots: for example, in their senses, their inability to produce positive experiences, or to regulate their emotions, or the many other reasons that are not necessarily visible to the observer. Their pathological evolution draws them to self-comforting behaviours, often related to the mouth: perhaps jamming a fist into it to suck on or bite. With the mouth used in this self-comforting way, it is difficult for the child to use it for smiling back at others or for eating well and with others. The mouth then becomes perverted and transformed into a tool of habitual sadomasochism. These fragile infants are driven to panic and rage at not finding peace and contentment; they become both overexcited and omnipotent, creating yet another series of habits or stereotypical behaviours that become tyrannical and effective with the parents.

Following these observations, it is not surprising that parents can become caught up in the fear–protection cycle and go to great lengths to control the persecutory frustrations their child brings out in them. Thousands of excuses appear to justify their care for the "dictator" installed in their home and lives. All the rules or principles disappear, to accommodate the loved child who is really frightening to them.

Psychoanalytic understanding has proved to be an effective approach to the complex condition of pre-autism, as every member of the family becomes a part of a system in which there is involvement, and even denial. This is the reason why treatment is provided to each family member, as well as to the family as a whole. The family learns to be with, observe, think about, and reflect upon the young child. They consider their ways of coping with their baby and how he or she affects them.

Early psychoanalytic intervention treatments have encountered much controversy given the lack of information surrounding this way of working. However, results are showing that the treatments lead to a long-term steady improvement in communication, socialisation, and imagination skills. It is clear that after early psychoanalytic intervention, and the emotional integration that it brings about, fragile babies become able to feel love for the mother and other people, to express that love, and, further, to understand feelings in both themselves and others. What is left of the autistic behaviours after treatment are personal characteristics such as extreme sensitivity, shyness, or a poetic nature. While there might always be a tendency to retreat at times of stress, life becomes lived within the family, not from the sidelines.

CHAPTER THREE

Neurobiological development and autistic behaviours

Isabel Jimenez Acquarone and Dominique Hawksley

The neurobiological basis of our approach

Our neurobiological make-up influences our state of mind and our behaviour, as there is a biological basis to, and direct interplay between, the processes that occur and our perceptions and corresponding emotions. Humans are able to reflect on, and talk about, their emotions, as well as experience awareness of the emotions of others. Such experiences add to and enrich our memory, providing an internal database that can later be used in different situations.

To gain an understanding of how neurobiological structures affect autistic behaviours, it is first important to look briefly at the neurobiology of normal development, at the brain's composition, communication, and growth. To obtain an insight into how our treatment can influence brain development, it is necessary to look in more detail at the possible disruptions that might hinder normal brain development.

What is essential to take into account is that two-thirds of brain development occurs within the first two years of life; therefore, the earlier we are able to diagnose, intervene, and treat disruptions to normal communication, the less damage there will be to the child, the child–parent relationship, and corresponding neurological systems (Schore, 1994). Research over the past decade has clearly illustrated the critical periods of brain development in an infant's life and confirms the value of early intervention.

The American neuroscientist Paul Maclean put forward the evolutionary model for understanding brain development by dividing the human brain into three distinct regions, which initially he named reptilian, mammalian, and human/rational regions. He called this the triune brain (Figure 3.1). Later, the three regions were changed to reptilian, limbic, and neocortex regions (as not only humans but also other higher mammals were shown to have some, if not all, of the features of this region).

The reptilian part of the brain evolved around 300 million years ago, and includes the brain stem, cerebellum, and vagus nerve. Its function is directly related to survival, such as the fight or flight response, and to control behaviours required for sustaining life, including circulation, breathing, hunger, digestion, body temperature, and balance. Key parts of the brain stem include the cerebellum and the vagus nerve. The cerebellum plays a key role in co-ordination, motor planning, and anticipation and, as we reveal below, develops differently in children with autism. The vagus nerve travels from the brain stem around the body, taking with it commands to regulate the function of the major organs, including the heart and lungs.

The mammalian brain, also known as the limbic system or the "emotional brain", evolved around 200 million years ago and is similar

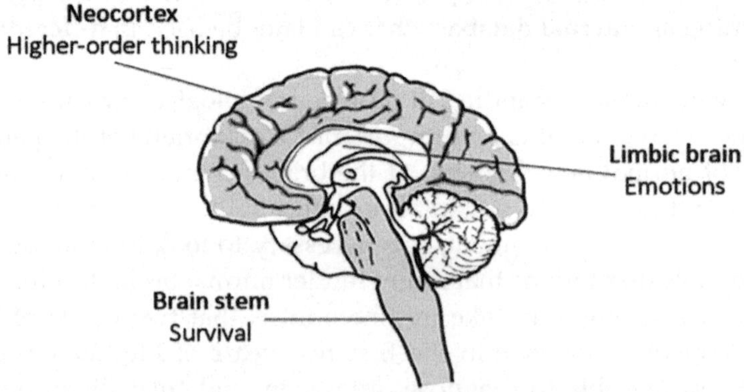

Figure 3.1. The triune brain.

to that found in other mammals (Reep et al., 2007). The limbic system triggers strong emotions, which need to be managed by the neocortex in order to prevent the emotions from becoming too overwhelming. Seven genetically engrained emotional systems have been identified via experimentation on rats (Panksepp, 1998). These emotional systems are: rage, fear, separation distress, seeking (the urge to explore), care, play, and lust (adults only).

As well as triggering strong emotions, the limbic system also has a role in helping control fight or flight responses. Key parts of the limbic system include the corpus callosum, the amygdala, and the hippocampus (Figure 3.2).

The amygdala is an alarm system that gives an emotional meaning to what is happening and warns other parts of the brain to initiate an appropriate response, which is calmed by higher brain activity. The corpus callosum links the right and left hemispheres of the brain and has a key role in physical and motor co-ordination, as well as organising and anticipating events. The hippocampus is a structure vital to memory. Here, all short-term memories are stored and sorted into which ones will be used for long-term memory retention.

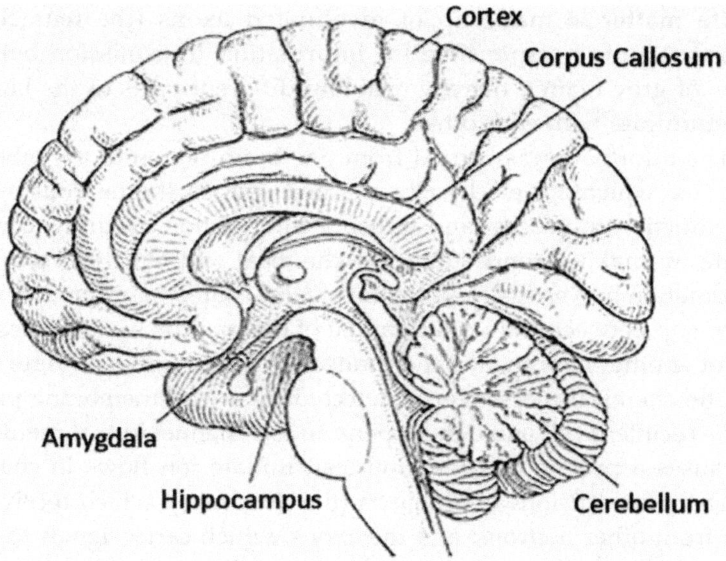

Figure 3.2. The hippocampus and amygdala of the limbic system.

The rational/human brain evolved around 200,000 years ago. It is known as the neocortex rather than the human brain, as not only humans but other higher mammals have some, if not all, of the features of this region. The functions of the neocortex include problem solving, sense making, and self-awareness. Vital to these functions is the role of the frontal lobes. These enable individuals to process sensations, feelings, and thoughts, rather than just experiencing them. They provide the capability to experience and process a subtle range of emotional responses (much more so than the limbic system). The neocortex plays an important role in the development of such skills as self-reflection, emotional regulation, and reasoning. Other vital parts include the parietal cortex, which registers and interprets body sensations, touch, and temperature, and the occipital lobe, which is the brain's visual processing centre.

Brain structure and communication

The brain is composed of grey matter and white matter. Grey matter is mainly found in the cortex and is densely packed with connected neurons (nerve cell bodies) responsible for information processing. White matter is made up of myelinated axons (the tentacles of neurons) and is responsible for information transmission between areas of grey matter, thereby enabling different parts of the brain to communicate with each other.

The information is carried from one brain region to the other via neurons, which are electrically charged cells in the nervous system that function to process and transmit information. Neurons communicate by making connections via chemical and electrical synapses. Information moves easily along the myelin-coated neurons. A synapse is the gap between the axon terminal of one neuron and the receiving cell of another neuron, and the connection made across it (Figure 3.3).

The chemical messenger is detected by a transmembrane protein in the recipient cell and either opens an ion channel in that membrane or causes a protein cascade. Both can initiate ion flows in channels along the protrusions of a neuron (the dendrites), which receive signals from other neurons, and the axons, which carry signals to other neurons. The longer axons are usually myelinated, which allows for faster message transmission.

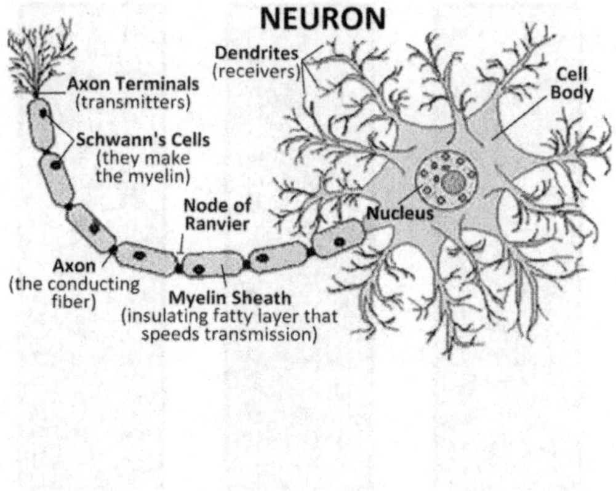

Figure 3.3a. Neuron.

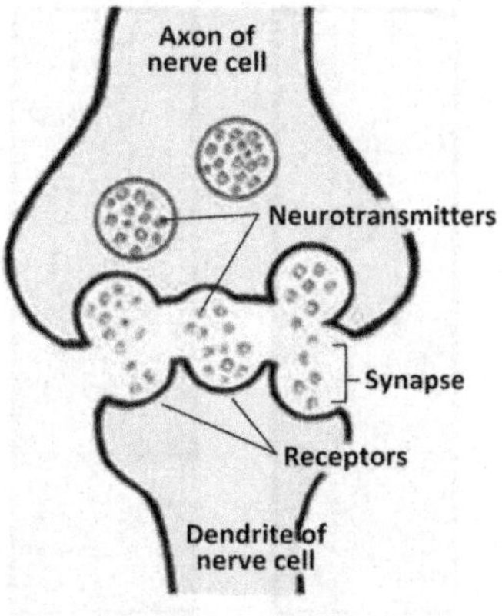

Figure 3.3b. Synapse.

Brain connections: the growth of potential

At birth, an infant has approximately 200 billion neurons (Sunderland, 2006). These neurons are, however, immature, their axons not yet sheathed in myelin, which means that signals cannot pass from one axon to another and, therefore, the brain cannot easily form connections. The most active areas of the brain in a newborn are those related to bodily regulation (based in the brain stem), sensation (the thalamus), and movement (the cerebellum). Myelination occurs as the baby becomes older, bringing areas of the infant's brain "online" by creating new connections across the gaps (synapses) between neurons.

After birth, the parietal cortex, which registers and interprets bodily sensations, touch, and temperature, becomes the most active part of the brain. By six months, early connections are being made from the limbic system to the frontal lobes; however, these are still immature. By one year, more robust connections are being made within the limbic system. The density of connections physically changes the composition of the brain as the areas of grey matter increase.

Scans of the brain at birth, at three months, and at two years reveal the increasing density and complexity of the connections between the neurons. In the first year of life, each neuron forms connections across about 15,000 synapses. By the end of the second year, the brain will have formed 1,000 trillion connections (Acquarone, 2007) (Figure 3.4).

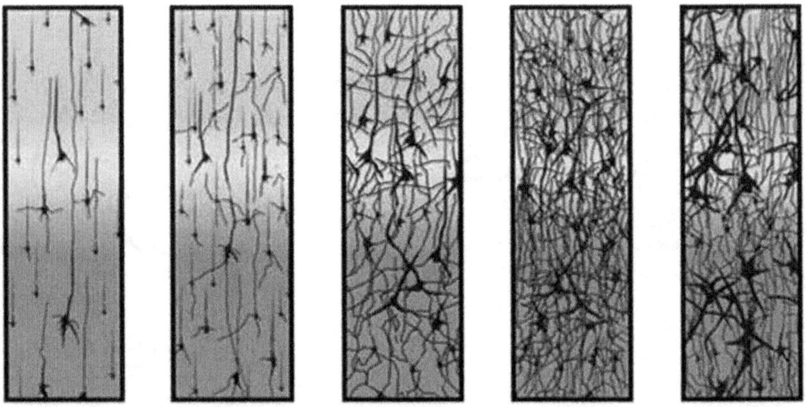

Figure 3.4. Neuron connections from newborn to adult.

Brain chemistry

The neurons and synapses in the brain are activated by the body's natural chemicals and hormones, which are also influenced in relationship to others.

First, there are the "feel good" chemicals: endorphins, such as oxytocin and opiodes. Oxytocin is released at birth to help the mother and baby bond, while opiodes are released through positive touch. Therefore, the infant who receives loving, tactile, comforting touch will be calmer and more relaxed, although comfort reduces the levels of acetylcholine in the brain. Acetylcholine is a neurotransmitter that assists learning, yet is potentially toxic when released in higher levels triggered by uncomforted separation distress.

At the other end of the spectrum is cortisol, a stress chemical released in reaction to fear. Cortisol helps promote energy efficiency in stressful situations; however, prolonged high levels of cortisol can cause cell death and impair immune function.

Brain development

Paralleling the growth of the ability to make connections is the pruning back of those connections that are rarely or never used. This "clean-up" phase must begin in order for the brain to wire up efficiently. Each neuron may prune up to 10,000 connections if not needed or not used. The pruning process, known as apoptosis, prevents the brain from literally becoming overstuffed with its own cells (Carter, 1998). Early events determine which circuits in the brain will be reinforced and retained and which will be pruned. New connections can, in fact, be formed at any time during life, whenever completely new situations demand it, but never with the same ease as in the early years.

Once connections have been severed, the unconnected cell dies. The number of brain cells we have decreases dramatically over time: from 200 billion at birth, to 120 billion at age one, 110 billion at age fifteen, 100 billion at thirty-five, and 95 billion at seventy-five (Sunderland, 2006). Ninety per cent of brain growth occurs during the first five years of life when millions of connections are formed, unformed, and reformed. Connections are made in direct response to the infant's experience of the world, in particular their experience of forming relationships with others.

In 1997, Chiron and colleagues found that there was right hemispheric predominance in infants up until three years of age. Asymmetry shifts to the left after this time; this shift follows the emergence of functions that were initially localised on the right, but later on the left hemisphere (i.e., visual, spatial, and, later, language abilities). The emotional, or affective, brain, which is located on the right hemisphere, slowly becomes connected to the left hemisphere, which involves rational and logical thought. While initial communication is through gesture, mirroring, touch, and vocalisation, it is the infant's "language" of mimicry, rhythm, and intonation that is the precursor to the verbal language that later develops and is located on the left hemisphere. This hemispheric distribution directly affects the neural, hormonal, and nervous systems and is the neurobiological basis of intersubjectivity.

Infants and their mammalian brain (limbic system)

While strong connections have yet to be made to the rational brain (neocortex), the mammalian brain (limbic system) is in control in infants. Central to the mammalian brain is the amygdala, the alarm system that gives an emotional meaning to what is happening and sends a signal to other parts of the brain to initiate an appropriate response. The amygdala is triggered by the emotional circuits within the limbic system and can be calmed by higher brain activity from the neocortex.

The power of the amygdala is not restricted to infants. In adulthood, for example, the amygdala can be triggered when a sudden movement is caught out of the corner of the eye. This immediately results in increased anxiety, raised heartbeat, and the release of cortisol. However, adults are able to use their neocortex, or "thinking brain", to reason with the situation and calm themselves down; the amygdala is quietened, calming chemicals are released, and the autonomic nervous system (which controls the internal organs, such as the heart, stomach, and intestines) is regulated. When the amygdala is triggered in infants—for example, by the separation distress felt on awakening in an empty room—they are unable to apply higher reasoning to the situation and so cry out for help to be calmed down.

The ability to think and soothe oneself

Infants are not able to control powerful emotions as the axons that connect the neocortex to the limbic system have yet to grow. "The young brain is . . . essentially unbalanced – the immature cortex no match for the powerful amygdala" (Carter, 1998, p. 19). As an infant's brain is underdeveloped, they need another person to think and reason for them and thus regulate their reactions to distress. By attuning to their infant's anxiety, and by responding with love and care, primary carers are able to teach their child how to begin to recognise and regulate their own uncomfortable feelings.

Attachment, attunement, and positive emotions

There is an evolutionary need and neurobiological basis for positive experience and patterns of relating which facilitate the connection of neurons and production of neural links, which is the basis for cognitive and emotional intelligence. Attachment, attunement, and positive emotions promote the release of the bonding hormones oxytocin and vasopressin, both of which are the neuroendocrine substrates for love (Panksepp, 1998). These "feel-good" hormones are released when social bonding behaviours occur, such as kisses and cuddles. The process of soothing a distressed child activates their vagus nerve, which, in turn, regulates the function of the major organs, rebalancing the autonomic nervous system's disruptions to the child's heart rate, digestion, breathing, and the immune system which had been caused by stress.

The function of joy, play, and passion

The expression of joy comes when there is connection between a need and a satisfaction; when there is an awareness of feeling good, and being able to relax and trust. When the baby is able to recognise others, feels loved, and is helped to understand what is happening around him, whether it is inside or outside of the body, he feels joy and excitement.

Play has its own distinctive neural motivational system and requires stimulation from another person or a carer. This is why social isolation has devastating effects on play, as infants become despondent and depressive, and, when reunited with the carer, engage in little play. Positive emotion and affective regulation are linked to those moments when parents are attuned to their infant's states. In the same way, the infant mirrors the parents' states and is attuned to them. This attunement is necessary and clearly beneficial for healthy relationships to develop and it also enables the infant to learn how to regulate themselves to their surroundings and adjust to new experiences (Table 3.1).

A healthy child's brain and a neglected child's brain

Figure 3.5 depicts, on the left, a PET scan showing the brain of a normal child, with regions of high (dark grey) and low (black) activity. The temporal lobes (top), which regulate emotions and receive and integrate inputs from the senses, show high activity, having become "wired" through positive early childhood experiences. The PET scan on the right shows the brain of a Romanian orphan who was

Table 3.1. The effects of having or lacking emotional attunement.

With emotional attunement	Without emotional attunement
There is positive social interaction—attunement, "the dance" (Trevarthen & Hubley, 1978; Stern, 1985)	There is a mismatched "dance"
Decreases hypothalamic pituitary adrenaline (HPA) reactivity, which modulates the autonomic nervous system function	Gross misattunement produces the opposite effect, resulting in high levels of HPA activity
Activates vagus nerve, which promotes infant's ability to self-calm	Dysregulation of autonomic nervous system—neurologically and physically unable to regulate themselves
Good relationships reduce experience of anxiety, and produce a sense of calm and relaxation	Negative interactions result in high levels of agitation and anxiety and lack of self-soothing mechanisms
Attunement and moments of misattunement are necessary for healthy interaction	The lack of release of opiodes in infants exposes them more readily to feelings of anxiety and panic

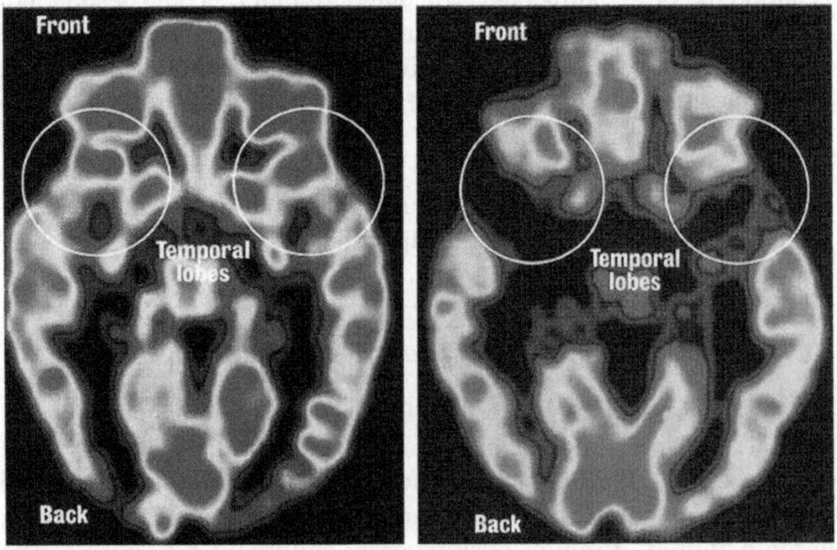

Figure 3.5. How the lack of a loving relationship affects brain development.

institutionalised shortly after birth. Here, the temporal lobes are almost completely inactive due to the effects of severe neglect and deprivation of physical contact. Such children suffer emotional and cognitive problems. While this comparison is an extreme illustration, it clearly highlights the value and importance of early intervention.

Mirror neurons: the neurobiology of empathy

In 1991, the Italian neurobiologist Giacomo Rizzolatti discovered that the same parts of the brain were activated when both observing and performing an action. While carrying out an experiment on primates, Rizzolatti noted that when one monkey picked up an apple and ate it, the area of the brain that was "fired up" was mirrored in the brain of another monkey who simply observed the action.

The neurons that do this are known as "mirror neurons" (Rizzolatti & Fabbri-Destro, 2010) (Figure 3.6). The same neural brain activity occurring implies that the emotion accompanying the action is also mirrored. Observing and mimicking another is the basis for empathy and the ability to relate to another's state.

The basis of empathy in early relationships

The American neuropsychologist Allan Schore (1994) argues that we place too much importance on mirror neurons and that what is important and necessary in an infant's life is positive relating, affective attunement, and containment through the modulation of affect. These

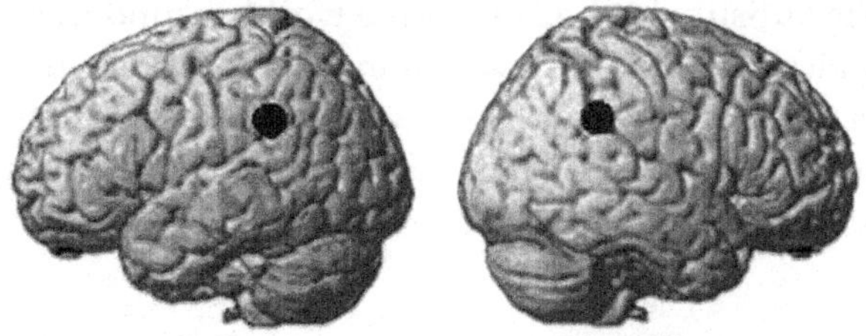

Figure 3.6. Mirror neurons.

behaviours lead to enriched neural networks, neural activity, and a procedural memory, which is later accessed by the infant. Procedural memory is linked to the interpersonal know-how of relationships and social relating, both of which are located in the right hemisphere of the brain. Such enriched attunement facilitates the link-up of the right and left hemispheres of the brain and integration of information into the cortex, which leads to the reflective function of lived experiences.

Neurobiological research seems to be validating our early findings that healthy bonds and healthy brains depend on quality relationships with the primary carers (usually parents) and on the consequent connections of neurons in the brain.

Since two-thirds of brain development occurs within the first two years of life, the earlier we can find and treat disruptions to "normal" communication, the less damage there will be to the child, the child–parent relationship, and the corresponding neurological system (Schore, 1994).

The autistic brain and how it differs

In early life, while nerve cell connections in the brain are rapidly taking place, large-scale pruning of unused cells is also occurring. At this stage, early traumas can result in secondary brain damage, while avoidant behaviours can become habits etched too deeply into the neurological pathways. The pre-autistic baby's subsequent experiences are layered on top of this first experience, and being excessively quiet or avoidant can quickly become not only a way of life, but also the only way that the growing baby knows and needs in order to feel safe.

Through their behaviour, we are able to observe the different ways in which the autistic child relates to the world around them. However, neurobiological research is now making it possible for us to see these differences on a neural level. There are significant differences in brain size, in the frontal lobes, corpus callosum, amygdala, hippocampus, and cerebellum, as well as in the functioning of the mirror neurons.

Size differences

An autistic child's head starts out smaller than average but then goes through a period of explosive growth, with severe cases growing the fastest. Studies based on magnetic resonance imaging (MRI) and basic tape-measure readings, by Courchesne and colleagues (2011), demonstrate that while children with autism are born with ordinary sized brains, they experience a rapid expansion by the age of two years, particularly in the frontal lobes, which are dedicated to logical reasoning. Perhaps these children were born with the potential to develop normally, but the lack of processing and synchronisation of the new experiences led to overstimulation and abnormal expansion of the brain size. Courchesne found that by the time autistic children are four years old, their brain size is that of a normal thirteen-year-old due to the excess connections and liquid.

Neural differences

Uddin and colleagues (2013) used a standard EEG test to compare the resting-state brain activity of children with autism to that of similarly aged youngsters without the developmental disorder. The autistic children showed a distinctive hyperconnectivity in a range of neural networks having an impact on many areas of development, including social and interpersonal cognition, episodic memory, speech perception, and motor control. The hyperconnectivity within networks results in limited connectivity between networks.

> The functional implications of hyperconnectivity within brain networks are far-reaching. If enhanced within-network connectivity is characteristic of autism, this may limit dynamic interactions among networks, which are necessary for successful navigation of complex real-world scenarios. Thus, we speculate that network isolation may account for some of the core symptoms of ASD, namely, difficulty with adapting to change, restrictive and repetitive behaviour, and increased sensitivity to visual, auditory, and tactile stimuli. (Uddin et al., 2013, p. 872)

Frontal lobes

Research (Carper & Courchesne, 2005) has found that autistic individuals have enlarged frontal lobes, due to an excess of white matter and an excess of connector axons, yet far fewer information-processing cells. Information can be received and sent around the brain but less sense can be made of the information itself. There are too many "local" connections between local brain areas and too few long-distance connections between different brain regions. As a result, information is captured but not processed in a manner that the individual can make sense of. While head size is larger, cognitive functioning is reduced.

Research shows that while autistic subjects show activity only in the media parietal region of the brain when processing familiar faces (Figure 3.7), non-autistic subjects used both medial frontal and parietal regions (Adolphs, 2001).

Corpus callosum

In autistic individuals, the corpus callosum is undersized (Frazier et al., 2012; Paul et al., 2014), which means that activity across hemispheres and diverse areas in the brain is poorly co-ordinated. Such poor co-ordination coupled with few long-distance connections results in a lack of synchronisation of information. Rather than the separate neural messages combining to make sense, like the different instruments in an orchestra, they sound discordant, like the pre-performance warm-up. In addition, there are delays in facial processing (Dawson et al., 2005), and so, rather than an autistic child seeing the full view of a face, they receive a muddle of differing aspects.

The amygdala

The amygdala is like an alarm system in the brain. In autistic infants, it is constantly being set off, like an oversensitive car alarm, hence its enlarged size (Mills Schumann et al., 2009). The amygdala is activated

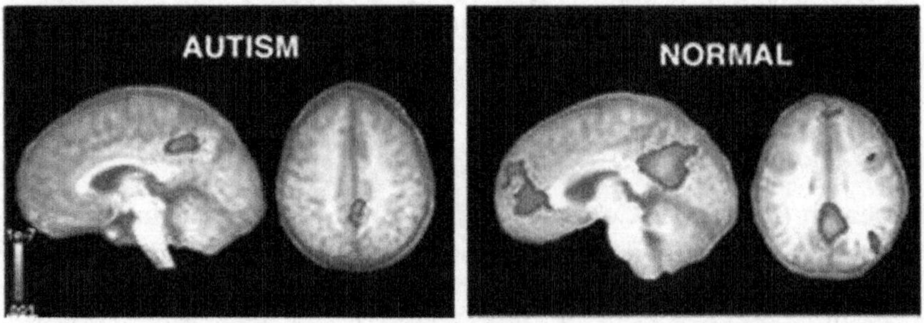

Figure 3.7. Media parietal region of the brain when processing familiar faces.

when looking at faces, as if perceiving whether or not the person presents a threat. The inability of autistic children to recognise faces (Adolphs, 2001; Schultz, 2005) is one possible reason for the continuous overstimulation of the amygdala, leading to its enlarged size. Research has shown that there are fewer cells in the amygdala of children and adults with autism. It is not known if this is a cause of emotional communication difficulties or due to a response to reduced social emotional interactions (Kleinhans et al., 2010).

Mirror neurons

The mirror neuron system is vital in the execution and observation of actions; however, these neurons are also involved in higher cognitive processes, such as language acquisition, and being able to imitate and learn from others (Oberman et al., 2005). Mirror neurons are vital for decoding other people's intentions and for being able to empathise with others. Autistic individuals have a deficit in the mirror mechanism, and so are unable to "decode" other people's movements or decipher the intention behind an action, which also explains the great difficulty they have in feeling empathy for others (Rizzolatti & Fabbri-Destro, 2010).

The hippocampus

The hippocampus is about ten per cent larger than usual in autistic individuals (Munson et al., 2006). This area is vital to memory and it is possible that the enlarged state is a result of autistic children relying on memory to interpret situations that other children process elsewhere in the brain. There is a strong superimposition of memory and wiring from the limbic system and amygdala directly to the hippocampus that almost bypasses the frontal lobes, which is responsible for reasoning and facial recognition. It is the relay to the frontal lobes and neocortex that allows the reasoning necessary in order to think rationally, reach a new perspective, regulate themselves, control the amygdala, and release calming neurotransmitters and opiodes (Lam, et al., 2006).

The connection between the amygdala, the frontal lobes, and the hippocampus is what regulates the autonomic nervous system (Kalat, 1995) (Figure 3.8). Without thought and a sense of calm, the infant's

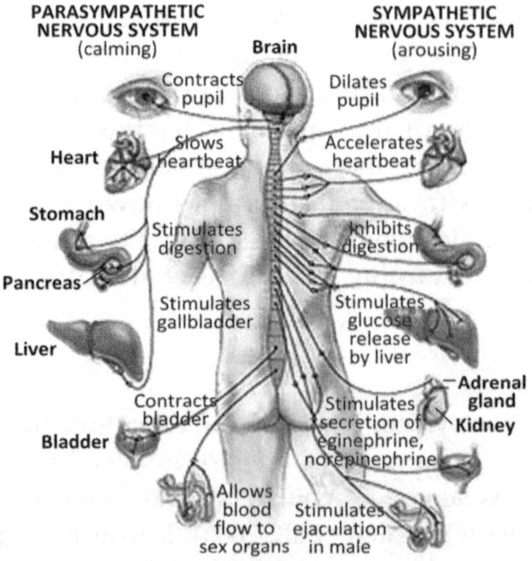

Figure 3.8. Autonomic nervous system regulation.

brain is permanently on a state of alert with high toxic levels of cortisol continuously reinforcing the perceived threat (Schore, 2001b). The constant firing of the threat alarm system evermore increases the infant's sensitivity; this is due to the properties of the neurons, which need less and less of a stimulus to fire (known as long-term potentiation). This leads to an internal state of tension that is evoked with increasing frequency, leading to the autonomic nervous system becoming unbalanced (Kalat, 1995). The autonomous nervous system is composed of the sympathetic nervous system and parasympathetic nervous system, which are in continuous interplay and in balance. However, in autistic individuals, the sympathetic system predominates over the parasympathetic, which then becomes impaired. This was confirmed by Xue Ming et al. (2005), who found a significant link between autism and the suppression of the parasympathetic nervous system.

How the capacity to think develops

The developing mind uses the states [of affect] of an attachment figure in order to help organize the operation of their own states [of love] (Siegel, 1991; Siegel & Hartzell, 2004). The primary carer psychobiologically regulates the maturation of the infant's limbic system through attunement to the emotional state of the child by providing containment, comfort, and understanding (Schore, 2001a). Attachment is the key to facilitating the regulation of the limbic and autonomic nervous system of a baby, resulting in efficient brain functioning and the ability to handle stress (Panksepp, 2001; Schore, 2001b; Siegel, 1991).

In psychotherapeutic interventions, therapists help carers contain and hold autistic individuals, providing them with limits within which the child feels safe and secure. Initially, the emotionally dysregulated infant might be unaccustomed to feeling secure in the carer's arms and so may try to wriggle free or lash out; yet, through the holding process, the infant gradually learns to relax and is able to reach a state of calm (Schore & Schore, 2008). The child slowly becomes aware that the carer has not entered into their panic and anxiety, and has been strong enough to provide them with a calm, secure environment. The infant, mirroring the inner state of the carer, feels safe, which has a regulating effect on his autonomic nervous system (Schore & Schore, 2008).

Cerebellum

Research has shown that the volume of white matter in the brain of an autistic child is 38% greater than in a child without autism (Noriuchi et al., 2010). While the amount of grey matter in normal children increases with age, the grey matter in autistic children does not (Courchesne et al., 2007). However, the increased white matter and decreased amount of grey matter disrupts the functions for which the cerebellum has key responsibility: notably, integrating sensory and motor activity (Allen, 2005). This appears to correlate to the difficulties autistic children have with physical and motor co-ordination, as well as in planning and anticipating events. The cerebellum is also involved in the body's balance and gait, and an abnormality in the cerebellum structure could explain the odd tip-toe walking observed in some autistic individuals.

Genetic chromosomal mutations

Certain chromosomal mutations can influence an infant's perception. However, this no longer means that all is lost, as recent studies show that genes are not as static as once believed (Doidge, 2007). Therapeutic intervention, experience, and rehabilitation can all change the proteins and core structures of our chromosomal and neuronal activity. For example, certain mutations on chromosome 2 can result in the presynaptic area not firing correctly, as there is intermittent transmission. Such synapses are called "silent synapses" and lead to the infant missing out when there is no conduction or connectivity. However, through cognitive exercising, functional learning, and psychodynamic early intervention and action, these synapses may start becoming active again. As they begin conducting messages efficiently and connecting the corresponding brain areas, the child is able to process stimuli correctly and take in their surrounding environment. Hence, the importance of understanding that genes and chromosomes can become activated or deactivated and can respond to therapeutic intervention. This is one of the most important reasons of how early intervention can literally change a child's destiny.

Conclusion

By gaining an insight into the differences in brain structures, connections, and mechanisms, one is better able to plan how best to help the autistic child make sense of the world around them.

Early childhood experiences determine which circuits in the brain will be enhanced and maintained and which will not. While the brain structures and neurological connections in children with autism may initially develop as normal, their experience of the environment will have made significant neurological differences by the time they are two years of age. This reinforces the importance of ensuring that early experiences are made as positive as possible, thereby reducing the risk of abnormal brain development occurring.

Some of the modifications that take place in the brain of autistic children (and adults) might result from the following:

- trauma;
- poor connection with parents (anxious/first parents) or mental health issues;
- disability;
- highly sensitive and fragile;
- genetic chromosomal mutations.

In these cases, normal processing is "sidetracked", the information shunted on to other neural pathways causing disruptions to brain connectivity. While this sidetracking might be easier to correct as the neurological system is maturing, and while synaptic pruning is still taking place, intervention becomes more difficult and less effective after three years of age. It is the very plasticity of the brain in the early years that provides hope of strengthening and reinforcing weaker areas and connections in the brain, in order for the autistic child to have a more normal neurobiological set-up and be able to integrate into society as they get older.

There is still scope for realigning the brain's normal processing after this stage, for making effective improvements to autistic behaviours, but the chances of the behaviours becoming irreversible increase significantly (Dawson et al., 2000), as they become a way of living and coping for the child and are, therefore, more deeply engrained.

Early intervention also helps parents assume the role of regulator, creating an emotional space that allows separation between themselves and their child to occur. Therapists gently guide the parents through the process, bringing about the necessary separation as well as helping establish the basic social links that the child needs for play to develop. Play is vital, as it engages and stimulates distinctive neural motivational systems and allows the child to develop a reflective function.

In conclusion, early behaviours and experiences need to be understood and altered to prevent unhealthy brain development, and, since pre-autistic behaviours are identifiable, they should be investigated as early as possible.

CHAPTER FOUR

How paediatric assessment helps in early diagnosis of autism

Denise Challis

Description

The symptoms of autism can be painfully florid when full-blown, yet subtle and difficult to diagnose in borderline cases, although no less traumatic for a child's parents. Autistic spectrum disorder (ASD), as autism is more commonly described clinically, is a behavioural syndrome, an imperfectly categorised disorder. According to the *Diagnostic and Statistical Manual of Mental Disorders* (*DSM*) *IV* criteria, there are three aspects to the diagnosis.

- First, there is qualitative impairment in social interaction. The child does not interact normally. There is reduced eye contact, lack of turn-taking and of shared enjoyment, and an inability to perceive other people's emotions. Sense of humour and imagination are also lacking.
- Second, there are qualitative impairments in communication. Autistic children do not use language normally. For example, they may not talk or may use phrases out of context. Their tone of voice is flat, and facial expressions are impaired and often misunderstood.

- Third, there is rigid thinking, leading to visible distress at changes in routine. Similarly, lack of social perception leads to withdrawal into repetitive, "meaningless" habits or behaviours (known as stereotypes). This might emerge as tip-toe walking, hand-flapping, or finger twisting, in addition to spinning. There may be preoccupations with parts of objects rather than the whole, or unusual sideways views of everyday objects.

Essentially, it is the inability to grasp the meaning of social communication that underpins all diagnoses. As Professor Simon Baron-Cohen so cogently describes it, the child has "mind-blindness".

Considering Asperger's Syndrome, which falls within the autistic spectrum, Gillberg has described diagnosis on the basis of six domains, classically after three years of age (Gillberg & Coleman, 2000). To meet criteria, they must show 2/4 social, 3/5 verbal communicative, 1/5 non-verbal communicative, 1/3 narrow interests, 1/2 rituals and routine, and 1 motor impairment.

In the *DSM V* classification, which was introduced in May 2013, these features all fall into two main categories of disorder to be considered when making a diagnosis. These are:

A. Persistent deficits in social communication and social interaction across contexts, not accounted for by general developmental delay and manifested by all three of the following:
   - A1. Deficits in social-emotional reciprocity
   - A2. Deficits in nonverbal communicative behaviours used for social interaction
   - A3. Deficits in developing and maintaining relationships, appropriate to developmental level (beyond those with carers).

B. Restricted, repetitive patterns of behaviour, interests, or activities, as manifested by at least two of the following:
   - B1. Stereotyped or repetitive speech, motor movements, or use of objects
   - B2. Excessive adherence to routines, ritualized patterns of verbal or nonverbal behaviour, or excessive resistance to change
   - B3. Highly restricted, fixated interests that are abnormal in intensity or focus
   - B4. Hyper- or hypo-reactivity to sensory input or unusual interest in sensory aspects of the environment.

In addition to the above, symptoms must be present in early childhood and affect or limit a child's everyday functioning.

Using *DSM V*, therefore, the separate definitions of Classical (76%), Asperger's (24%), and Pervasive Developmental Disorder (PDD, 16%) are merged into one overall diagnosis. A recent paper by Mandy and colleagues (2012) shows, by factor analysis using the structured developmental, diagnostic, and dimensional interview (3Di) with parents, that the dyadic model fits diagnosis better than the traditional triadic model. Also, the inclusion of sensory abnormalities—hyper- or hyporeactivity to sensory input or an unusual interest in these stimuli—increases specificity of diagnosis. They might be a form of repetitive behaviour because they cluster with that aspect in factor analysis. Research overall so far shows that *DSM V* is not likely to under-diagnose ASD as compared with *DSM IV*.

Aetiology

Autistic individuals comprise 0.7–1.2% of the population, with boys outnumbering girls in terms of prevalence. The causes are many, especially where learning difficulties with epilepsy is concerned. Acquired brain lesions, such as those arising in tuberous sclerosis (which is located on chromosomes 16p and 9q) or in herpes encephalitis, have been causally associated. Children who already have attention deficit hyperactivity disorder (ADHD) or tics are more likely to show autistic symptoms.

Signs of other psychiatric disorders, such as obsessive-compulsive disorder (OCD) or anxiety/depression as a bipolar disorder, can present with autistic symptoms also.

Other conditions have been described independently but are considered by many to be under the autistic umbrella. These would include Rett's Syndrome, which is a regressive disorder on the MEPC2 gene, arising in girls during the second year of life. Atypical Rett's on the CDKL5 gene is also implicated, presenting often with early epileptic seizures. Oppositional defiant disorder (ODD), originally described by Dr Elizabeth Newsom as a distinct disorder, is now considered a subtype within the spectrum. Similarly, non-verbal learning disorder, described in the USA by Bourke, is an autistic disorder characterised by particular difficulty in distinguishing the meaning of facial expressions.

Verbal cognition is more than fifteen intelligence quotient points above non-verbal ability—the equivalent of one standard deviation and, therefore, a significant difference.

Other significant paediatric neuroses that can present antecedent to autistic criteria are selective mutism, post traumatic stress disorder, personality disorder, eating disorders, and even sleep disorder (raising the theoretical suspicion that melatonin might be connected to autistic neural pathway dominance).

When considering the many conditions in which the autistic criteria occur, it is helpful to imagine a daisy with the central autistic spectrum disorder represented by the central corolla and with outer petals attached to the centre all representing the primary conditions that manifest as autism. Such petals might be primary Kanner's autism, but also Asperger's Syndrome or "high-functioning" autism, in which children are verbal but do not meet the criteria for Asperger's. Also, there might be petals representing post traumatic stress disorder, severe learning difficulties of known or unknown aetiology, particularly with epilepsy, the occasional effect of blindness from an early age, ODD, and non-verbal learning disorder.

The aetiology of autism remains obscure, but important underlying genetic vulnerability is being steadily and progressively identified from familial and twin studies. At the time of writing, it seems that chromosomes 2, 7, and 16 are implicated. The genes involved are thought to be neuroligin, neurexin, SHANK -2, -3, and glutamate genes. It seems that the DRD3 gene is involved in children with a predisposition to stereotypic behaviour. Clearly, there must be a problem affecting neuronal circuits of the "social brain", probably in the prefrontal cortex, amygdala, or superior temporal regions, which also link to the cerebellum and to the hippocampal region (where emotional memories are stored). Synapse dysfunction and anomalies in the clock genes (which control the body's sleep–wake cycle) then lead towards an abnormal default mode network.

It is known that, in addition to the genetic vulnerability, there are environmental risks that, if present, are more likely to lead to autism. Some precipitating events or disorders have been outlined already. Others are prematurity, gestational alcoholism in the mother, maternal gestational thalidomide ingestion, "TORCH" viruses during pregnancy, and vitamin D deficiency. It is known that autism is more common among first generation children of parents who have moved away from their own kin to other parts of the world. Whether this is a characteristic of some of those who move to another culture (perhaps autism risk gene carriers who are less attached to their indigenous social networks) or whether it is a bruising, isolating experience suffered on arriving in the adopted culture is not yet clear.

Clinical features

At present it appears that two patterns of presentation of autism are evident. The first occurs in infants who have never demonstrated "normal" eye contact, maternal bonding behaviour, or interpersonal interaction. The second is in toddlers who started well and who might even have developed early language skills but who then started to regress from around thirteen to twenty-four months, before slowly regaining some of their lost skills.

Of additional concern is the frequency of co-morbidity with autism. This is distinct from those conditions that may appear to be antecedent causes. Most common are:

- epilepsy, which is present in 25–50% of cases over time. Although only 10% may show seizures in childhood, by forty-five years of age Gillberg (2007) reports 45% of cases showing epilepsy. In a fresh presentation of seizures and loss of speech in three- or four-year-olds, one should consider Landau–Kleffner Syndrome (a rare form of epilepsy);
- ADHD, which has 30–60% co-morbidity. The variants are ADD (30–50%) and hyperactivity alone (10%);
- disorder of attention and motor perception (DAMP) is another frequently encountered variant.

Treatment

Perhaps most important to parents is the quest to find the most successful treatment, or at least to minimise the signs and symptoms of what is otherwise a life-long condition. It is widely accepted that currently treatment should be based on a co-ordinated care plan with targeted intervention. This intervention should include at least fifteen hours per week of teaching support with direct involvement from a speech and language therapist.

Different styles of treatment are recommended, depending on the age of the child at presentation and the severity of the symptoms. Core principles include: (a) the avoidance of the causes of distress by carefully preparing the environment; and (b) a positive behaviour reward management programme. Specifically, such a programme may use applied behavioural adaptation (ABA): for example, as in the PEACH (Parents for the Early intervention of Autism in CHildren) or TEACCH (Treatment and Education of Autistic and Communication-related handicapped CHildren) methods.

Other methods described are:

- Sonrise: non-directive use of a child's secure room for all activities, both those of learning and of everyday living. This is often incorporated with hugging;
- Hanen: a non-directive communication therapy, often taught to parents by speech therapists;
- early psychoanalytical psychotherapy for parents and child: this emphasises the crucial aim of all interventions, which is the earliest possible detection. It is an intense and supportive treatment exemplified by the work, among others, of Stella Acquarone and her international pre-autistic network (ipAn).

Along different routes are attempts at diets to exclude any potential irritating or allergenic factors. In practice, they may only be useful where there are definite gastrointestinal symptoms or clear evidence of gluten or dairy sensitivity on immunoglobulin and coeliac disease screening tests. However, where a child's diet is extremely restricted, there is good reason to believe that taking supplementary vitamins and minerals may be prudent, particularly omega III oils. There is evidence to show the harmful nature of chelation of heavy metals (such as lead and mercury) as a form of intervention, and that other "way-out" anecdotal treatments, such as the use of the hormone secretin, are to be avoided.

Pharmacologically, the use of serotonin selective re-uptake inhibitors (SSRIs), such as fluoxetine, has a sound theoretical base. In the UK, this is licensed only for use in adults at present. Other medications might help specific symptoms. For example, treating the comorbid ADHD with methylphenidate may help language to emerge. If children are so distressed as to become psychotic, then risperidone is indicated, and not chlorpromazine or haloperidol.

Diagnostic methods

As with most neurodevelopmental conditions, early detection and confirmation of diagnosis lie with paediatricians with a special interest in neurodisability, also known as developmental neurologists. The most reliable method is to use a neurodevelopmental observational assessment schedule (or a specific autism observation method such as the autism diagnostic observation schedule, ADOS). In the less obvious cases, this should be coupled with a parental structured interview and a behavioural report from the different settings in which the child experiences daily life, such as a nursery class.

Perhaps the most helpful observation is that provided by the Griffiths mental development scales (GMDS). These scales were originally devised by the pioneering work of Ruth Griffiths, an eminent psychologist (1954, 1970) whose observations of children growing up from birth to eight years of age—the full duration of brain maturation—were unparalleled in her day and have scarcely been advanced upon since. Her scales from birth to two years were revised by Michael Huntley of the Institute of Child Health, London, in 1996, and from two years to eight years by Dolores Luiz and colleagues of the University of Nelson Mandela, Port Elizabeth, South Africa (the GMDS-ER), in 2006.

The principles underlying the scales are that the developmental profile is a reflection of the maturation of the brain, and that developmental trends might be influenced by both environment and inherited disposition. It is implicit in the continuing myelination and maturation of the brain during the neurodevelopmental process that there are opportunities arising from brain plasticity. Thus, opportunities for remedial intervention occur following injury and perinatal oxygen starvation and during critical periods of maximal learning potential. When considering therapeutic intervention to restore function after neurological injury, the foremost independent variable is age, followed by type of injury, and last by genetic substrate.

Parents are clear in their expressed views that "the assessment profile helped us to develop a sense of what is best to help our child". There can be modification of inappropriate parental expectations, avoiding unnecessary behavioural problems or unwarranted anxiety. Neurodevelopmental diagnosis may clearly indicate the need for further specific investigations. One of the main advantages of the use of the Griffiths scales over other observational schedules is that it gives a cognitive description as well as an autistic one, thus helpfully guiding towards the appropriate provision of resources in reflection of the underlying overall abilities of the child.

The Griffiths scales look at five distinct domains in children from birth to two years. This is broadened further to six domains for children functioning over two years. The domains, or subscales, are as follows:

1. Locomotor = posture, balance, graded co-ordination, movement competence, economy of effort.
2. Personal–social abilities = growing self-awareness, independence, and social integration.
3. Language = ability to hear, listen, comprehend, formulate verbal response with intelligibility in correct language code for the listener.
4. Eye–hand co-ordination = visual competence with fine motor precision functionality.
5. Visual performance = analyses visuo-perceptual awareness and praxis with speed of location as proxy.
6. Practical reasoning = a measure of the child's ability to use past learning experiences with generalisation in both visual and auditory tasks.

Early detection of autistic behaviour is facilitated in the first year of life, particularly when using the personal–social and language scales, which can help identify possible warning signs, or "red flags", if the child fails to demonstrate the following:

- visually recognises mother;
- returns examiner's glance with smiling or cooing;
- friendly to strangers (at around four months);
- anticipatory movements when about to be lifted;
- differentiates strangers from family and friends (at around seven months old);
- shows peer interest;
- stretches to be taken up;
- responds socially to mirror image;
- gives affection;

- plays interactive games;
- asocial interest.

In the second year of life, there are more criteria, which, if not demonstrated, are flagged as warning signs. These include:

- obedience to request with gesture;
- likes adult to show them a book;
- identifies parts of a doll's body on request;
- begins to co-operate in play with other children.

In the language scale during the first year of life, failure of the following may be significant, particularly in combination with other measurements in this scale and in the personal–social scale:

- ability to listen to conversations socially;
- give an immediate response to name call;
- use of two or more words in communication;
- use of early varied jargon with intonation of more than four syllables.

During the second year, lack of any or all the expressive language or speech items may be seen. However, the early development of speech should not necessarily be seen as contraindicating autism, as regression of speech may be a feature after thirteen months of age.

In the other non-verbally mediated scales, the autistic child might show unusual behaviour interpersonally or with the test equipment. For example, he/she:

- might use equipment in an odd way, not for the purpose intended;
- is often unwilling to follow verbal instructions;
- might persist and insist on holding one special toy throughout, beyond the age when this might normally be expected;
- might line up cars obsessively;
- might be unable to follow examiner's directions with formboards; alternatively, may be exceptionally quick with them.

Subtle later findings, especially with Asperger's syndrome, include:

- responds throughout to examiner's requests or language in a strangely literal way, illustrating semantic–pragmatic language disorder. This can be detected by careful questioning over the large picture scenario and with the comprehension questions—"What if . . .?" is responded to with "I'm not";
- often fails personal–social questions relating to playmates or, more specifically, to naming a sole friend;
- usually shows motor co-ordination difficulties, delaying overall results in locomotor and eye–hand co-ordination scales (but not usually in visual performance);
- in practical reasoning, might have conceptual difficulty: for example, seeing parts as disparate rather than as a whole;
- might respond to minute details in picture sequences: for example, the side of the door handle or colour of the door in sequential pictures of a house being built.

Thus, diagnostic confirmation for overt autism can be confidently made using the GMDS plus the meeting of *DSM V* criteria from that qualitative observation. ADOS is unlikely to give further clarification in these cases. However, subtle autistic spectrum disorder needs a structured parental questionnaire in addition to the GMDS. Ideal for this purpose, in children who have reached their third birthday, is the 3Di structured parental interview. Other commonly used assessment tools include the diagnostic interview for social and communication disorders (DISCO) and the autism diagnostic interview-revised (ADI-R).

Below are two case illustrations showing the diagnostic use of the GMDS in this disorder.

Case illustrations

Jim

Jim, a quadruplet born prematurely at twenty-nine weeks, was twenty-one months old. His parents and grandparents reported social regression from the age of sixteen months, with repetitive spinning of toys and of himself. The other siblings were reported to have normal social development (Table 4.1 and Figure 4.1).

Griffiths-elicited atypical features:

- no observed communicative vocalisation;
- lacked peer interest;
- failed to listen to conversations socially;
- failed responsive anticipatory arm stretch;
- failed response to name call;
- lacked two words of communicative speech;
- lacked early jargon with intonation;
- lacked obedience to request with gesture.

Table 4.1. Jim's developmental age abilities and quotients.

	Motor	Personal–social adaptive	Receptive language	Expressive language	Eye-hand co-ordination	Visual perform-ance
Developmental age	19.8 months	12 months	13 months	10 months	20.5 months	19 months
Developmental quotient (DQ)	90 DQ	54.5 DQ	60.5 DQ	46.5 DQ	93 DQ	86 DQ

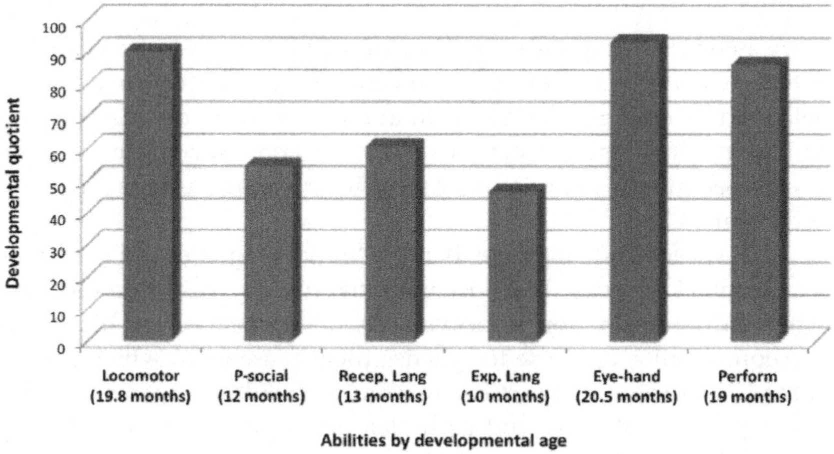

Figure 4.1. Jim's developmental quotients and abilities by developmental age.

Griffiths-elicited favourable features:

- observed smile at mirror image;
- imitative clap with smile;
- anticipatory behaviour on pick-up (no arm movements);
- interest in picture book;
- Parents reported head-shake for "no", affection, "peep-bo", interest in others, but these were not observed.

Descriptively observed:

- qualitatively impaired social eye-gaze;
- failure to elicit eye-gaze monitoring;
- swifter focus to sounds other than human voice;
- lack of proto-imperative pointing.

Thus, early identification of delayed disordered autistic characteristics enabled early intervention. Disproportionate personal–social, play and communication delay or disorder were elicited as core autistic features. Social delay or disorder accounted for the scattered delayed nature of the personal–social scale. Detailed autistic assessment and treatment is indicated.

Mark

Mark had ASD diagnosed by the use of GMDS and observational criteria when he was aged two years and eleven months. He had been delivered by emergency Caesarean at term for foetal distress. He had had an inguinal hernia repair at six months and a severe ear infection at eighteen months, but no other significant medical events (Table 4.2 and Figure 4.2).

With speech and language therapy, Mark's language and personal–social skills kept pace. With occupational therapy, his locomotor and eye–hand co-ordination improved. As he learned to use his visual perceptual skills, he chose to practise them ceaselessly, which greatly helped his progress. Practical reasoning steadily improved as his language concepts rose and as he learned to reason using visually mediated working memory. Mark now attends a mainstream school and is coping well in a small class with individual learning assistance.

Table 4.2. Mark's developmental age and quotients.

Chronological age	Locomotor	Personal-social	Language	Eye–hand coordination	Performance	Practical reasoning
41.7m	—	60 Q	60 Q	70 Q	84 Q	74 Q
48m	60 Q	63 Q	70 Q	92 Q	122 Q	95 Q
48m	1st percentile	1st percentile	1st –5th percentile	25th percentile	90th–95th percentile	25th–50th percentile
56m	71 Q	57 Q	70 Q	Not tested	139 Q	103 Q
56m	1st–5th percentile	1st percentile	1st–5th percentile	—	95th percentile	50th–75th percentile

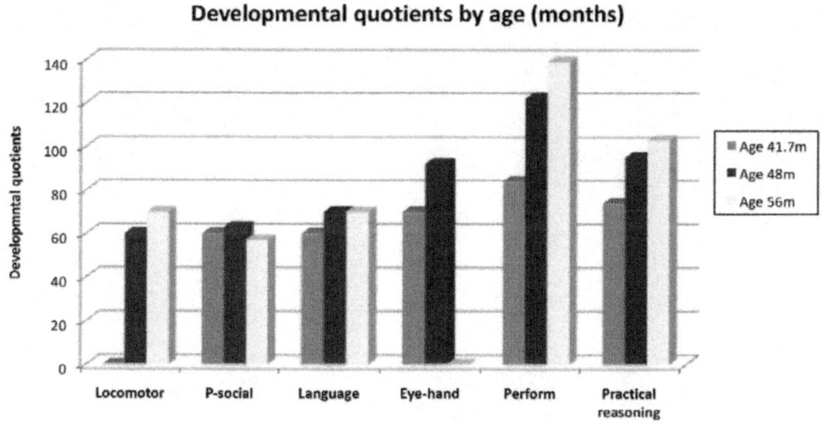

Figure 4.2. Mark's developmental quotients.

Conclusion

In summary, people with autism are people first, regardless of their understanding of our views about them. They need respect. They need early recognition and multi-disciplinary assistance. Our focus of service to them, once identified, should be on changing the environment around them to minimise distress and to foster their adaptive skills.

PART II

A MODEL FOR TREATMENT

CHAPTER FIVE

Re:Start: an infant–family treatment programme for young children displaying pre-autistic and autistic behaviours

Stella Acquarone with Isabel Jimenez Acquarone

At the Parent Infant Centre in London, we treat the child within their family. We believe that pre-autistic behaviours can be identified from birth and we offer a specifically designed assessment and treatment programme for infants aged from four months to four years.

The idea of involving the whole family in the treatment process was developed as a consequence of two observations I made over many years of practice, both in the NHS and in private clinics. First, I witnessed the angry reaction of many parents who felt that their early concerns regarding the absence of expressiveness and communication skills in their child were not listened to, or were not taken seriously enough by the medical profession. Parents spoke of their frustration at being told to "wait and see", and their anxiety that the delay in services might have hindered their child's development. Second, many siblings of autistic children were being referred to either the NHS Child and Adolescent Mental Health Service or private clinics for behavioural and emotional problems. This led me to question the possible impact of living with an autistic child and the need for siblings to be considered part of the treatment.

The history of our treatment model

In 1980, while working for the local Child Guidance Clinic (an NHS-run multi-disciplinary facility for families with children who had emotional and behavioural difficulties), I was allowed to attend the Under-Fives Clinic in the local health centre for three hours a week. At this NHS facility, where babies are checked physically and developmentally by paediatricians, health visitors, and other professionals, I was available for parents who were worried about their baby's behaviour. As my involvement was determined by parental concern, I was able to see many infants far sooner than if they had had to wait to be formally assessed and referred. In agreement, and sometimes together, with the community developmental paediatrician, I met with families who expressed a somewhat vague-sounding concern that something about their baby's behaviour seemed "different" to their other children's. When, after an initial meeting, we could see why the parents might be concerned about their infant's lack of interest or inability to relate or communicate, we planned a programme of intervention.

The intervention involved weekly meetings with the infant and parents, lasting between one and a half to two hours, for a period of up to three years. During these sessions, we would observe the infant's behaviour and the dynamics of the relationships within the family and find ways to enhance or motivate communication. Of course, not all parental concerns involved early autistic behaviours, but it was my experience with these infants and their families that increased my dedication to the field of early detection and treatment of autism.

During the sessions, the ability to enter the world of the child with poor communication skills was key to developing an understanding of their lack of motivation to engage in meaningful relationships with others. Over the years, the amount of time spent working with these infants and their parents gradually increased as the complex nature of entering the infant's world was more fully appreciated. In 1990, now working outside of the constraints of the NHS, I was able to extend the intervention period to twice a week for two hours, then to four times a week for three hours. Ten years later, I was offering three week-long treatments of thirty-six hours a week, and then once a week for a year, with additional support in the nursery for a year or two.

The Re:Start infant–family programme

Our early intervention model involves at least six hours of intervention or observation a day for five or six days a week for a period of two to four weeks, depending on the age of the child and any additional issues. The idea is to spend long enough with the infant and his family "to break the ice" and be able to delve deep into their dynamics and help them bring about change. The intense involvement means that the world can be seen from the infant's perspective in a shorter time frame, thereby enabling the appropriate intervention to be put in place more quickly, preferably before the age of three. Families are enabled to engage and interact with their child in more meaningful ways and obstacles are tackled together.

The intensive treatment programme is offered after a thorough paediatric assessment which is explained in Chapter Four. It is only the beginning of a new way of thinking, understanding, and acting, as we continue to meet weekly with the child and his family for at least another year. The aim is to consolidate and enhance the changes achieved during the intensive part of the programme, and for the autism to be modified early enough so as to be manageable for the rest of the child's life. In addition, we seek to help the child return to, and maintain, a path of healthy cognitive and emotional development. The name of the programme is Re:Start because we go back to the beginning and try to restore the first missed steps of the parent–child "dance".

Working with the whole family

Most families we see have just become aware that their child is exhibiting pre-autistic behaviours, and are desperate for help. Due to their young age, such children might not necessarily have been diagnosed with autism spectrum disorder (ASD).

We introduce the idea that we only work with the child if the whole family is involved, that is, parents, siblings, and the child with ASD. We also add that after the intensive programme we want to include any other adults involved in the child's day-to-day life, such as grandparents, nannies, and key staff from the child's nursery. This often comes as a surprise to the families, and reactions range from delight to total scepticism, anger, and resistance. However, those are our conditions. All our work with children in the autistic spectrum includes the whole family, as we strongly believe that to help a child change we need to help the family change, too: to identify and shift patterns of relating internally and as a unit. There is a saying about autism being a "family affair", and, in our experience, treating the family is fundamental to breaking the vicious cycles of bad habits and oppression within which the whole family inadvertently become entrenched.

At first glance it can seem as if the "problem" lies solely with the child, and that the adults and siblings are being "dragged" into the treatment process. Therefore, we have to be careful, sensitive, and very precise when describing our methods of working, and why involving the whole family is so important. We explain that our work is based on gaining an understanding of the behaviours presented and the underlying emotions behind them. Hence, we need to examine not only the child's seeming reluctance to communicate, but also the dynamics between that child and those with whom he "should" communicate, and who try to communicate with him. We do not consider that a "problem" or "blame" lies with any individual member or the family as a whole, but view their present difficulties as an unfortunate consequence of a wide combination of factors: environmental, circumstantial, and personal. We do not take lightly the commitment shown by a family that agrees to follow such an intense programme as ours.

Once the initial referral is accepted and the suitability assessment is done, we draw up a timetable of the required sessions with the different psychotherapists and therapists as needed (see Figures 5.1–5.3 for an example).

The intensive model

Our intensive Re:Start programme is a three-phase treatment, underpinned by psychoanalysis and neurobiology, which aims to help infants, parents, and siblings find a new way of relating to one another.

Phase I: assessment and formulation

- We carefully observe and identify what physical, environmental, relational, or emotional obstacles might be hindering an infant's

ACQUARONE INTENSIVE INFANT FAMILY INTERVENTION®

3-WEEK TIMETABLE

name: **FAMILY** *dates:* **DD MMM to DD MMM**

WEEK 1 – EXPLORATION OF FAMILY DYNAMICS

WEEK 1 – EXPLORATION OF FAMILY DYNAMICS		MORNING SESSIONS				AFTERNOON SESSIONS		
date		SESSION 1	*break*	SESSION 2	*lunch*	SESSION 3	*break*	SESSION 4
DAY 1	PARENTS	*Welcome & Introductions* *Family Assessment* *Expectations* [all therapists]		*Thoughts in my head...* [mother] [father]		*Observation of Parents & Child* [therapist]		*Observation of Parents & Child* [therapist]
	CHILD		*½ hour*	*Getting to know child* [therapist]	*1½ hour*		*½ hour*	
	SIBLINGS			*Further Assessment* [therapist]		*Creative Activity* [therapist]		*Creative Activity* [therapist]
DAY 2	PARENTS	*Family Assessment* *Parent Art Therapy* [all therapists]		*Family Assessment* *Exploration of Feeling through Art* [all therapists]		*Hopes & Expectations* [couple therapy]		*Hopes & Expectations* [individual therapy]
	CHILD		*½ hour*		*1½ hour*	*Sibling(s) with Child* [therapist]	*½ hour*	*Sibling(s) with Child* [therapist]
	SIBLINGS							
DAY 3	PARENTS	*Family Understanding* [father]		*Exploration of Child* [father]		*Family Understanding* [father / mother observing w/camera]		*Parents Playing Game* [couple therapy]
	CHILD	*Exploration of Child* [mother]	*½ hour*	*Family Understanding* [mother]	*1½ hour*	*Music Therapy* [mother with child]	*½ hour*	*Exploration of Child* [father]
	SIBLINGS					*Sibling Therapy* [therapist]		*Sibling Therapy* [therapist]
DAY 4	PARENTS	*Family Understanding* [father]		*Family Understanding* [mother]		*Storytelling* [father]		*Family Understanding* [mother]
	CHILD	*Exploration of Child* [father]	*½ hour*	*Exploration of Child* [mother]	*1½ hour*	*OUTING* [mother]	*½ hour*	*Exploration of Child* [mother with therapist]
	SIBLINGS					*Sibling Individual Therapy* [therapist]		*Sibling Individual Therapy* [therapist]
DAY 5	PARENTS	*Exploration/Trials of child* – [father]		*Exploration/Trials of child* [mother]		*Issues needing to be explored* [mother w/camera watching]		*Issues needing to be explored* [mother]
	CHILD	*Issues needing to be explored* – [mother & baby]	*½ hour*	*Issues needing to be explored* [father & baby]	*1½ hour*	*Music Therapy* [father]	*½ hour*	*Exploration/Trials of Child* [father]
	SIBLINGS					*Sibling Individual Therapy* [therapist]		*Sibling Individual Therapy* [therapist]

Figure 5.1. Timetable for week 1 of the intensive treatment model.

WEEK 2 – FINDING A WAY FORWARD

WEEK 2 – FINDING A WAY FORWARD		MORNING SESSIONS				AFTERNOON SESSIONS		
date		SESSION 1	*break*	SESSION 2	*lunch*	SESSION 3	*break*	SESSION 4
DAY 6	PARENTS	*Parents and child* [all therapists]		*Thoughts in my head...* [mother] [father]		*Individual work.* *Couple Art, other*		*Observation of Parents & Child* [therapist]
	CHILD		*½ hour*	*Getting to know child* [therapist]	*1½ hour*		*½ hour*	
	SIBLINGS			*Further Assessment* [therapist]		*Individual Therapy* [therapist]		*Understanding of Child* [therapist]
DAY 7	PARENTS	*Arts Therapy* [mother] [father]		*Family Assessment* *Exploration of Feeling through Art* [all therapists]		*Arts Therapy* [mother] [father]		*Arts Therapy* [mother] [father]
	CHILD	*Exploration of Child* [therapist]	*½ hour*		*1½ hour* NANNY	*Relationship with Nanny* [therapist]	*½ hour*	*Relationship with Nanny* [therapist]
	SIBLINGS					*Individual Therapy* [therapist]		*Individual Therapy* [therapist]
DAY 8	PARENTS	*Couple Therapy* [therapist]		*Couple Therapy* [therapist]		*Family Meeting* [all therapists]		*Individual Reflections* [mother] [father]
	CHILD	*Developing Trust* [therapist]	*½ hour*	*Developing Trust* [therapist]	*1½ hour*		*½ hour*	*Individual Reflections* [therapist]
	SIBLINGS							*Individual Reflections* [therapists]
DAY 9	PARENTS	*Exploration of Dynamics* [mother] [father]		*Exploration of Dynamics* [mother] [father]		*Exploration of Dynamics* [mother] [father]		*Exploration of Dynamics* [mother] [father]
	CHILD	*Developing Communication*	*½ hour*	*Developing Communication* [therapist]	*1½ hour*	*Developing Communication* [therapist]	*½ hour*	*Developing Communication* [therapist]
	SIBLINGS			*Individual Therapy Support through Art/Talking/Play*		*Individual Therapy Support through Art/Talking/Play*		*Individual Therapy Support through Art/Talking/Play*
DAY 10	PARENTS	*Exploration of Dynamics* [mother] [father]		*Exploration/Trials of child* [mother]		*Individual Therapy* [therapist]		*Individual Therapy* [therapist]
	CHILD	*Developing Communication*	*½ hour*	*Developing Communication* [therapist]	*1½ hour*	*With Sibling...* [therapist]	*½ hour*	*With Sibling...* [therapist]
	SIBLINGS					*With Child (going/doing)* [therapist]		*With Child (going/doing)* [therapist]

Figure 5.2. Timetable for week 2 of the intensive treatment model.

WEEK 3 – PUTTING IT ALL TOGETHER

WEEK 3 – PUTTING IT ALL TOGETHER		MORNING SESSIONS				AFTERNOON SESSIONS		
date		SESSION 1	break	SESSION 2	lunch	SESSION 3	break	SESSION 4
DAY 11	PARENTS	*Couple Exploration* [CCTV]		*Couple Exploration & Changes* [CCTV]		*Review & Adjustments* [mother] [father]		*Review & Adjustments* [mother] [father]
	CHILD	*Developing Communication*	*½ hour*	*Developing Communication* [therapist]	*1½ hour*	*With Sibling...* [therapist]	*½ hour*	*With Sibling...* [therapist]
	SIBLINGS					*With Child* [therapist]		*With Child* [therapist]
DAY 12	PARENTS	*Couple Exploration* [CCTV]		*Couple Exploration & Changes* [CCTV]		*Review & Adjustments* [mother] [father]		*Review & Adjustments* [mother] [father]
	CHILD	*Developing Communication*	*½ hour*	*Developing Communication* [therapist]	*1½ hour*	*With Sibling...* [therapist]	*½ hour*	*With Sibling...* [therapist]
	SIBLINGS					*With Child* [therapist]		*With Child* [therapist]
DAY 13	PARENTS	*Individual and child work* [therapist]		*Individual and parent child work* [therapist]		*Individual Work with Child* [mother] [father]		*Individual Reflections* [mother] [father]
	CHILD	*Improving Communication*	*½ hour*	*Improving Communication* [therapist]	*1½ hour*	*With Sibling...* [therapist]	*½ hour*	*Individual Reflections* [therapist]
	SIBLINGS					*With Child* [therapist]		*Individual Reflections* [therapists]
DAY 14	PARENTS	*Strengthening Relationships*		*Family Observing & Interacting* [family] [therapists]		*Family Interactions* [family] [therapists]		*Family Interactions* [family] [therapists]
	CHILD	*With Family*	*½ hour*	*With Family*	*1½ hour*	*With Family*	*½ hour*	*With Family*
	SIBLINGS			*With Family*		*With Family*		*With Family*
DAY 15	PARENTS	*Family Reflection* [family] [therapists]		*Family Reflection & Evaluation* [family] [therapists]		*Thinking to the Future* [family] [therapists]		*Thinking to the Future* [family] [therapists]
	CHILD	*Family Reflection* [family] [therapists]	*½ hour*	*Family Reflection & Evaluation* [family] [therapists]	*1½ hour*	*With Family*	*½ hour*	*With Family*
	SIBLINGS	*Family Reflection* [family] [therapists]		*Family Reflection & Evaluation* [family] [therapists]		*With Family*		*With Family*

Figure 5.3. Timetable for the week 3 of the intensive treatment model.

willingness to communicate. For this purpose, we watch for every subtle form of communication, when it happened, and what is transmitted to the observer. We are there with carefully chosen toys, soft and hard, waiting to see how they behave with their parents and on their own. We observe their attitude towards their siblings. We note their comfort or discomfort, their abilities and likings, their specific sensitivities. We go slowly, allowing time and space for the manifestation of all non-verbal and verbal signs with respect and a positive attitude.

- We carefully observe and explore the interfamily patterns of relating and of managing emotions that might be affecting the parents' ability to successfully connect with their child. We do this by inviting parents to tell us stories of their own childhood and to describe their hopes and expectations on becoming the parents of this and any other child they may have (or wish to have). Art materials are used at times as a way to facilitate self-expression, while storytelling is encouraged to exercise imagination.
- We carefully observe and investigate the whole spectrum of child development to see what areas might be lagging, to identify sticking points, and to ensure that the integrated approach we put together properly addresses bottlenecks in communication, behaviour, and emotional development. We refer the child on for

further assessment if necessary: for example, to speech therapists, neurologists, etc. We make sure that we are aware of each child's individual circumstances when evaluating their language acquisition: for example, children brought up bilingual may develop language at a slower pace than monolingual children.

At the end of the assessment period, we have an idea about the child's individual sensibilities; how/by whom they are triggered; and how they manifest themselves: physical reactions, posture patterns, motor difficulties. We have an understanding of how the child perceives the world; any attachment patterns, to what or to whom; their emotional states; and how they regulate their feelings.

Having gained an understanding of the infant's way of being in the world, we then try to establish the following:

- his motivation to communicate: awakening his wish to be in relationship with others;
- his sensory defensiveness and how to help integration;
- his motor abilities and his stance towards a separate identity;
- his stages of emotional development: areas affected, and the existence or absence of a mind that can hold thoughts, memories, mental representations;
- his relationship with the parents;
- the quality of attachment.

We also have a picture of how each individual parent observes and treats the child, their understanding of their child's sensitivities, and their reactions to them. We begin to see how each parent relates to the other and to their child/children, and form some idea about their own past difficulties, and any intergenerational patterns of attachment and feeling.

In the case of siblings, we get a sense of whether they need any specifically tailored activities, as well as individual psychotherapeutic help, that would allow them to form an understanding of, and positive relationship with, the brother or sister with autistic behaviours.

Phase II: therapeutic intervention

- We work with the child to both understand his avoidant or repetitious behaviours and to expand his repertoire of skills, his motivation to communicate and his expressions of desire and need. We adjust our strategies according to how or where the infant is "stuck". Led by our countertransference (the reaction in the therapist to the child's or patient's behaviour), we serve as facilitators of actions that have never occurred to the child. For example, we might sit side by side, to share their view on the world, look in the same direction they do, and comment on what "we" see. Sometimes, we "scaffold" the child, sitting behind them to move their arms as they play with the ball, or to help them hold playdough or a rattle or to touch their mother's skin. Finally, we attempt to sit opposite the child, face to face, taking turns and laughing about the same things, having fun, and feeling joy and trust.

- We work with the parents and child together to help them identify and formulate close and sensitive ways of being together and to expand on these relating skills.

We focus on the infant or child's sensibilities, body posture, and individual ways of responding, or not responding. This can take many hours of observation, sharing of states and experiences, and of helping them to feel themselves in their skin, body, psyche, and emotional climate in different circumstances. These circumstances may not seem dramatic to us. They can be physical (for example, changes in light, texture, sound, volume, pitch, or touch) or emotional (for example, spending time with different family members). Any changes in these circumstances can be experienced as catastrophic in an overtly sensitive baby.

In our individual work with the infant, we try to create the foundations for all future learning by helping to restructure his mind so that it is better able to receive clear thoughts and feelings. Some babies are born more sensitive than others to different stimuli, while others have individual characteristics that do not allow them to integrate their awakening senses, leading to confusion and isolation.

The therapist therefore engages the child in activities that most children naturally do on their own through self-motivated, effortful, independent, and enjoyable early play and exploration. These activities encourage what is natural in most babies: eye contact, imitation, and exploration of surroundings, as well as movement towards tasks or toys.

Using simple toys and materials (such as large plastic buttons or cotton reels, balls, animals, cars, string, playdough, etc.), we create situations in which the child can explore and organise them in different ways (by size, colour, form, gender, or roles—such as mother and baby). We generally encourage this using "scaffolding", where the child is supported. This is sometimes done on a long, low table, with a raised edge so that objects do not fall or roll off, with a mirror at one end so that the child can see and incorporate himself and someone else in the activity. There are different levels of scaffolding that we use.

- *Full scaffolding*: this is where the therapist is behind the child supporting his whole body and guiding his hands. This is for body awareness and for instilling an incipient sense of self by helping the child recognise that parts of him are capable of making different movements, with her arms and her hands.
- *Half scaffolding*: as the child progresses, his arms are held only up to the elbows, and the child uses his hands to do the activities.
- *Quarter scaffolding*: here, the therapist is either behind the child, and indicating from the shoulders, or in front, and guiding the arms. The child becomes motivated by the positive emotions he experiences when successfully finding an object, achieving an activity, concentrating, and learning more and more about the power of doing something with somebody and changing the environment.

We spend time enjoying with the child those moments of understanding what is going on around them through the use of simple explanations. We place much emphasis on the understanding of gestures and signals in others, and we stick to the use of the four basic emotions: happiness, sadness, fear, and anger. The constant use of these basic emotions, first via simple drawings and then through different members of the family and other children at nursery or school, reinforces their importance and gives the child more security in social interactions. Re:Start means to make these little children develop attachments and interest in others in a way they can understand and relate to.

As the treatment continues, we bring in the parents and help them to involve their child in everyday domestic activities. They learn to be with their child while carrying out everyday tasks and are taught to explain to them in advance what they are going to do: for example, a trip to the supermarket, cooking, or some other domestic activity. In the case of babies who isolate themselves, we encourage the use of a baby seat that can be placed on top of a table or on the floor while the mother or father is cooking or doing an activity. While in the seat, the child can be sung to, talked to, or read to by the parent, encouraging interest in and connection to the parents or siblings.

We place great value on parents holding the baby in their arms when their child is having a prolonged temper tantrum, is inconsolable or moving around in an overexcited manner, as if looking for limits. We support parents who have difficulty doing this, or who find it hard to be firm. Likewise, we put limits on repetitive behaviours and help the child alter his behaviour through clear and coherent explanations from both us and his parents. Extreme emotions such as rage and fury are talked about, and we prevent aggressive behaviour by deciphering the cause behind it, which in turn helps to restart play and vocalisation on the part of the child.

In addition:

- we work with parents individually to explore any learnt patterns of managing emotions that might stem from their own childhood and might be hindering them from communicating with their infant in a way the infant can best respond to;
- we work with the couple to explore any current or past relationship issues that might have a bearing on their ability to effectively co-parent effectively;
- we work with siblings to explore their emotional needs, and the particular difficulties that arise from having a sibling with perceived special needs. We expand upon the siblings' strengths in managing their own feelings and frustrations effectively and to model new ways of relating to their sensitive sibling and other family members.

The treatment programme uses structured times and unstructured times with all family members. Structured times act as a container of internal exploration. They are extremely important for creating a space in the mind where thoughts can be thought and retained, and where emotions can be felt and/or recognised, compared, observed, and expressed (for those old enough to do so). Unstructured times provide an opportunity to develop and stretch the imagination in order for new ideas to emerge and sustain the processes of understanding new situations and forming relationships.

Below is a list of the seven main elements of the therapeutic process of parent–infant psychotherapy (as suggested by Paris et al., 2009) that we incorporate into our practice.

1. Narration of the experience and observing the parents and their baby or child.
2. Processing the experience—being "in the moment".
3. Connecting past and present—making useful links to the family's current situation.
4. Modelling something new within the baby (or small child).
5. Promoting new affective behaviours through encouragement when a parent shows positive interactions.
6. Opening future possibilities—letting the imagination run free and allowing changes to occur.
7. Building reflective function, encouraged by a mutual desire to find other solutions or thoughts to share.

All of these processes overlap, but are useful to tease out separately.

Phase III: integration

By its very nature, this intensive therapeutic process involves the experience, or re-experience, of strong emotions for all family members. There might be grief, when parents mourn the "ideal" early infant they were not able to discuss or be open about with that particular child, distress, when the infant is separated for a time from the parents with whom the child has begun to experience a more dynamic attachment, and even anger, when siblings compete for their parents' time and attention. However, there are also moments of great joy and happiness, such as when parents experience being "felt" by their child for the first time.

The team accompanies the family on their journey, supporting them through the diverse emotions, experiences, and changes along the way. We carefully measure and document any progress. At the same time, we remain aware of the areas requiring further attention or development, and prepare the family for the challenges ahead.

The intensive programme involves a strong commitment from the family, not only in terms of time, but also in terms of trust, emotional involvement, and hard work. Families attend the clinic almost daily for approximately three weeks. This often involves staying in nearby accommodation away from family and friends. The family receives at least six hours of therapeutic intervention each day, usually from 9 a.m. to 4 p.m. (including breaks and lunch) five days a week for (on average) three weeks. An additional day each week is spent observing the family as they go about their daily routine. It is important to note that while a clear timetable is in place, the clinic remains flexible and responsive to the needs of the young children we treat. Breaks for feeding and naps are built into the daily programme, and full advantage is taken of them. For example, parents may have time for couple therapy while their baby is asleep and in the care of member of staff.

The treatment itself aims to bring about substantial changes in the infant's readiness and keenness to emotionally relate to others; an increased understanding and sensitivity in the parents; and greater acceptance by, and awareness in, the siblings. The treatment is not, however, a "solve all" programme, and follow-up measures are necessary to consolidate changes, face possible future obstacles, and provide continuing support.

Follow-up treatment includes weekly (or sometimes twice-weekly) sessions at the clinic for the infant and parents for a year, as well as weekly therapy sessions for siblings if required. In addition, there are liaisons with nursery school staff as well as other professionals, such as speech, language, and occupational therapists.

Further follow-up meetings with parents requiring continuing support can be arranged if they wish to maintain a relationship with the clinic. This continues for the next year or two, with subsequent annual follow-ups if possible during the infant's childhood.

Cost

This intensive treatment is not cheap, but this is due to the large team of qualified and experienced staff needed. While the costs are but a small fraction of those involved in providing life-long specialist support for an autistic child, they might still be prohibitive to many families. We wish to stress that while some families have the treatment covered by their insurance or pay for it themselves, a significant proportion receive funding, in whole or part, from the charity International pre-Autistic Network (ipAn).

Short-term treatments

The three-week programme of intensive treatment aims to address the relational deficits of those infants who have already significantly distanced themselves from the world around them. However, since not all the infants we see show such extreme behaviour (for example, babies only a few months old), alternative treatments are available. These include short-term intensives, which can last from three to five days. They offer a condensed version of the three-week programme, with up to eight hours a day of observation and assessment, intervention, and integration for the parents individually and as a couple, and for the infant individually and with the parents.

The infants for whom we consider this kind of treatment to be more appropriate include those who might fixate on repetitive behaviours but who can be more easily distracted from them by encouragement from persistent parents. We also use the short-term treatment for those infants whose fleeting contact with the world has shown a greater range of variety and flexibility. We aim to enhance the understanding and skill of those parents whose perseverance and awareness have already helped them make and retain some contact with their child. It offers a model of recognition of their good observation skills, support for what does work, and a new perspective on what else could be beneficial.

We continue to see these infants and their parents once a week for a year, or two. In some cases, if we consider it to be more beneficial to the child to maintain a long-term relationship with us rather than have them undergo a short, intense treatment programme, we see the family regularly over a few years. This is sometimes the case with families whose child has additional special needs or who do not have a large support network.

The team

Central to every kind of treatment is the experience and commitment of our team of practitioners, each one offering their expertise and understanding to the families. Our team is made up of professionals from a range of backgrounds, including parent–infant psychotherapy, adult psychotherapy, child psychotherapy, developmental therapy, occupational therapy, couple psychotherapy, music, speech, and language therapy. We also employ a paediatric physiotherapist, and a nutritionist is available if the need arises.

The treatment sessions are a dynamic process and provide families and therapists with unique, intense, and sometimes challenging experiences. The intensity is a natural consequence of breaking through the autistic barrier and entering into the child's world, finding a way to communicate with them, and help them feel less overwhelmed by emotions or experiences. The team must work together to be able to hold the emotions and information they encounter in these instances. Therefore, the therapists not only support the family as they progress through the treatment, they also support each other.

We believe that the function of the team is to contain and digest each family's difficulties and to then assist in bringing about transformation. Essential to this are the twice-daily supervision sessions. This is the space to "debrief", share, and discuss issues that have arisen during the therapy. Talking about the work enables the therapists as a team to identify wider themes within the family dynamics, to recognise what the patient brings from their past relationships into the consultation, and how the therapist reacts to the transmission of feelings (transference–countertransference). By thinking with the family and for the family during the supervision, the team acts cohesively: the group mind has the strength and the capability to think clearly on many different levels and to contain the intense, and, at times, conflicting, emotions that are evoked in the parents and in the professionals involved with them.

Dynamics are re-enacted within the team during the treatment, and our experience and awareness of them further inform our understanding and choice of intervention. There are times when different family members, usually unconsciously, try to dissociate themselves or project paranoid thoughts about us and the treatment process. It is only by reflecting together and trusting each other that it is possible to bring any feelings of conflict into the open and integrate them into the process, rather than leaving them unspoken and unresolved. It requires a lot of trust from the family to bring up hidden resentments and negative thoughts, but, by being at the heart of the team who work with and support them, these thoughts can be voiced and understood. Thinking together as a group enables us to manage, digest, and make sense of the barrage of primitive and painful feelings and experiences that are brought out in the intensive treatment process.

Summary

The key to understanding a baby's or young child's internal world, with their unknown and unmet needs, fears, anger, and rage, is a combination of the following:

- Observation: being with and thinking with the child.
- Exploration: expressing (verbally) the baby's experience of the world: emotionally, sensorially, posturally/motor or interpersonally, and rehearsing new ways of being.

Central to our interventions is the understanding that

- the development of language and communication skills, socialisation, and the imagination are based on the development of a relationship that gives meaning to the child's life and which he or she can use for survival and growth of emotional love with other human beings;
- we have a conscious life that we are all mostly aware of, and we have an unconscious, the part of our mind that keeps trauma, memories, fantasies, needs, desires, and other aspects of our life hidden and out of reach; and
- the relationship between the mother, father, and infant—known as the eternal triangle—forms the basis for other relationships. Even in the event of the father not being present (for example, due to death or serious illness, or frequently away on business), it is the relationship with the father's mental representation and the relationship the mother had with her own parents that allow for the process of separation and individuation to occur in the mother's mind (Ogden, 1992).

Key to bringing about lasting change is engaging with committed parents, individually and as a couple, to help them examine their own fears and anxieties and to help them to understand their child and have a relationship with them, in spite of any previous experiences of rejection. By analysing their own behaviours and feelings, as well as learning more about their baby's behaviour and feelings, parents are able to become more resourceful, and more patient, in finding new ways to be with and "find" their child.

While we have tried to present the essence of our work in a theoretical manner, we believe that only by considering the "real" work can we share the value of this way of working. In the following chapters, we present examples of the Re:Start programme at different ages: Joseph, two years old; Geronimo, almost three years old; Nicola, eight months old; Filippo, eighteen months. For each case study, we will share the practical experiences, the theoretical understanding, and the emotional relationships as they developed. We would like to clarify that, due to our sincere obligation to protect the identity of those children and families with whom we have worked, these case studies have been created out of an amalgamation of clinical experiences. While fictional in terms of circumstance and compilation, they are true in terms of clinical insight and intervention.

Acknowledgment

I would like to thank Isabel Jimenez Acquarone for her contribution to the writing and thinking of the Re:Start model.

CHAPTER SIX

Joseph (aged two years): an in-depth case study

Stella Acquarone

> "Walking silence, like a phantom in the midst of his family. Rolled up in a corner moving gently from side to side. Sometimes under a table or chair. Trying to catch the light through the curtains. Fixated on a frail, gentle movement in the air, or on the lines in the fabric. It seems so interesting to him: the motes of dust suspended in the beam of light; all the lines of the textile interweaving. Or perhaps it's the blankness of it all, or simply the consistency of colour and structure—something that provides calm and safe feelings. He hides himself in an invisible space, one that nobody knows about and where no one can reach him."
>
> (Clinical notes, Stella Acquarone)

I began this book with the same description of Joseph. This is how I saw him at his first consultation after being diagnosed with autism.

This chapter is all about where we start, and how we continue, to help a child and his family relate to one another by giving them an understanding of their inner way of functioning and their different emotional states. This understanding will activate and develop a capacity to love in the child and parents, fundamental for their relationship to become fulfilling, enjoyable, and full of creativity. It is also important in promoting healthy cognitive development within the child.

Family background

Joseph was aged two years and one month at the time of referral. His parents were John, aged thirty-eight, and Louise, thirty-five. He had one older sister, Sue, aged five years and nine months. Joseph's parents were both British: his mother was from a small village in Yorkshire, his father from outside Edinburgh. They had both lived in London since moving there for work after university. They met through mutual friends at a party twelve years ago, and were married three years later.

Joseph's father worked in a bank, and often travelled abroad for work. His mother was in the fashion industry but gave up work to care for the children. She has plans to return to work part time when the children are older.

Father's family history

The eldest of four boys, John described a rural upbringing in a loving family. He very much liked being part of a large family, and his memories of childhood were happy. He described being competitive at school and having a desire to do well academically. He met his wife and they had many years together without having children. When they decided to start a family, he took a job in the City and began working long hours.

Mother's family history

Louise was the youngest of three girls and was brought up in a small village. She described a happy childhood spent playing with her sisters and was unable to recall any "bad" things or unhappy memories from this time. As a teenager, she had good friends and she did not have problems with her parents. She gave up her job to look after her children and was very proud of being a stay-at-home mother. However, she felt devastated by the increasing awareness that Joseph was not responding happily to them, that he did not smile, and was unwilling to interact with his older sister.

The birth of the two children

Sue was born after a planned pregnancy. It was a natural birth without any complications. She met routine developmental milestones and no concerns about her development have been raised. Sue is at primary school, and though she initially found it difficult to settle, is now doing well.

Joseph was conceived as soon as his parents decided to try for a second child. The pregnancy was uncomplicated and the natural birth without note. The maternal grandmother came to help care for Sue for a fortnight during the period of Joseph's birth.

Routine tests for deafness came back with no signs of any impairment.

Concerns, assessment and diagnosis

By the age of one, Joseph's parents began to worry about his behaviour: his lack of eye contact and preference to play with objects rather than people. Louise took their concerns to their GP, who initially told her that she should not be worried, that she should relax, as perhaps she was too tired, and that Joseph would surely grow out of it. They were advised to "wait and see". The family sought private medical opinion and arranged to see a developmental paediatrician, who noted their concerns. A reassessment at the age of two confirmed that Joseph's behaviours were on the autistic spectrum, according to the autistic diagnostic observation schedule (ADOS) and the Griffiths mental development scales (GMDS). After thorough testing, no organic contributing factors or coexisting disorders were identified. The paediatrician recommended that Joseph and his family would benefit from relational treatment to help with his emotional development, and they were referred to the Parent Infant Centre. This was one month before Joseph and his family came to see us.

Assessment and formulation

On receiving the referral from the paediatrician, we contacted the family to arrange an initial consultation, involving the whole family. We requested copies of any home videos of Joseph, which we could use to assist us in our understanding of him prior to our first meeting.

The early videos showed a passive baby, often staring at hanging mobiles and happiest when alone. He did not seem to enjoy being picked up and would recoil like a snail.

Assessment of Joseph

In later videos, Joseph seemed largely oblivious to the chaotic family interactions around him. He sat on the rug looking through books or lining up toy train carriages. Attempts to engage with, or expand on, Joseph's play resulted in him turning around and turning his back on the person in question. Joseph sometimes seemed to be watching his family from a distance.

What was interesting to note was how the mother behaved. She seemed strongly influenced by Joseph's lack of response and, compared to the early home videos, was no longer trying to connect with her son. She had ceased calling his name or finding things for him to do.

Initial family consultation

The first meeting was held in a large, calm room with toys and art materials laid out. Three psychotherapists were present (parent–infant, child, and adult psychotherapists), so that all family members could be attended to. Joseph was carried into the building from the car by his father and put down on the floor of the waiting room, his beautiful face half hidden behind long, uncombed hair. He had a noticeable lack of muscle tone and drooled all the time. When the family were called in, he moved cautiously into the room, glanced sideways, then, swift as a cat, headed for a corner of the room. Joseph spent much of the ninety-minute consultation in that corner, crouched down, as if part of the furniture, immobile. At times he might look through the window or the glass door, perhaps absorbed in the movement of the leaves in the trees or just in the air, silent.

From the selection of toys, Joseph only seemed interested in the cars, not even the whole of the cars: just the wheels spinning round and round. Like hypnosis, this focus was calming to him, as if he could find a space in the air that allowed him to be in a state of suspension, trance-like and floating, a space that existed at his will, and which I call autistic space.

Joseph's parents were extremely willing to get involved in understanding this mysterious member of the family. Joseph seemed oblivious to his parents' voices, completely immune to his name being called. He did not react when an adult sat close to him, to talk to him or show him something he might like. However, if their voices got louder when he did not respond, he would start emitting a grunting noise, and to rock or spin. When stopped, he would enter into a panic, his face fearful, and would start to cry or knock himself in a painful way. He was not crying because of the pain he was causing himself but almost distracting himself with an external pain to control or regulate his primitive anxieties. It seemed that he was crying because his "psychic skin" had been penetrated, something secret to him had been violated and it had dismantled his capacity to regulate his strong emotions, which had become uncontained. Real panic appeared in his face, far removed from his calm expression when playing repetitively with the toy car.

Joseph's sister, Sue, was lively and keen to play with the toys and art materials provided. However, at times, she seemed resentful of the amount of attention being given to her brother. Her approach to Joseph alternated between ignoring him completely and being overtly physical with him: picking him up and turning him upside down or throwing him on an armchair. Joseph did not appear to react to her treatment of him; he just maintained his blank face and tried to escape to his quiet corner or to the window. Without a response from Joseph, we observed that sometimes Sue tried to elicit reactions from her parents, either by "being kind" and kissing Joseph, or by physically placing herself between her parents and Joseph.

Our understanding of Joseph

Joseph showed in his first meeting a sense of being lost in a silent space with no understanding of time other than his own. Retreating to the corner was not a reaction to being in a new place, but echoed behaviours from home and nursery, where he would play by himself or "spend the whole morning under a table". It seemed that by being immobile or moving around in circles, he was taking control of his sensations and keeping any chaotic feelings at bay. He might not be able to acknowledge any changes of place, of routine, or of games, but, thanks to the space under the chairs or table, he could always find peace. He used such small spaces to try to escape the deep feelings of turbulence he experienced when around people: the unintegrated, overwhelming sensations and fear. At times I felt, in my countertransference, such increasing trepidation as if my/his chest was fibrillating, non-stop.

Joseph was unable to acknowledge requests; he could not even catch his name. Although we knew he could physically hear the sounds, they were indiscriminate sounds that he could not unify or make coherent. So, for him, language was a noise not understood. Similarly, he seemed unable to understand what the expectant gazes of others demanded of him. From Joseph's perspective, it seemed as if he found "the expectant eyes and expressions difficult to read and so uncomfortable". He could not look at other people's faces, as they made him feel so uneasy. We wondered if he was unable to process the whole face of those who looked at him, or whether such information was processed by him piecemeal.

I did not feel I existed for him; I was just something to be avoided or denied. He looked at people sideways simply so that he could softly move around them. I, full of interest in this boy, was treated by him no differently than a piece of furniture. (I did wonder whether my sense of inquisitiveness could in part stand as countertransference for his non-autistic aspects.) The transmission of affect was clear, reflected in his difficulty in being with us, of receiving and returning a greeting, a smile, a look. He was able to express his avoidance, his vigilance, and fear by finding a quiet, alone place. It gave him comfort, and was his way of adapting to the new place. The words and movements around him, the room, the decor, the toys, faces, floating feelings, actions, and activities were all too much.

According to our emotional screening scale (Acquarone, 2009), which is represented for Joseph and his mother (Figures 6.1 and 6.2), and which we filled in after the first consultation, Joseph displayed twelve signs of alarm: more than four is already an indication that early intervention is required. The mother's scale showed that she did

ACQUARONE DETECTION SCALES FOR EARLY RELATIONSHIPS®

EARLY SIGNS OF ALARM – pre-Autism

ASSESSMENT – INFANT/CHILD

name: **JOSEPH**

age: **2 years 2 months** *date of this observation:* **DD MMM YYYY**

	NEVER	RARELY	FREQUENT	ALWAYS	OBSERVER REACTIONS
INTERPERSONAL					
1. GAZING *Eye-to-eye contact within a relationship and the maintenance of this contact*		●			*Overall ... avoidance of contact of any kind*
2. BABBLING *Making sounds for the benefit of the partner in the parent-infant relationship*	●				
3. CALLING *– The facial expressions – Noises or gestures that seek to produce an affectionate response from the partner*	●				*... attitude*
4. IMITATING *– Moving mouth, tongue, etc., in imitation of mother's (or another) – The repetition of a sound or a movement heard or seen by the child*	●				*Not able to imitate behaviour*
5. PROVOKING *Inciting the person into interacting, not just to use as an instrument to do something for him/her*	●				*Was withdrawn and not interested in persons or things*
6. POINTING *Indicating with index finger to a person about an object of interest*	●				
7. FEEDING *Child's attitude during the intake of food, including anticipatory behaviour (e.g. head-turning, moving arms the food/breast)*		●			*Drank only milk ... given regularly ... no need to ask*
8. JOINT ATTENTION *Looking in the same direction*	●				
9. PLAY *– Capacity to play the same game for more than 5 minutes, and share with another person – Take turns and stay with a person – Children*	●				*Only by himself*
10. ALONE				●	
11. RELATING *Behaviours indicating the capacity to relate & accept emotional warmth.*					*Showed and felt ... frightened ... confused*
– Mother, Father	●				
– Other caregivers	●				
– Other unfamiliar adults	●				
– Siblings	●				
– Other unfamiliar children	●				
12. REACTIVE BEHAVIOURS *tolerance to frustrations, including: – a) Capacity to accept emotional warmth – b) Capacity to bounce back after stressful event – c) Capacity to adapt to changes...please indicate*		●			*No signs of frustration as he was allowed to be calm by himself*
SENSORIAL					
TOUCHING					
13. *Skin-to-skin contact initiated by infant for play or affection*		●			*Looked disassociated*
14. *Does the child touch paint, foam, sand, water, playdoh, plasticine and other messy substances*	●				
RESPONSE					*... retracting*
15. *Response to sounds*	●				
16. *Response to noise*		●			
17. *Response to name*	●				
18. *Response to light & patterns*				●	
19. *Response to smells*	●				
20. COMFORTING *Child's ability to find relief from distress by themselves (e.g. thumb sucking, touching hands, playing with one car, others)...specify*		●			
MOTOR					
HOLDING					
21. *The posturing of the child when he is supported in the arms of the mother (e.g. floppy, rigid, restless) – General muscle tone when sitting or standing*				●	*... floppy*
22. *Stereotypic movement of arms, eyes, etc. – Walking: on tiptoes or sluggish*				●	
23. *Use of hands: for grasping, for helping himself – Use of body: to reach, to climb, to hide, other...*				●	
AFFECT					
24. EXPRESSIVENESS *The body or facial expression of emotional states (e.g., sad, worried, anxious, bland, happy, or others)...specify*	●				*... anxious*
25. SELF HELP DEVELOPMENT *– Ability to cope independently with the environment, (e.g., dress) – Eating – Being careful with him/herself or others*		●			
ANY OTHER OBSERVATIONS NOT LISTED ABOVE:					

Figure 6.1. Joseph's assessment.

try to engage and play with her son, but her score lowered as her attempts were met with disinterest and rejection. The pale grey dots reflect the lack of affection and enthusiasm in the behaviours shown by both mother and child.

ACQUARONE DETECTION SCALES FOR EARLY RELATIONSHIPS®

EARLY SIGNS OF ALARM – pre-Autism

...affecting the baby or being affected by the baby...

ASSESSMENT – MOTHER/caregiver

name: **NAME**
child: **JOSEPH** *age:* **2 years 2 months**

		NEVER	RARELY	FREQUENT	ALWAYS	OBSERVER REACTIONS
INTERPERSONAL	**1. GAZING** *Eye-to-eye contact with the baby and the maintenance of this contact*		●			*Mother ... appeared anxious*
	2. BABBLING *– Making sounds for the benefit of the parent-infant relationship – Talking*		●			*... unable to connect with the child*
	3. CALLING *Facial expressions, noises or gestures seeking to produce an affectionate response from the infant*			●		*... very resistance and busy with work*
	4. FEEDING *Mother's attitude towards infant's hunger and need to feed: – Does she anticipate behavior and have meal or breast easily available? – Does she pay attention, talk with the baby and enjoy feeding? – Does she interrupt with any excuse (e.g., talks to others and looks away)? – Is she fearful, full of anguish or has she any delusions? – Is she apathetic?*	●				*In the hands of nannies ... Mother had no idea ... Mother felt guilty*
	5. GAMES / PLAY *– Playful encounters, including songs and teasing*	●				
	6. RELATING *Behaviours indicating the capacity to relate & accept emotional warmth towards the baby*		●			*Mother tried to relate*
	7. REACTIVE BEHAVIOURS *including: – Tolerance to frustrations – Capacity to accept emotional warmth – Capacity to bounce back after stressful event – Capacity to adapt to changes*			●		*... felt rejected and became distant*
SENSORIAL	**8. TOUCHING** *– Skin-to-skin contact initiated by infant for play or affection*		●			*... busy with the other children*
	9. COMFORTING *– Mother's ability to find relief for the baby's distress*	●				*... high pitched voice ... jerky movements, as if angry*
MOTOR	**10. POSTURE** *The posturing of the mother when the infant is supported in her arms or any other way (e.g., other, rough, balanced precariously)*		●			
AFFECT	**11. EXPRESSIVENESS** *– Expression of emotional state (e.g., sad, worried, anxious, bland, happy, others)...specify*		●			*... worried*
	12. UNDERSTANDING OF EMOTIONS *– in themselves*		●			*... resistant*
	– in the baby	●				
	13. PAST *– Psychiatric illness*	●				*... difficult to reach*
	– Other difficulties	●				

ANY OTHER OBSERVATIONS NOT LISTED ABOVE:

Showed anger towards who looked after the child and showed difficulty in engaging with her 3rd and difficult-to-reach baby.

Figure 6.2. Joseph's mother's assessment.

Until recently, the family had had a strong identity of being a unit, with a "wonderful" daughter and an ideal baby. Joseph had been the "perfect" baby who never cried, able to be picked up by anybody, never complaining. The family thought they had been blessed. When their gradual concerns about Joseph's lack of interaction were confirmed by the paediatrician as a possible sign of autistic behaviour, the family were shocked, but were willing to do whatever it took to help him and to "save" the family. Consequently, they agreed to our intensive treatment programme, and to follow up the process for as long as necessary. A start date of one month's time was set. This quick timescale highlights our view that the earlier the intervention, the better the prognosis. Joseph was aged two years and two months when he started the treatment.

A timetable for Joseph and his family was drawn up. It included the following sessions: infant psychotherapy for Joseph, to explore his use of the autistic space and to expand on his way of being in the world; child psychotherapy for his sister, to explore her relationship with Joseph, and his impact on her; couple and individual adult psychotherapy for the parents, to explore their personal issues reactivated by the newfound commitment to "rescue" Joseph from the world he had learned to exist in. It was important to offer this support to the parents, to give them the strength to be able to act together when times became "rough". Family sessions were primarily timetabled for the third week, as we first had to understand Joseph's behaviour and emotions.

The timetable also included music therapy, speech therapy, and paediatric physiotherapy.

Intensive treatment process

Getting to know Joseph

Joseph's mother chose his name because she liked the biblical character of Joseph. It was after seeing a performance of *Joseph and the Amazing Technicolor Dreamcoat* that she came to this decision. She imagined Joseph as intelligent and resourceful, someone who could not only survive the hatred of his brothers, who were envious of the special affection the father had for him, but who grew up to be trusted, insightful, important, and rich. However, the child brought to us had little in common with the biblical Joseph. He was silent and unresponsive, as if he was barely alive. He gave the impression of having nothing to offer, and of being deeply frightened of feeling.

Our work with Joseph consisted of exploring the conditions in which he would feel ready and able to "meet" us relationally. We did this by waiting and talking about it, even when seemingly he was not listening, letting him know that we were there. We were going to "seek out" and work on the cut-off parts of Joseph, the parts that were interested in others, in forming relationships. To do this, we had to be patient. We waited, with a watchful curiosity for his signs, his cues, his own curiosity in us. At first, Joseph resisted being drawn out of himself. He displayed a stubborn determination to carry on with his immature ways of relating: silent, quiet, alone. Yet, soon, chinks began to appear, and our words and interest in him were met with a half-smile or a fleeting eye contact.

We also explored further his object relations (how he had internally formed his relationships with others): whether they existed in a symbiotic manner for him, whether they had not yet been "born", hence his lack of interpersonal interest, or whether his emotions regarding others were conflictive, oppositional, grabby. Perhaps Joseph was interested in only one of his parents as a protective shield or as a possession to protect him from harm? In fact, from our observations, Joseph seemed not to distinguish between family members externally or internally. He identified himself with inanimate objects rather than living plants or people. He did not seem to respond to experiences that were frightening. When he was roughly held upside down by his sister, his face remained expressionless and blank. He could have been paralysed with terror, but appeared to be like a stuffed toy that could be carelessly tossed around: like A. A. Milne's Winnie the Pooh, he was "a bear of very little brain", cut off from his own capacity to think and react.

This strategy of cutting himself off had been long used, and now had to be fully explored by us. Joseph did not take up any more space than where he was sitting, and it seemed that he was working very hard to keep himself under control, for hours if necessary. (We often hear that in the first and second year of life, these children prefer to be alone for hours, entertaining themselves.)

Our immediate reaction (the countertransference) was a tumult of sensations, similar to being at sea in a storm. This sea could only be calmed or managed by moving somewhere more peaceful, where a sense of control and self-preservation could be achieved, but only when alone. This is what we saw Joseph doing when he retreated to a peaceful corner. It felt as if an internal order could be found, and clung to amid the chaos. We wondered how we would be able to help Joseph risk letting go of his "life jacket" (with which he floated, able to breathe, but dangerously alone) and climb aboard the "lifeboat", to trust other people to know and help him. We needed to find a way to let Joseph know that we could understand the sensations he was experiencing, and that this process of sharing the experience could take time, like adjusting to seeing in the dark.

I wanted to know him, but did he want to know me? Could he pick up on my intentions? Could he perceive me or us directly, as a whole or in fragments? Did he want to join us or did he feel better staying where he was? Did he have the perseverance to continue trying to respond to his parents? It was almost certainly impossible when he could not understand or make sense of the situation.

Like most children with difficulties, Joseph came to us because he was brought by parents who wished him to be integrated into the family and who wanted to know him better. His physical development was quite normal, but his emotional development seemed to have been arrested at a very early stage, with a pseudo hyper-vigilant modality of keeping the "other person" at bay with fleeting looks. Joseph's way of thinking was yet to be discovered, though it seemed he could predict the behaviour of others and so be able to avoid "them". The common denominator was the lack of shared meaning and of shared experiences.

At the start of the treatment, there were two different systems of reflection in action: Joseph's seemed defensive, on the retreat, while mine (and his parents) seemed towards interaction. We were both thinking about the other but with different purposes.

An illustration of day one

Joseph lay on the floor, his left arm extended, holding a toy car as far from his face as possible. He was looking, sideways, at the car, his eyes fixed on the tiny movements of a wheel. How far did he have to escape into this spinning wheel to be able to avoid his surroundings, his family? In the large room his sister was shouting, his parents laughing with her as a large ball was bounced around. The atmosphere felt chaotic, and yet so distant, concentrating hard, like Joseph was doing. He was in a numbed state of being, having gone into the car's wheel, the ceaseless spinning distracting him from both the surrounding sensorial bombardment and the deep feelings of fear. It felt like a type of self-hypnosis. I voiced what Joseph might be feeling at this time, but Joseph showed no reaction, not even an acknowledgment of having heard something.

Joseph's mother was suddenly reminded of her son, and hurried to the floor to be near him, calling his name softly. He did not respond, so she said his name over and over, her anxiety increasing. She stretched out her arms to embrace him but he moved away. Joseph's expression seemed both puzzled and fearful. I found myself wondering how he saw his mother: whether as a person or simply as an encroaching moving hole (her mouth, if perceived unassimilated to her face). His mother then retreated, saying, with a note of anger in her voice, "How can I have him as my boy? Is it me? Well, I was not bad for Sue, so what happened? He's not deaf or blind and still he doesn't look at me, or say anything."

With remorse and love, she elaborated further on her feelings when she gets close to Joseph. She described feeling at a loss at not being able to please her baby, and how "everything started to be upside down in my head as if I was mad". In a desperate tone, Joseph's mother described wanting to "shake him into the family", into her reality, into her love. Joseph's mother's words convey the desperation of not being noticed by him, of not being taken into account, as if she were another child in the family, powerless in the face of Joseph's behaviour and diagnosis.

Shunned by her son, Joseph's mother turned round and started singing. Her voice was not melodic but abrupt, rough, loud, almost like tearing her and everyone's soul. Her husband and daughter laughed at her singing; John commented that it sounded as if she was trying to make herself feel better, to assuage her sorrow.

Joseph moved further away from his family. Soon his father moved near him, sat cross-legged on the floor and played peek-a-boo: putting his hands in front of his eyes and peeking round them saying, "Where is Joseph? Where is Joseph? I can't see him and I want him. Oh dear me, oh *there* is Joseph. Oh no, where is Joseph?"

Joseph remained unresponsive. He lay on the floor looking at the fray in the carpet. He was moving gently from side to side, as if trembling. His focus changed and he seemed to be gazing at the air, or the light. His father then lay next to Joseph, but the boy pulled back and went to another corner of the room, his back to us, looking at the shadow created by his body blocking the light. It was as if every time his parents tried to engage him, or to simply be close by, Joseph moved. I wondered whether he was moving away from his father or from something he had not been able to identify as his father: a bulk, a big moving thing. By removing himself, he was vetoing any form of interaction. Solitary pursuits make for a peaceful life.

Some minutes passed and another person approached Joseph, this time a psychotherapist. Joseph seemed to fold himself away from this a new sound and shape that was close, too close. The psychotherapist moved back to allow a little more space between them, while keeping close enough to show Joseph her interest in him. It was time to find a channel of communication between them.

The therapist began by playing hide and seek with a small toy. She hid and found it herself, saying "peek-a-boo" each time. She did not demand that Joseph interact with her, and yet he watched her, from the side. Soon, he shuffled a little closer, then, after a few more repetitions, he started to repeat her words, "peek-a-boo". There was no eye contact, or sense of engagement, only a half-smile that showed his pleasure at the sound of the words in his mouth—and maybe the feeling in his head? He walked away looking blank but repeating over and over "peek-a-boo . . . peek-a-boo". His parents showed their immense relief: "See, he *can* speak!"

"Peek-a-boo", the first words coming out of the "walking silence", were sounds that could resonate for Joseph in a way that felt pleasurable, exciting, that were directed at himself. We took these words as an invitation to find him.

Let's imagine

To understand how to reach Joseph in his autistic state we had to ask ourselves seemingly impossible questions: how to catch the wind, how to see the world in our own reflection, how to be held by a leaf. We had to try to view the everyday world from a different perspective. In Joseph's world, ordinary events are experienced as if in a different dimension: time moves at a different pace; the air is more viscous; light has greater depth and luminosity; sound has exaggerated volumes and rhythm. Different needs can be satisfied by attention to tiny details and, in Joseph's world, he hangs on to these details: the resonance of a sound; the suspension of a mote of dust.

In Joseph's world, he keeps within his own space: always on the border or in the cracks, never in the middle, in the midst of others. Yet, while absorbed in his own dimension, Joseph is aware of the wider space around him. He continues to scan and check changes in movements, the surrounding atmosphere: he knows something is there (people, expectations), but it is not easy to know what.

Let's try

In my wonder I went to the piano and played a note, middle C, and let its sound hang there. While the note was still resonating, Joseph came closer to me and played a note a few keys higher, and looked briefly at me, his mouth open, dribbling and in a sort of half smile. It was a discovery for us both! Joseph was there in the moment, the single sound going around. Sue then came to the piano and began playing notes, laughing, pushing Joseph aside. Her parents stopped her, but Joseph moved softly away.

Joseph's mother saw what had happened, and started humming a nursery rhyme, very softly. She seemed to be inviting Joseph to join in with her and, after a moment, he did, hesitantly putting words between his teeth, dribbling. Louise started to cry, saying that until then she had not realised how slow and fragile Joseph was. It seemed that he could see and hear but had difficulty processing the sights and sounds within the noise of his family world. It was as if the natural flow of the family did not allow for individuals that were struggling to integrate different aspects from different senses or even from a single sense. So, it seemed important to slow down, when catching the sound was possible and fishing around for clues of Joseph's little pleasures, even if they seemed ridiculous, could work.

There were many things Joseph could not do, so the task was to find out what he could do. We had to think in different terms, in order to perceive the dimensions of his world. Maybe we needed to perceive and experience the world differently, as if we could become, for example, wallpaper or a leaf, or a feather or a bird, or be as light and brief as a soap bubble. As a consequence of being too sensitive and unable to mix modal communications, Joseph had not been able to understand others' communication with him, or enable them to understand him. We had to identify his specific sensitivities and then try to communicate with him with respect for these sensitivities, in the hope that he could finally meet us, and his family, in a way he could comprehend and integrate, and even delight in.

An illustration of day two

Joseph sat on the floor like a six-month-old, his curved back towards me and his mother, dribbling. He was looking at a hair on the floor (was it his mother's? was it mine?), long and black, lying on a dark carpet. He seemed mesmerised by the single hair and when we gently moved towards him he would rock momentarily, looking frightened. The room was darkened, the curtains closed to create a muted environment. It was quiet, the rest of his family elsewhere. Joseph seemed lizard-like, immobile, as if wary of something about to happen, in a state of hyper-vigilance. After a while, the curtains were opened and sunlight entered the room. Joseph was fascinated by the tidal effect, and raised his hand to catch the fine dust particles that suddenly appeared in the ray of light.

It felt as if Joseph and I were suspended in space and time, waiting together. His legs were stretched out in front of him, and I began talking very slowly and gently about his feet. I could feel his fear going through my body and my mind. I could feel his mind was in panic mode, his body ready to retract or flee or freeze, so my gentle talk was about being there in the room and feeling the same as him. I thought that perhaps he was sensitive to my reaction (that I might be feeling a bit irritated) to his attitude of being engaged in a kind of twisted way (seemingly perverse): enjoying being watched, but maintaining a social and emotional detachment. Yet, it seemed as if he knew what he was doing. Somewhere in me it hurt; it was as if I did not matter, and as if I was not likeable, desirable, or even interesting, as if I were no different from the others.

I talked about the need to keep me in sight, to look at me for as long as he could, and in doing so to be able to take in all aspects of my face, or my movements. I also talked about my being quiet so that he could take in my face and my presence, and how we were both scanning each other. At that, his ears suddenly pricked up, though there was no direct gaze at me. Somewhere I felt him, for a second, engage: was he waiting for more?

And so the terms of engagement started. By understanding and entering his world, going at his pace, and helping him put experiences together, we could find a joint purpose. It was my intention to offer a transitional container and a transitional structure in which he could order and classify his feelings. It seemed that Joseph did not yet have an internal space that could store experiences, either positive or negative. (It might have been that for him all experiences were negative, to be discarded, but we did not identify any negative projections.) It seemed that he needed to be helped at a more basic level of creating a container (an overall "skin", according to Bick) for his psychological experiences to develop; to help his feelings become something that could be integrated.

Joseph's parents

John and Louise were in shock when they came to see us. Their relief at having their concerns validated had been replaced with a sense of despair that their son had been diagnosed with autism. What happened to him? They had parented both their children the same, so how could he have turned out differently? They initially told us that they did not want to be part of "a treatment", or for Sue to miss school, but after feeling that they had no choice if they wished to be helped, they agreed to the programme.

Not long into the first couple meeting, Joseph's parents tearfully discussed his diagnosis. They explained that they knew what it meant to be autistic, that it was a disability, and that his future as an autistic adult was too terrible to imagine. They discussed their determination to help him, describing themselves as "fighters". They wanted to learn more about this disability and would do everything possible until "the day [they] die". As well as being a place to consider their commitment to Joseph, the couple and individual sessions gave his parents an opportunity to consider the feelings of ambivalence, disappointment, and anger they experienced. It was a place to reflect on what they knew about Joseph, and their family, and to discuss the impact of the new knowledge and experiences that emerged as the treatment progressed.

It seemed that, in the father's mind, it was his responsibility to bring in the money, and that it was the mother's role to look after and play with the children. John was loving, but seemed uncomfortable in managing the children or playing with them. Despite being caring, attentive, and supportive to his wife, he did not realise that it was important for the family as a whole that he be an active participant, not just the breadwinner. Louise did not show any resentment towards her husband, but did seem to be the far more anxious of the two parents about Joseph and his future; she seemed, at times, "stuck in his stuckness".

During the sessions, John and Louise were encouraged to use different art mediums as a way of exploring and expressing their fears and desires, and as a way of fostering their imagination and creativity.

They also underwent dream analysis, which brought to light many unconscious themes. The adult psychotherapists supported the parents, holding them, so that they in turn were more able to support and hold their family.

Patterns of relating within the family

Meetings with Joseph and his sister revealed issues that had been denied or not seen. For example, the "love" of his big sister was quite often cruel and nasty, rather than caring. Because Joseph never complained, the family seemed to assume that he enjoyed it. His parents rarely intervened and, during their sessions, it became apparent that they did not want to stop the interactions between the siblings, even if they were one-sided, as "at least" they were interactions.

During their therapy, the parents considered their children's behaviour, the causes, and how they could be changed. They discussed in more detail their own childhood experiences. Both parents had been brought up by a series of nannies, as Louise's mother was a manic-depressive and John's mother worked. They considered their deep-held "truths" in the light of their actual feelings. For example, Louise talked a little more about her happy memories of playing with her sisters, but, through her descriptions, revealed that they had actually treated her like a doll, making her do as they wished rather than letting her contribute to the games. For them to become parents, they had to look back on the parenting they had received, develop the type of parenting they would have liked to have had, and consider the parenting each of their children needed. They had a hard job to do, but they were determined to change. They had to learn to play as children and with the children, facing the grief that this implied, both for their own childhood and for the perceived losses regarding the "ideal" baby years they had dreamed of for Joseph. They had to find resilience, strength, and, most of all, humour to help them have "fun" and to meet the needs of their children, constantly adapting to each child's changing requirements.

Feeling the power of worrying his parents

Joseph started to feel the power of the concern he was causing in his newly alert parents. While the parents learnt to slow their thinking and reflect on their feelings, they also learnt about their child's states of mind and emotions. This emotional awareness was coupled with new techniques of sensitisation and ideas about how to keep the slow but gentle progress going. As his parents worked harder to understand Joseph, his repertoire of engagement grew. This included "helpful" interactions, such as increasing eye contact, smiling, and displaying humour, as well as less helpful mechanisms, such as "playing dumb"', manipulating others, and entering power struggles.

The understanding and development of Joseph's emotional states

As his parents and the therapists increased their own and, by reflection, Joseph's emotional states, so Joseph's awareness and experience of them increased. The different emotional states were illustrated by the therapist, described, drawn, and acted out in games and play. For example, the therapist held up pictures of feeling states, or acted out a story with puppets in which feelings were the central theme. In response, Joseph began to react by embodying the same feeling states. Should the therapist have been enacting angry feelings with a doll, Joseph would begin to become angry himself, throwing the dolls around.

What is interesting to observe is that as the child starts feeling that he has emotions, he goes forward and backwards in his development. One can see that as he incorporates new experiences and skills in his repertoire, they become disconcerting to him, and he reverts back to his old behaviour. New ways of perceiving and feeling promote trepidation and a desire to put a stop to the novelty. Yet, at the same time, curiosity starts to develop, fuelled by the power of a relationship that can be experienced and even enjoyed. Depending on the degree of dissociation and delay, we want the new insights to be retained, to be used appropriately, and to develop, as in other children. We start being hopeful and Joseph might feel it as a burden, unless we say to him that is he who is starting to hope and he might be observing what happens in us with his hope.

Joseph did not dare to think that *he* could wish, want something, and bear the wait without being overwhelmed. He tried through us to see what we did with his want, with the disillusion of not having, with his efforts about not going back to previous behaviours.

So, we watched as he took a few steps forward and then a few back. His face had a tender expression, as though he was requesting patience, time, and not to be left alone, needing to join in, yet terrified of emotional contact, dependence, and recognition. The tenderness in his look when connected became a growing asset. It appeared in glimpses in the intensive treatment and we followed it as we best we could.

There is a common aspect in all the young children we see, and it is the enormous depth in the connection shown in encounters, as if they cannot bear the strength of their perceptions; perhaps because it is slower and more complex, or perhaps because they hang on to details that are irrelevant to us, but when they can look they seem to see our thoughts and feelings.

An example was when I saw Joseph at the end of the second week. I had just received a letter telling me about the sudden death of a close friend. I was not crying when the session began, but Joseph started crying inconsolably. I said that I was sad and that he was crying, and I wondered whether he was crying to accompany me. He looked at me and I talked to him about the immense sadness and overwhelming feelings that he carried from other people and which he did not understand. I was silent for a time, during which Joseph mostly kept his eyes on me. There was a feeling of him being like the howling dog when the master is dying, and I understood that it is in that fine line of terrifying sympathy that Joseph sometimes felt caught and which made him want to run away.

From our minds and being, to our reactions and reflection

How do we start again? How do we find that our wish reflects their hope? Our states of mind and being (the countertransference) are the principal guides that can reflect part of the landscape of their minds. And when we want something for them, we might be projecting our own wishes and expectations, which might have been what overwhelmed the child in the first place (the wishes and expectations of other people), since they are too difficult to process or to carry.

Would that be the origin of the rebellious, stubborn attitude shown in the recovery? Is it strength or defence?

A container for his thoughts

The individual work progressed. During one session, when we were all sitting around the table to start playing with playdough (to sensitise Joseph's hands, which were idle and floppy), Joseph was looking down, floppy and drooling. We described our actions and the sensation of moulding the dough. We described his difficulty in doing this activity. It seemed as if he did not know what his hands were for. It was not that he did not want to participate, he simply did not know how. So we "scaffolded" him by sitting in front of him, or behind him if he was reluctant. He did not refuse. It was as if he could not put together in his mind the opportunity of playing with the dough, but, with our support, he allowed the activity to take place. Gradually, over the next few sessions, Joseph started rolling, shaping, copying, and interacting by pairing up different coloured dough, and eventually taking turns with us.

By concentrating and paying attention, he learnt to put together the pieces, as if he were allowing himself to put together the pieces of his world. Finally, integration was taking place in his mind, but it was a slow process, and would require the full commitment of his parents in the years to come.

The new awareness of his mother as a person, separate to himself, who could hold his feelings, brought with it delight and pain. Playing peek-a-boo under a translucent veil of fabric, Joseph smiled, seeming full of passion whenever his mother returned to view. He began to reach forward to touch her face through the material. As Joseph's awareness of his mother as a separate being increased, so did his attachment to her. The consequence of his new-found love and delight in his mother was a new-found fear and pain at separating. When his mother had to leave him to do something else, Joseph howled: terrible, despairing screams. His infantile fears appearing for the first time were hard to bear: for him, for his mother, who experienced feeling "torn apart", and even the therapists, witnesses to a primal grief. It can be difficult for the parents to bear the process of rebirth, of literally allowing their child to start over and undergo the process of building a "membrane that can contain all the aspects of the personality", as Bick describes it (1968). Prior to object relations, the skin offers that overall containment that probably starts in the mother's arms and serves as a foundation for allowing healthy relationships to develop. Some children find it more difficult than others to create that first overall container of their emotions, sensations, perceptions, and needs. They feel at the mercy of the fragments of their experiences that appear and disappear without staying to form a whole. So, the work done by us is very much like building a container for the self that can integrate the parts, and then use them in functional and creative ways, externally as well as internally. Maybe sometimes the force that kept them apart was the fear of not understanding the array of sensations, or being oversensitive from the beginning.

The entire process is difficult to speed up: putting together experience after experience, perception after perception with an integration that makes sense is a very slow and complex process. However, it is only in this way that the mind can form friendly figures, objects, and representations that are reliable. Only then, once the self has a thinking mind, is the child able to fully relate to others.

The programme timetable

Helping a child begin to build internal structures (his own mind) and external structures (relationships with his family) involves a whole team who understand the principles of development and who can adapt their interventions to match the progress and delays. As the child needs structure and containment, so does the treatment process. A clear timetable is created that incorporates a range of approaches, activities, and techniques.

Structured and unstructured times

We spend time with the child alone as well as together with the parents. The individual time together is generally structured time, to help create a mind that is able to hold thoughts in the form of ideas, memories, and representations. We talk gently and slowly about what we are doing and why. We sit with the child on the carpet or at a table when doing a specific task. Tasks are chosen with an understanding of developmental stages, kinaesthetic experiences, psychoanalytic theory, and a need for fun. The therapist might fan a little interest in a toy or some other object in the room, in order to generate interest in the child or demonstrate something interesting or meaningful.

The aim is to help the development of different stages of the mind, creating the foundations for object relations to occur. It is as if we are "jump-starting" the mind out of the undifferentiated state in which it got stuck at the beginning of life, when the separation between the psyches of the mother and the child had not occurred. This very important work needs to be carried out by a developmental therapist who will aim to adjust the bias. We want to create a container for thoughts to be produced, held first in an external space before becoming internalised.

We taught Joseph the basics of taking in experiences, learning from the experiences, and creating and remembering his own experiences. We sat him at a table and gave him activities to do that would help his brain accommodate knowledge, by exercising executive functions that appeared absent in this child. For this process to happen, we needed to build basic skills such as analysing, classifying, pairing, piling up, taking turns, and recognising the basic emotions of happiness, anger, fear, and surprise, then looking at them in their relatives. In this slow, calm way, Joseph learned to start and finish different activities. We believe that the repetitive actions of an autistic child are limited in nature because of the reduced number of experiences they have to draw on, due to fear or lack of imagination.

Therapeutic techniques

It took time for us to really get to know Joseph. We spent the first twenty-four hours of treatment (over three days) observing and being with him, moving in front of or beside him to share his view, his breathing, his experience. We were careful not to move too much so that Joseph was able to perceive us. Gradually, Joseph became accustomed to our still, close, quiet presence. Once he had got used to us, we could start experimenting, guided by our knowledge of child development, with comments and actions to see what reached him. We talked gently, modulating our tone. We offered a range of playthings in different textures, colours, and sizes. We started by trying to get his attention by doing full scaffolding, supporting his body from behind (whether sitting on the floor or on a chair) to indicate that we were there to help him feel the weight of his whole body first, as well as to explore the different things he could do with his hands, such as rolling out the playdough. We did not allow Joseph to lean on us or use us as a chair; we talked about being considered as a person, not as a piece of furniture, and that our goal was for him to be a person as well, that there was a part of him that wanted to be like everyone else but did not know how. By scaffolding him physically (and psychologically by commenting on what we were doing), we taught him "how to do it". Soon, he was being supported only by the arms, then with just his hands, to do tasks like moulding playdough, or playing with the ball or foam or paint.

Joseph learnt from his encounters with his therapists that we were predictable, not necessarily in our actions, but in our calm, containing presence. With this new predictability, and an associated reduction in fear, Joseph appeared to find the sessions with us, and his parents, a pleasant novelty. His drooling stopped and a mischievousness started to appear. The pull to return to the brainless teddy bear state had not disappeared, but the new experiences were making him curious. The power of the relationships was making a difference and he no longer wanted to escape.

We used drawing to talk about the four basic feelings (happy, sad, scared, angry), and to help Joseph start differentiating faces and gestures. For this, we also used photographs of other children and adults. We started employing a content that required verbal explanations and that could be dramatised.

We also used holding by the mother or father when Joseph started to wander around and around when feeling anxious. This consisted of one of them holding Joseph in their arms, close to their body and containing him while talking about his insecurities and fears: a dread of a sensation of an endless fall, or of bad things happening. This physical, verbal, and emotional containment was an opportunity for the parents to assuage and give meaning to developmentally immature anxieties. The fear transmitted physically from Joseph's skin and nerves was met by "muscle talk" from his parents; they showed him that they were stronger, and that they could hold his fears and fury and not be overcome by them; that they could stand this activity for as long as it took to see positive results. Of course, the good results are always the impetus for calming a child. Providing a secure container for a child's bodily terrors is highlighted by Winnicott (1949) and Bick (1968, 1986), who talk of the parents' desire to quell their own fears when they see their distressed child: for example, the falling for ever, spilling out, different skin sensations, or losing parts of the body. So, even though it looked at times as if the parents identified with the terrified part of the child, by exercising the holding, supported by us, they could identify with the part of the child that craves having strong parents to keep them safe in their arms, mind, and heart.

In our work, we also use teddy bears or toys to enact the child's everyday experiences. We first put words to ordinary events to facilitate the process of interpretation and understanding, and later incorporate the toys so that, through symbolic play, the child can "reproduce" the events.

In addition, we talk in the third person when describing atmospheres of feelings. Alvarez (1992) observes that some children cannot cope with the direct feeling in themselves but can, instead, look and talk about something that is outside of them, and will be able to identify with the feelings once they can integrate them or piece them together internally.

During our sessions with Joseph, if he refused to accompany us in trying to play or to use his hands in different ways, he would express his rage with grunting sounds and temper tantrums. We felt happy when "real emotions" started appearing, even negative ones, as they were an indication that he was bothering to respond, to put up a fight. By the middle of the second week, by the sixtieth hour, Joseph was saying the odd word. By the eightieth hour, he was stringing two words together, and by the hundredth (end of the third week), he was saying whole phrases—sometimes copying, sometimes to request something.

It was interesting to see Joseph begin to "tease" his therapist with jokes, or by hiding toys, or using her name in puns. These and other normal childlike behaviours slowly began to replace the self-comforting repetitive actions, as he was able to have feelings and hold them in his mind and heart without experiencing much, or even any, panic.

Unstructured periods were timetabled for the family in the second and third weeks. These included art sessions, helping prepare lunch and then eating together, going food shopping, library trips, cooking, playing games, and trips to the park. Everyone involved was engaged in the planning, preparation, and actual activity. We facilitated communication and reflection during these times. For example, in family meetings, so that everybody could have space and respect, we used a spoon to take turns: whoever had the spoon could speak.

The unstructured sessions allowed us to work psychotherapeutically on the family systems, on issues such as boundaries, conflict, control, and defences. This type of work demands more time than the three weeks of the treatment allow, but we are able to start the process. In the family group, the children in particular are encouraged to express and reflect on their own desires and feelings. We support the parents in supporting their children to manage their own feelings. For example, in the case of Joseph's family, rather than feeling overwhelmed by their daughter's temper tantrums, Louise and John had the time, and support, to develop their own resourceful solutions and coping mechanisms. We also helped the parents to understand their children better, and to allow for individuality to flourish. In this way, Joseph had a more caring and versatile environment in which to grow and develop, and to understand the process of trust.

We allowed the older child, Sue, to regress during the games, playing the baby and talking about it, and we allowed her to behave as the older child, to rehearse coping mechanisms, becoming characters or playing as different animals, and dealing with the creation of anticipation. Joseph was slow to come to terms with the process of change in his sister, but he managed, and, as the different stages of play matured, it allowed for symbolisation to appear—a positive step towards normal development.

The progress

Various personal topics were revealed as being important to the parents. John disclosed that he was the only adult male in employment in his family, and that his financial responsibilities to support his own and his extended family (father, mother, and brother) had resulted in him "giving up" joy and fun with the family. A key theme in his individual and couple sessions was the importance of his "paternal function" and his role in supporting Louise, as if needing to reclaim her from the torrent of emotions generated by their sensitive son.

Louise explored her identification with a "useless" mother who kept having children—her mother had had four children and numerous miscarriages. She expressed the fear she felt surrounding her mother's bipolar disorder and the disconcerting behaviour and rules she enforced in the childhood home. Louise thought about intergenerational patterns affecting her own mothering skills: for example, her obsession about everybody having to be extremely slim. Louise revealed that the name "Joseph" had been chosen because she had briefly thought about having an abortion and, feeling guilty about those thoughts, had chosen the name of somebody who had survived.

The couple sessions helped John and Louise rekindle their relationship, to learn to enjoy it again, with the sense of maturing in their parenthood together and sharing their personal desires and needs.

With support from us, Joseph's parents took responsibility for the outcome of the enterprise. They accepted our clear boundaries and were able to speak openly, bringing to us all their dislikes, negative thoughts, grievances, and any other feelings they had against us (most of the time authoritative transferences, while at other times infantile transferences that needed to be worked out). In doing so, they avoided acting out any uncertainty or resentments and enabled us to resolve tensions quickly.

Joseph's older sister, Sue, received individual psychotherapy, as well as taking part in the family programme. Her individual sessions were focused on helping her express and explore her feelings, in particular, the impact on her life of having a brother who seemed to occupy so much of her mother's mind. We gave her a safe space to vent her resentment and anger, as well as her sadness that "Joseph doesn't want to play with me". In her therapy and in joint sessions with her parents, Sue began to realise that she had not been replaced in her parents' affections. As she felt a renewed confidence, she began to better understand the fragility of her brother and his autistic behaviours. Sue's behaviour towards Joseph became more tender, as if wanting to find and help him, rather than use him as a prop, vying with him for her parents' attention.

When the treatment programme was over and the parents were not being supported all the time, Joseph started to regress. However, due to his parents' commitment to weekly follow-on support, they were able to halt the regression and resume improvement. The new mental representations need help stabilising as functional internal representations, which gradually become more benign as the new state of the mind continues to develop; this is why we see follow-up as an essential part of the treatment. The whole family received individual and family help for a year and half. Joseph received additional one-to-one help in the nursery from a member of our team during this period.

Joseph is now eleven years old. He is able to make and maintain friendships and has even been on sleep-overs at friends' houses. He is in the middle range of achievement in the class. His parents have described their delight at Joseph "rejoining" their family. He has been reassessed by the paediatrician, who was happy to consider him out of the autistic spectrum.

Analysing the results of the three-week intensive treatment process

The scale depicted in Figure 6.3 shows the changes in Joseph after the three-week programme. We not only see the progress in his behaviours—from Never or Always to Rarely and Frequently—but how the acceptance and growth of his interpersonal relationships added warmth and emotion to his encounters. There is an acceptance in the interpersonal area of people (his family and other children), but Joseph remains a little shy with regard to initiating contact with others and in his reactive behaviours.

All other behaviours in the motor, sensorial, and expressive areas saw much improvement.

These results demonstrate the enormous developments that can occur once the ability to relate to others has been learnt. In Joseph's case, this happened first with the developmental psychotherapist and then with his mother as the container of his newly felt fragmented emotions. Similarly for his parents, when they learnt to understand him and when he responded to them, it was as if a window opened on to a whole new world. Love and affection were felt, as evidenced by the black dots on the scale depicted in Figure 6.4.

Conclusion

In this chapter, I illustrated in detail how we treat a child and his family in the Re:Start intensive programme. The purpose of our work is to start again, to go back to the beginning, in an effort to provide a foundation from which the child can explore the thoughts, ideas, and

ACQUARONE DETECTION SCALES FOR EARLY RELATIONSHIPS®

EARLY SIGNS OF ALARM – pre-Autism

FOLLOW-UP – INFANT/CHILD

name: **JOSEPH**

age: **2 years 2 months** *date of this observation:* **DD MMM YYYY**

		NEVER	RARELY	FREQUENT	ALWAYS	OBSERVER REACTIONS
INTERPERSONAL	1. GAZING			●		*Attentive when called and when he requests something*
	2. BABBLING			●		
	3. CALLING			●		
	4. IMITATING			●		*Played with other children ... is able to copy his siblings and other children*
	5. PROVOKING		●			
	6. POINTING			●		
	7. FEEDING			●		*Eating well and all sorts of vegetables, fruits and meats*
	8. JOINT ATTENTION			●		
	9. PLAY			●		*His play is varied and creative ... reached representational level*
	10. ALONE			●		
	11. RELATING *– to other children*			●		*Frequent with ... siblings ...*
	– to adults			●		*Frequent with ... Mother/Father ... other caregivers ... other unfamiliar adults*
	12. REACTIVE BEHAVIOURS *capacity to... a) accept emotional warmth b) bear stressful event c) adapt to changes*		●	●		
SENSORIAL	TOUCHING					
	13. *Skin-to-skin*			●		
	14. *Textures*			●		
	RESPONSE					
	15. *Sounds*			●		*Still very sensitive to loud noise ... usually when loud speakers are involved*
	16. *Noise*		●			
	17. *Name*					
	18. *Light & patterns*			●		
	19. *Smells*			●		
	20. COMFORTING			●		
MOTOR	HOLDING					
	21. *Posturing*			●		
	22. *Stereotypic movement*	●				
	23. *Use of hands/Use of body*			●		
AFFECT	24. EXPRESSIVENESS			●		
	25. SELF HELP DEVELOPMENT			●		

ANY OTHER OBSERVATIONS NOT LISTED ABOVE:

The treatment continued for another 6 months. Same results.

Figure 6.3. Joseph's follow-up assessment.

ACQUARONE DETECTION SCALES FOR EARLY RELATIONSHIPS®

EARLY SIGNS OF ALARM – pre-Autism

...affecting the baby or being affected by the baby...

FOLLOW-UP – MOTHER/caregiver

name: **NAME**
child: JOSEPH *age:* 2 years 2 months

		NEVER	RARELY	FREQUENT	ALWAYS	OBSERVER REACTIONS
INTERPERSONAL	1. GAZING			●		*Mother*
	2. BABBLING			●		*... showed overall interest and joy about knowing more about her child and the others*
	3. CALLING			●		*... gave importance to her role*
	4. FEEDING		●			*... relaxed and ... showing pleasure in holding the baby*
	5. GAMES / PLAY		●			
	6. RELATING		●			
	7. REACTIVE BEHAVIOURS		●			
SENSORIAL	8. TOUCHING			●		*... showed feeling*
	9. COMFORTING		●			*... relaxed ... showing pleasure ... doing things with him*
MOTOR	10. POSTURE		●			
AFFECT	11. EXPRESSIVENESS			●		
	12. UNDERSTANDING OF EMOTIONS					
	– *in themselves*			●		
	– *in the baby*			●		
	13. PAST					
	– *Psychiatric illness*			●		
	– *Other difficulties*			●		

ANY OTHER OBSERVATIONS NOT LISTED ABOVE:

Figure 6.4. Joseph's mother's follow-up assessment.

sensations that result from his experience in the external world. We involve the parents in our work because they must learn about the quality of the child's processing and how to help him to form relationships. Various techniques are used to achieve this. These techniques are in the realm of "vitalizing experiences", as Alvarez (2012) describes them, and initiate the process of structuring the mind, which is accompanied by explanations. Later on, interpretations can be verbalised to further the psychic progress of the young child. The structured mind is then able to contain thoughts, ideas, and feelings, and the child is eventually able to voice and talk about them.

By working with the whole family, we not only help the child face his anxieties and feelings of panic during the treatment, but also enable the parents to understand and to help their child face these emotions in the long term. The autistic tendency does not disappear entirely, but the earlier the treatment, the better for knowing how to recognise and deal with it.

Figures 6.5 and 6.6 summarise the changes in Joseph's behaviour from when we first saw him to when he'd completed the three-week treatment. The pale grey lines indicate the flat, uninterested, unmotivated young child we saw at the start, unable to form an interesting relationship with others. Black indicates Joseph's behaviour at the end of the programme, when he was able to integrate the activities in his brain and complete tasks on his own, without the therapists needing to scaffold him; this gave him a wonderful sense of satisfaction. On top of this, Joseph was able to perform and communicate with others, which helped him to overcome the confusion and isolation of autism and which showed him that having enjoyable relationships was possible.

The following statement by Trevarthen and Delafield-Butt (2013) is relevant to how we treated Joseph, and how we approach all such cases:

> Understanding of the fundamental and deeply felt disorder in autism as failure of integrative brain activity for carrying out sensori-motor intentions with ease and creativity, that it is a disorder that also affects communicative expression and perceiving the motor intentions of others, may help explain how intensive, imitation-based therapies attentive to emotions may be effective and may foster enjoyable response and interest (Nind, 1999; Nadel, 2006; Nordoff & Robbins, 2007; Zeedyk, 2008; Caldwell, 2010; Field et al., 2002, 2011; Frank & Trevarthen, 2012; Lüdke, 2012; Solomon et al., 2012).
>
> By consciously "attuning" to the motor acts of the autistic patient and feeling their affective and intentional content in "intense interaction", before re-enacting creative collaborations with adaptation to responses, the therapist provides an exterior pattern of actions that are timed and directed sensitively to compensate for repetition of uncertain, anxious attempts. A responsive "listening" makes communication possible, as well as progress to new self-confident and joyful experience, which may free an exceptional talent (Ockleford, 2013) . . . Such therapy can aid not only the autistic child to achieve communication, but can be of great help to a parent.

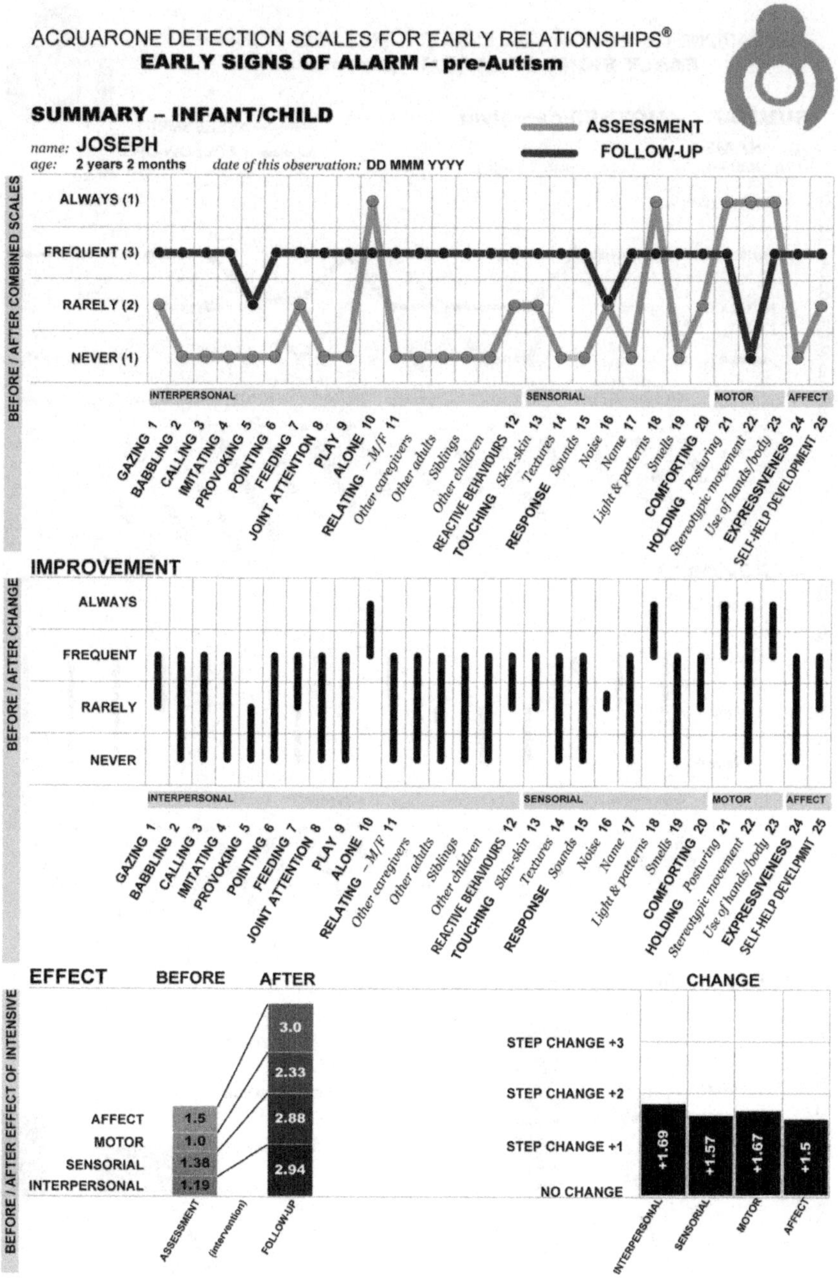

Figure 6.5. Follow-up summary report for Joseph.

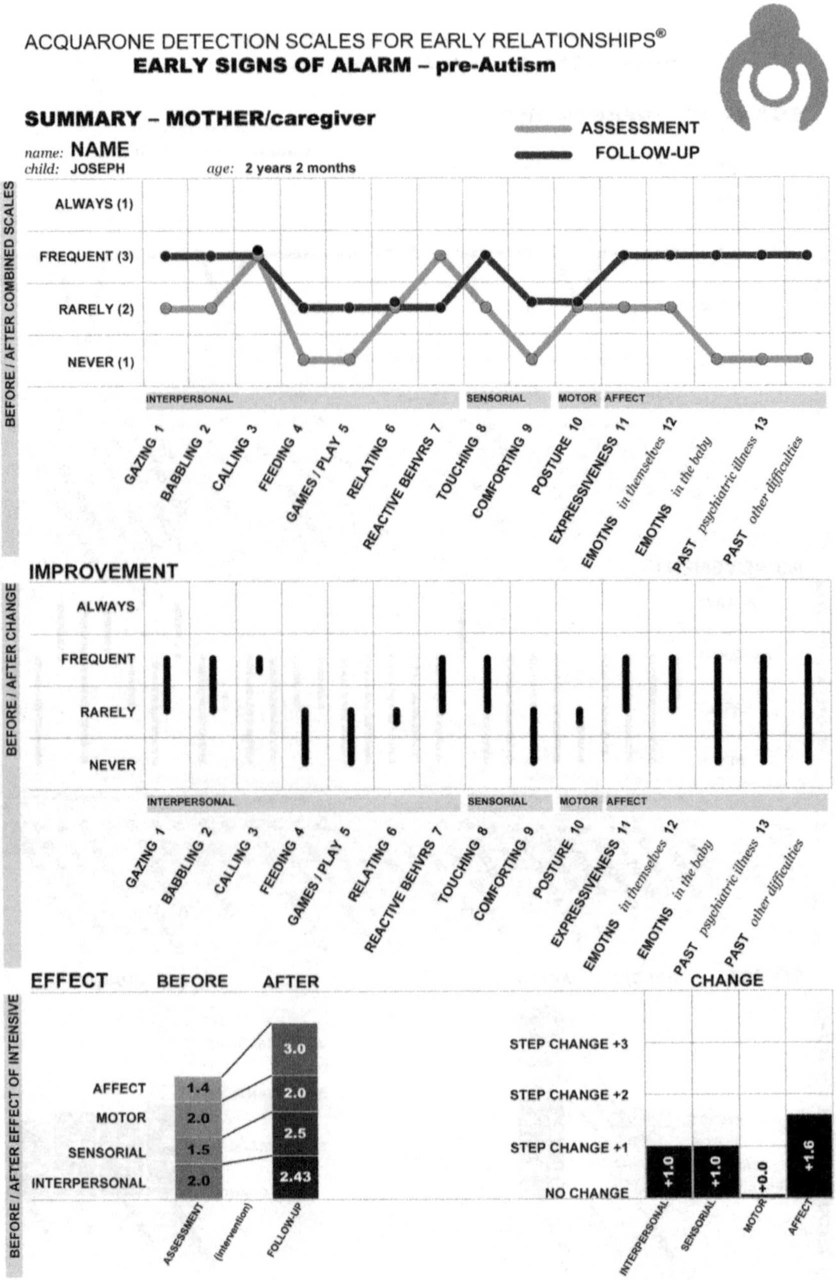

Figure 6.6. Follow-up summary report for Joseph's mother.

CHAPTER SEVEN

Geronimo (aged three years, two months): a complex child

Stella Acquarone

"Inside a pushchair covered with a black cloth, the boy lay silent. The parents spoke quietly about him, as if frightened of his reactions, explaining that he was autistic—'the poor child'. If the cloth was removed, a pair of wide, anxious eyes appeared in a face surrounded by long, messy curls. He was sucking his thumb while holding a piece of muslin, on the alert in case anything changed, because if it did he was ready to scream inconsolably. His clothes were clean but creased, and he had mucus coming out of his nose that he would rub with his hands into his hair."

(Clinical notes, Stella Acquarone)

Geronimo was aged three years and two months when he was brought to us. He was an only child, and had not yet started to speak. He did not want to be with his loving parents, he did not want to look at them, or anybody else, in fact. He simply preferred to be in his pushchair, under its black sunshade—the blanket behind which he could hide. The sunshade was always on, whether out on the street or inside the house. If Geronimo was taken out of the pushchair, he demanded to be held in his parents' arms, but never cuddled up inside them. He stared at the floor and whined constantly. To stop the whining, Geronimo was usually given a dummy to suck on.

The young boy never slept at night, only during the day, spending hours in a quiet lethargy. His grandparents were worried about his behaviour and tantrums. He could not be left alone with them, or with anybody, because he would cry so bitterly that his parents felt totally under his control. They described feeling that Geronimo was "under their skin".

Despite having suspicions about it for more than a year and half, and the referral for a paediatric assessment, his parents were in disbelief when Geronimo was diagnosed with autistic spectrum disorder (ASD). They thought that his behaviour was "OK", except for the fact that he did not utter a word.

Background

Geronimo's parents looked alike, as if they were brother and sister. His father, James, was American, his mother, Orla, from an Irish family. They had met in high school in the USA and moved to London when Geronimo was two years old, as Orla was completing her PhD in English Literature. Although the parents were best friends, they had different approaches to managing their child. While James "knew all about children" because he came from a big family, he spent most of his time immersed in his computer. Orla was an only child, and with little experience of being around young children and feeling insecure in her role as a parent, leaned on the father's "expertise" when it came to dealing with Geronimo.

Geronimo and his mother were a unity that could not separate. Geronimo was awake most of the night and Orla had begun to feel unwell due to the lack of sleep and her uncertainty about what to do. She told us that she had read and followed all the parenting books she could find, but none of the advice had helped. James had resorted to sleeping in the lounge to get some rest, but was in total agreement that the child should not suffer or be alone if he was awake at night.

The pregnancy had been a terrible ordeal for Orla; she suffered from debilitating morning sickness, and was even hospitalised on three occasions due to dehydration. The birth was also traumatic. Orla had found it hard to cope with the constant changeover of midwives throughout the twenty-four-hour delivery. Once the baby was born, her physical problems subsided, and with relief she found that the child was of normal weight and eager to feed. However, breastfeeding was painful and, as Orla did not want to cope with yet another struggle, she quickly switched to giving him formula. Even though she initially claimed to be "happy" about the birth, later sessions revealed an underlying resentment towards the child who had made her feel so sick.

Geronimo was named after the great warrior and prominent leader of the Bedonkohe Apache who fought against Mexico and the USA for their expansion into Apache tribal lands. As a newborn, Geronimo slept most of the day, allowing his mother to get on with her studies. When awake, Geronimo played by himself. Her only complaint was that he was a "fussy eater"; he refused most solids, his diet consisting mainly of milk drunk from a bottle. The mother thought she had been blessed with an independent sweet character, and was greatly surprised when she was told that he was on the autistic spectrum. She was deeply affected by the diagnosis, as she could not imagine anything worse. Researching into what might help, they took Geronimo to a speech therapist, but the child had not been interested at all. During the therapy, he had been constantly distracted. His mother described how he would look in the air as if relating to something or somebody, and would open and close his mouth as though having mute conversations, almost hallucinatory.

We saw this for ourselves during the initial consultation, and realised that this was a sign that Geronimo was experiencing some form of conversation in his mind, even though there were no words and no interest in interacting with real people. At times, he would even flap his arms when spoken to, as if filled with discomfort.

According to the paediatric assessment he had thus far received, it had been found that Geronimo had a slight chromosome disorder—an extra tail on chromosome 5. This does not generally cause any significant problems, although can result in some developmental delay. Geronimo was physically very normal in height, weight, vision, and hearing, but his emotional and cognitive development had not caught up. According to the Griffiths scale, the child was on the autistic spectrum.

On the Acquarone scale, Geronimo scored twenty signs of alarm (Figure 7.1), a strong indication that he was in need of our intensive infant–parent programme, for four weeks rather than the usual three.

ACQUARONE DETECTION SCALES FOR EARLY RELATIONSHIPS®

EARLY SIGNS OF ALARM – pre-Autism

ASSESSMENT – INFANT/CHILD

name: **GERONIMO**
age: **3 years** *date of this observation:* **DD MMM YYYY**

		NEVER	RARELY	FREQUENT	ALWAYS	OBSERVER REACTIONS
INTERPERSONAL	1. **GAZING** *Eye-to-eye contact within a relationship and the maintenance of this contact*	●				
	2. **BABBLING** *Making sounds for the benefit of the partner in the parent-infant relationship*	●				
	3. **CALLING** *– The facial expressions – Noises or gestures that seek to produce an affectionate response from the partner*	●				
	4. **IMITATING** *– Moving mouth, tongue, etc., in imitation of mother's (or another) – The repetition of a sound or a movement heard or seen by the child*	●				
	5. **PROVOKING** *Inciting the person into interacting, not just to use as an instrument to do something for him/her*	●				
	6. **POINTING** *Indicating with index finger to a person about an object of interest*	●				
	7. **FEEDING** *Child's attitude during the intake of food, including anticipatory behaviour (e.g. head-turning, moving arms the food/breast)*	●				
	8. **JOINT ATTENTION** *Looking in the same direction*	●				
	9. **PLAY** *– Capacity to play the same game for more than 5 minutes, and share with another person – Take turns and stay with a person – Children* 10. **ALONE**	●				
	11. **RELATING** *Behaviours indicating the capacity to relate & accept emotional warmth.*					
	– Mother, Father	●				
	– Other caregivers	●				
	– Other unfamiliar adults	●				
	– Siblings	●				
	– Other unfamiliar children	●				
	12. **REACTIVE BEHAVIOURS** *tolerance to frustrations, including: – a) Capacity to accept emotional warmth – b) Capacity to bounce back after stressful event – c) Capacity to adapt to changes...please indicate*	●	●			
SENSORIAL	**TOUCHING**					
	13. *Skin-to-skin contact initiated by infant for play or affection*	●				
	14. *Does the child touch paint, foam, sand, water, playdoh, plasticine and other messy substances*		●			
	RESPONSE					
	15. *Response to sounds*	●				
	16. *Response to noise*	●				
	17. *Response to name*	●				
	18. *Response to light & patterns*	●				
	19. *Response to smells*	●				
	20. **COMFORTING** *Child's ability to find relief from distress by themselves (e.g. thumb sucking, touching hands, playing with one car, others)...specify*	●				
MOTOR	**HOLDING** 21. *The posturing of the child when he is supported in the arms of the mother (e.g. floppy, rigid, restless) – General muscle tone when sitting or standing*		●				
	22. *Stereotypic movement of arms, eyes, etc. – Walking: on tiptoes or sluggish*		●			
	23. *Use of hands: for grasping, for helping himself – Use of body: to reach, to climb, to hide, other...*	●				
AFFECT	24. **EXPRESSIVENESS** *The body or facial expression of emotional states (e.g., sad, worried, anxious, bland, happy, or others)...specify*	●				
	25. **SELF-HELP DEVELOPMENT** *– Ability to cope independently with the environment, (e.g., dress) – Eating – Being careful with him/herself or others*	●				

ANY OTHER OBSERVATIONS NOT LISTED ABOVE:
Continues twisting fingers constantly. In a pushchair for sleeping or for not walking. Crying continuously indicating to the parents tiredness and managing to fall asleep often. Not wanting to eat. Extremely select in the food eating - chips with ketchup and baby food in front of the TV.

Figure 7.1. Geronimo's assessment scale.

ACQUARONE DETECTION SCALES FOR EARLY RELATIONSHIPS®

EARLY SIGNS OF ALARM – pre-Autism

...affecting the baby or being affected by the baby...

ASSESSMENT – MOTHER/caregiver

name: **NAME**

child: GERONIMO *age:* 3 years

		NEVER	RARELY	FREQUENT	ALWAYS	OBSERVER REACTIONS
INTERPERSONAL	1. **GAZING** *Eye-to-eye contact with the baby and the maintenance of this contact*				●	*... mother and father were watching the child with fear*
	2. **BABBLING** *– Making sounds for the benefit of the parent-infant relationship – Talking*				●	
	3. **CALLING** *Facial expressions, noises or gestures seeking to produce an affectionate response from the infant*				●	*... anxiety about lack of response*
	4. **FEEDING** *Mother's attitude towards infant's hunger and need to feed: – Does she anticipate behaviour and have meal or breast easily available? – Does she pay attention, talk with the baby and enjoy feeding? – Does she interrupt with any excuse (e.g., talks to others and looks away)? – Is she fearful, full of anguish or has she any delusions? – Is she apathetic?*				●	*... always chips and in front of ipad*
	5. **GAMES / PLAY** *– Playful encounters, including songs and teasing*	●				
	6. **RELATING** *Behaviours indicating the capacity to relate & accept emotional warmth towards the baby*	●				*... child did not want to relate*
	7. **REACTIVE BEHAVIOURS** *including: – Tolerance to frustrations – Capacity to accept emotional warmth – Capacity to bounce back after stressful event – Capacity to adapt to changes*	●				
SENSORIAL	8. **TOUCHING** *– Skin-to-skin contact initiated by infant for play or affection*	●				
	9. **COMFORTING** *– Mother's ability to find relief for the baby's distress*				●	*... continuous*
MOTOR	10. **POSTURE** *The posturing of the mother when the infant is supported in her arms or any other way (e.g., other, rough, balanced precariously)*	●				
AFFECT	11. **EXPRESSIVENESS** *– Expression of emotional state (e.g., sad, worried, anxious, bland, happy, others)...specify*				●	*... anxious and frightened*
	12. **UNDERSTANDING OF EMOTIONS** *– in themselves*		●			*... a lot of difficulty*
	– in the baby	●				
	13. **PAST** *– Psychiatric illness*		●			
	– Other difficulties		●			

ANY OTHER OBSERVATIONS NOT LISTED ABOVE:

Comments about never felt valued by her mother and fear of having a bad relationship with her son.

Figure 7.2. Geronimo's mother's assessment scale.

Geronimo was delayed in his response to other people, delayed in his speech and communication capacities, and in his play—which was not visible at all since he was either asleep or drifting in and out of sleep. He also presented delays in several other areas, such as feeding, toilet training, and motor and sensory skills. We agreed that we could offer an intensive treatment to help the child. We could help him to stay awake, to structure his mind in such a way that would enable him to look, pay attention, concentrate, take turns over activities, start the natural process of classifying and analysing, to use his hands for more than just sucking his thumb, to walk and move around with purpose, and to slowly become part of the family.

From our observations, it was clear that each parent required individual therapy so that they could learn to separate properly from one another and to cease projecting and reintrojecting their own negative emotions to each other and to Geronimo (projective identification). They also needed help with their feelings of hopelessness and to learn how to mature into the type of grown-up parents that Geronimo needed.

When we communicated our conclusions to Geronimo's parents, they were delighted with the prospect of therapy for the three of them. We agreed on four weeks of intensive treatment due to child's age and the habituated strength of his autistic behaviours.

The process

As usual, we began the process by asking the parents what they hoped to gain from the Re:Start programme. They replied that they simply wished to be able to live as everybody else, to sleep through the night, and to have a son who responded to their love. From the initial assessment we could see that Geronimo was used to sleeping much of the day, and that he enjoyed it. He refused to walk, preferring to be wheeled around in his pushchair while he sucked on a dummy. In the first meeting, we allowed Geronimo to carry on doing this to see how the parents reacted to him. They give in to his demands immediately, which caused them to feel both sadness and fear.

It was this underlying fear that led them to justify his behaviour with, "Poor child, he doesn't understand", or "Poor child, he's autistic". As a result, it seemed as if Geronimo was to be put up with rather than brought up; to be pampered rather than told off if he hit either of them, or if he threw his food on the floor or refused to eat. He had not yet been toilet trained as his parents believed that "he couldn't understand".

Treating Geronimo

Geronimo's treatment began with three days of assessment. At first, Geronimo did not want to be separated from his mother, or from his pushchair or dummy. He would cry inconsolably if his pushchair was not in the room with him, or the dummy not to hand. He brought a teddy with him—dirty, smelly, and threadbare—and sucked on that instead. We discovered that he took it to bed with him every night. It was interesting to note that while many children use a cuddly toy as a transitional object to help them separate from their parents, Geronimo, fused with his mother, had not yet begun to separate. We talked with Geronimo about the fact that he wanted to bring his teddy to show us how he felt about himself and how its dirty, smelly state reflected his difficulty in staying awake.

We discussed with the parents the fact that we could not allow the pushchair or the dummy during the treatment, that we needed to remove Geronimo's "escape routes" if we were to successfully engage with him. We needed, together with his parents, to try to keep him awake—whether playing or even crying—so that we could help him understand his situation. James and Orla were both reluctant to take such a firm stance, but we reminded them that they were paying the price of giving in to him with their sleepless nights, no sex life, a gradually diminishing social life, and the worrying possibility that their child was not getting any better but worse, despite all their care.

After the initial three days of assessment, we started working with Geronimo. We kept him awake by engaging him in activities, allowing him only a short nap after lunch (forty-five minutes). As a result, Geronimo was soon sleeping through the night. It took a week for Geronimo to go "upstairs" to the clinic's playroom without feeling distressed. "Upstairs" was a place where he could not hide from his own fears and pain. It was, however, a room in which everything was explained and contained, where he was helped to do things, and, little by little, acquire a new awareness of his body and what he could do with the different parts. For example, if he sat on the chair looking at the playdough with his arms hanging limply by his sides, we would place ourselves behind him, with a mirror at the other end of the table, for him to start to be able to see himself and us, to understand that there was a "you and me". We call this activity "scaffolding". We guided his arms and hands to achieve the rolling, shaping, and cutting actions with the playdough. The aim was to show him how to make these actions on his own, and, by being in front of the mirror, he could see that he was being helped. We did the same with a paintbrush or shaving foam, explaining that his hands were not only for covering his eyes or for rubbing and poking his nose, but could be used for doing things with external objects or to caress people.

We also played with different coloured cotton reels, showing him how to thread them or classify them by colour, and how to build towers or bridges with them. We extended each activity in many different forms so that Geronimo would not get stuck in repetitive actions out of not knowing what else to do. Slowly, we incorporated representational games into the activities, until the boy learnt to use his imagination on his own.

Sometimes, Geronimo sat on our legs on the floor and, without insisting on him looking at us, he would be helped to touch the face of the psychotherapist for the purpose of acknowledging another person: eyes with lashes that opened and shut; the mouth that spoke and could kiss; the nose that could smell. Then we changed over and did the same touching actions with him. What was interesting was that an incipient interest started appearing, possibly because the length of time we spent on this activity allowed Geronimo to catch the form of the face, to feel the calmness and patience of the therapist.

We introduced simple drawings made by us of faces showing the four basic emotions: happiness, sadness, anger, and surprise or fear. We discussed them with him, imitating the faces in front of the mirror. We even took the faces to the dining room for him to express his feelings by showing us the appropriate drawing. We would make the same expression with our own faces, indicating the eyebrow movements and the shape of the mouth to help him to understand how other people felt. We moved on to family photographs to help Geronimo interpret emotions in people he was familiar with, rather than just learning how to imitate facial expressions from drawings.

During the second week Geronimo began to say the odd word clearly. His parents were amazed. Our efforts consisted of speaking slowly and clearly, in simple phrases, and we used motivational language to help him express his wishes: for example, before switching the light on or off, or opening the door, or washing his hands, we would wait until Geronimo uttered a word of the request. By week three, Geronimo was using even more words unprompted.

Geronimo found it difficult to make eye contact, choosing to look at things and people sideways out of the corners of his eyes. However, by the second week (the eightieth hour) the first signs of him being able to look directly at us appeared, often accompanied by a sweet smile. We spoke about mummy and daddy having eyes as well that were easier to look at.

We used teddy bears to act out going to the toilet and getting rid of nappies. Soon Geronimo was asking to go to the toilet, too, and doing so on his own successfully. We did not wish to potty-train him, but to help him take responsibility for his own body and what he needed to do on his own. We wanted him to show us that he "can do it", and find the motivation to want to do it, so as not to remain stuck as a baby forever.

Despite all the progress, there were days when we were taking two steps forward and one step back. The child had a strong tendency to regress, at times resorting to his old defensive behaviours. His parents were easily discouraged by the apparent lack of sustainability and durability in his progress. It was, therefore, very important to help them understand how far they and Geronimo had come in such a short time: they were now sleeping through the night, walking everywhere (the buggy had been discarded), going to restaurants, and seeing their son eat a much wider variety of foods. The sense of discouragement was reflected in the parents' individual sessions, when their resistance to change was tackled in more depth.

In consultation with the paediatrician, we agreed to bring in other professionals as necessary, to find out if there were any possible organic factors that might be influencing Geronimo's behaviour. We consulted with, among others, a neurologist (due to the severity of his "fit-like" temper tantrums), an allergy specialist, a nutritionist, a geneticist (due to his mutation in chromosome 5), and a physiotherapist. The physiotherapist discovered that Geronimo had joint hypermobility in his feet, and the discomfort he felt might well have been the main reason behind his refusal to walk. The physiotherapist worked with Geronimo on several occasions during the treatment to help with his movements and walking, and to advise his parents on the most suitable footwear and what they could do to help.

Treating the parents

James and Orla met with their individual and couple psychotherapists while Geronimo slept under our care. The stories that unfolded from their sessions revealed intergenerational issues in Orla's capacity to mother. Her own mother had been a manic-depressive and her father was mostly absent. She had not wanted to live at home and went happily to a boarding school as soon as it was suggested at the age of seven. After boarding at middle school, she asked to go to an ordinary high school near her parents, and it was there that she met James. All her home-family memories were in a jumble and she wanted to find peace with herself and her mother, who was now dead (she died young of cancer). Her happy memories were associated with the time spent with Geronimo's father before she became pregnant. It was then that her happy memories ended, as the sickness she experienced during pregnancy had made her feel frightened and had brought on a misery that had gradually worsened. It was as though the pregnancy had awakened the feelings of discomfort and terror that she had never experienced as a child. Orla had "survived" mentally by dissociating the helpless baby-self in the arms of her mother, with whom she never felt secure and who, from the very beginning, had not helped her to make sense of the world around her. It seemed that there was a grandmother she was close to and from whom she probably got some sense of security and peace.

As Orla appeared to be suffering from depression, we asked a psychiatrist to see her and to be available if needed. She was grateful for this, as it confirmed that we understood how frightening it was for her to relive her difficult childhood and the ordeal of her pregnancy. Orla had become confused about her role as a mother. She had, as she put it, "fused with" Geronimo's own needs as she had no functional mother figure with whom she could identify or turn to for help.

Orla underwent hours of therapy with Geronimo, as well as on her own and with her husband. As she became aware of the root causes of her own emotions, she learnt to claim a space for herself to face her internal conflicts. She allowed Geronimo to form a relationship with his infant developmental psychotherapist, so that he could have his own space for individuality to emerge.

The father, James, came from a wealthy farming background. He was the second of six children, and felt confident about "knowing more" about children, having been brought up in such a large family. His own father was a very laid-back man, who had made no demands on his son to find a job as there was plenty of money. James's life had been one of pleasure up until his wife's pregnancy, when she had become so cut off from the world. But it was Geronimo's diagnosis that had been most shocking to him; having a son who behaved differently to others was not something that he was able to deal with.

There was a hint of identity confusion about James's personality, as though not fully formed. It was apparent that he had not moved on from his teenage years of no responsibility: that role had belonged to his parents, who were happy to provide from their business and investments.

It was difficult to start work with James. He had little awareness of boundaries and often asked inappropriate questions of the therapists. We used art as a tool to help him to feel relaxed, to express himself, and to tell us stories. He began to tell us about his dreams, which were vivid and sometimes frightening. In them, he was always flying very high above Earth, over high mountains, over tsunamis. There were no boundaries in his dreams but they conveyed a sense of manic denial of time passing, family responsibilities, and growing older.

On one occasion he dreamed of entering a house, one very similar to our clinic. There he met with the prostitute who had donated the egg for their baby to be conceived. She and her boyfriend wanted to take Geronimo away to bring him up properly, because they had done such a bad job. The dream was full of anxiety and despair, and could be interpreted thus: James felt that we, the paid prostitutes, were taking his child away, for us to bring him up our way. He viewed us as people of authority (coming from his parental representations) who were judging him as bad. His dream showed how little he trusted us; he felt persecuted by us and so could not relax in our presence or accept the help we were offering. Voicing these fears brought James great relief, and his new sense of ease allowed him to reflect further. He admitted that at times he felt as if his own mother was like a prostitute, one who kept having children whom she did not look after properly. He felt ashamed of these thoughts, but also became aware of the strong and possessive feelings he had towards his mother and the anger he had really felt as a child for not being "held" by her.

Couple sessions explored the unspoken issues of James and Orla's relationship: their hidden agendas, their unvoiced expectations of each other, the negative experiences from the pregnancy, and Geronimo's diagnosis. Added to this were the ghosts of their own childhoods and the trauma of having to deal with unexpected pain and danger. The unconscious walls that had gone up between them had restricted their capacity to understand their own child.

Discussion

How to start again

Geronimo was a complex child with many challenges that had to be explored. He had managed to get "under the skin" of his parents, especially his mother, and it was if both James and Orla had become entangled in their son's emotional and cognitive development.

Throughout the pregnancy, Geronimo had held on inside the womb, in spite of his mother's constant sickness, her dehydration, and hospital admissions. At the same time, his mother had managed to keep the baby inside her. It was as if both were in "survival mode", one that prevented them from living life to the full. The strong mother–child bond that had formed was of a negative nature.

Once born, Geronimo did not seem able to separate from his mother, and therefore started out life with a mother not differentiated from him. They were in a state of "one-ness" that did not allow him to form an individual mind able to develop emotions and thoughts. Geronimo had to be taught how to disengage himself, physically and psychologically. He had to be shown that he could have a mind, that he could understand and achieve things, and that he had to allow us to show him how.

Internalisation of experiences

Geronimo found it difficult to internalise positive experiences, as he was so preoccupied with blocking out the negative sensations he experienced. This left him deprived of a mind that could exercise the power of relating, playing, having fun. It seemed as if by choosing the name of a heroic leader, the parents might have projected a subconscious desire to find an advocate for their own childhood difficulties. But now they had to be leaders themselves. They had to help Geronimo find strength to overcome his fears.

Over the four weeks of treatment, Geronimo made great progress: from sleeping through the night almost straightaway, to eating properly, to using single words, and, by the end, to constructing whole phrases. As Geronimo's parents became more aware of his capabilities, and more insistent on his growing independence (throwing away his dummy, giving up the pushchair), so Geronimo tried harder to pull them back. He wanted to regress, and to have less "work" to do by himself. Life was easier when everything was done for him.

Geronimo seemed not to have been born with a social interest, or with a curiosity about others, as if he had not finished his time in the womb or had entered the world with something missing. We did wonder at times if the difficult pregnancy (not just the constant vomiting, but the worry, annoyance, and all the other negative emotions that had been reactivated) combined with Geronimo's genetic tendency (to be slower) and need to involve the mother and father in his anxieties and fears might have contributed to his inability to interact socially and engage with the external world, separate from his mother.

However, when Geronimo's parents began actively to separate themselves from him and to present a united front when it came to dealing with his behaviour (for example, when he was having a tantrum), Geronimo took this as an opportunity for individual growth. He toilet-trained himself, walked everywhere, and started a relationship with his father and mother separately, one that involved gentle teasing and joking about the other parent. There was pain in the separation but also joy. He was able to experience the advantages of growing up by developing a sense of self and others.

In the last week, his grandparents came over to learn how best to treat and play with Geronimo. A nanny whom the parents had started using also attended for a day, so that we could observe their relationship and advise her on additional tactics to promote the child's incipient curiosity and creativity.

Figures 7.3 and 7.4 are the Acquarone scales completed for both Geronimo and Orla after the four-week treatment programme. Geronimo's scale shows the dramatic change in his ability to feel emotions and warmth. He arrived presenting severe autistic behaviours: not walking, not talking, not sleeping at night, not relating to other people, and dominating his parents' lives. When he left, he was able to start processing and integrating sensory experiences, and was allowing adults to regulate his behaviours. He walked everywhere, slept soundly through the night, and was able to experience a sense of satisfaction, the desire to socialise, the joy of play, and a feeling of security that his parents could contain him.

The mother's scale (Figure 7.4) shows how she gained a far better understanding of what lay behind Geronimo's behaviours. This

ACQUARONE DETECTION SCALES FOR EARLY RELATIONSHIPS®

EARLY SIGNS OF ALARM – pre-Autism

FOLLOW-UP – INFANT/CHILD

name: **GERONIMO**
age: **3 years** *date of this observation:* **DD MMM YYYY**

		NEVER	RARELY	FREQUENT	ALWAYS	OBSERVER REACTIONS
INTERPERSONAL	1. GAZING		●			
	2. BABBLING		●			
	3. CALLING	●				
	4. IMITATING		●			
	5. PROVOKING	●				
	6. POINTING	●				
	7. FEEDING			●		*... when promted* *... can eat by himself*
	8. JOINT ATTENTION	●				
	9. PLAY		●			
	10. ALONE					
	11. RELATING *– to other children*	●				
	– to adults		●			
	12. REACTIVE BEHAVIOURS *capacity to... a) accept emotional warmth b) bear stressful event c) adapt to changes*		●			*... tolerance to frustration*
SENSORIAL	TOUCHING					
	13. *Skin-to-skin*			●		
	14. *Textures*			●		
	RESPONSE					
	15. *Sounds*		●			
	16. *Noise*		●			
	17. *Name*		●			
	18. *Light & patterns*	●				
	19. *Smells*			●		
	20. COMFORTING		●			*... still he resorts easily to touch her face, head, and ears*
MOTOR	HOLDING					
	21. *Posturing*		●			
	22. *Stereotypic movement*	●				
	23. *Use of hands/Use of body*			●		*... he is able to grasp when he wants*
AFFECT	24. EXPRESSIVENESS		●			*... of emotional states* *... he smiles when he finishes having an interaction*
	25. SELF-HELP DEVELOPMENT	●	●			*... delay in being pampered (different styles, e.g., perfumed, massaged, etc.*

ANY OTHER OBSERVATIONS NOT LISTED ABOVE:

There are a lot of behaviours that need more intensive help and it has been requested an extra week

Figure 7.3. Geronimo's follow-up assessment.

ACQUARONE DETECTION SCALES FOR EARLY RELATIONSHIPS®

EARLY SIGNS OF ALARM – pre-Autism

...affecting the baby or being affected by the baby...

FOLLOW-UP – MOTHER/caregiver

name: **NAME**
child: **GERONIMO** *age:* **3 years**

		NEVER	RARELY	FREQUENT	ALWAYS	OBSERVER REACTIONS
INTERPERSONAL	1. GAZING			●		
	2. BABBLING		●			*... talking to replace noises*
	3. CALLING			●		
	4. FEEDING			●		*... all sorts and raised good*
	5. GAMES / PLAY			●		*... in a directed way*
	6. RELATING			●		*...firmly*
	7. REACTIVE BEHAVIOURS		●			
SENSORIAL	8. TOUCHING			●		
	9. COMFORTING			●		
MOTOR	10. POSTURE			●		
AFFECT	11. EXPRESSIVENESS			●		
	12. UNDERSTANDING OF EMOTIONS					
	– in themselves			●		
	– in the baby		●			
	13. PAST					
	– Psychiatric illness					
	– Other difficulties			●		

ANY OTHER OBSERVATIONS NOT LISTED ABOVE:

Figure 7.4. Geronimo's mother's follow-up assessment.

allowed her to help Geronimo move on and trust the process of change. Her own behaviour greatly improved as her son began responding positively to her demands—even during the times when she had to show firmness towards him "no matter what"—and the bond with her son switched to being a positive one.

Just as Geronimo had to go back to the beginning, so, too, did Orla and James when it came to parenting. They had to undo their old ways and learn to recognise and deal with their child's needs in a positive manner, using the tasks they learnt in the programme as support.

Follow-up

Geronimo continued having individual child psychotherapy three times a week for three years as he had to integrate two ways of being: the nascent newborn child in the treatment and his old habits, such as having imaginary conversations with himself. His parents continued with their individual therapy and fortnightly couple therapy for more than three years. Geronimo had one-to-one help in a mainstream nursery for two years, and a classroom assistant was made available to him when he started primary school. His sensitive nature meant that he struggled as a teenager at secondary school and so his parents decided to move him to a small private school, where he thrived and was able to attain A-levels, though over a longer period of time than was normal. It was at this time that he came back to see us for a year. It was interesting to witness how the autistic traits of his personality had taken a back seat, revealing a gentle, sensitive soul who was aware of other people's "stuff", meaning "their conflicts". He was particularly popular with the girls as he was a boy in touch with his feelings.

After finishing his education, Geronimo went into media, making short films for companies. He enjoyed being behind the camera because from there it was possible to change what was not done properly.

Discussion

I could see when we first started to treat Geronimo that, at age three, his bad habits (autistic behaviours) had become deeply entrenched. He had grown physically but not psychologically, his psychic development stuck at the prenatal stage. Geronimo had "fused" with his mother; he not only had to learn to separate from her, but also to cope with the separation. Only by doing this could he create the space in which to form relationships, develop language, and respond to positive experiences.

Both James and Orla had to overcome their fear of becoming adults and take on grown-up responsibilities, such as taking care of their parents, taking care of their child, planning for the future, balancing budgets, and managing their own lives. In addition to the existential, ordinary anxieties of everyday life, they had to find a way of coping with a child that had difficulties in internalising parents that provided care and constant love.

Urwin mentions, in respect to language development, that it is as much the mother's difficulty in being able separate from the infant as the infant's difficulty:

> It is probably generally accepted in psychoanalysis that language development is an aspect of separation–individuation, and that there is something crucial about the Oedipal situation, or the place of the father. Where a mother apparently anticipates a baby's needs too completely, for example, or where the baby merges with the mother to a marked degree, there may be little incentive for the baby to learn to talk. Most would also accept, with Lacan, that the presence of the father may not just disrupt the exclusivity of the mother–child dyad but also provide another object for identification through which self and other can be differentiated. (Urwin, 2002, p. 74)

However, as an explanation for what motivates language development, Urwin goes on to argue that

> . . . the emphasis on loss in psychoanalytic accounts smacks of what, in the 1970s, Bruner (personal communication) used to call "get you out of trouble" theories of language development, in which the apparently unpleasant process of acquisition is somehow explained by an advantageous end product, which the baby cannot know about in advance. For example, a commonly stressed advantage of language is that it allows us to communicate about events which are remote from us in time and space. (Urwin, 2002, p. 74)

Autistic children find it difficult to understand their emotions: they are easily frightened and overwhelmed by a world that comes at them too fast or is too full of anxieties and sensations. Bion's theories place great emphasis on the capacity of the parents to contain, transform, and make sense of these emotions for their highly sensitive child. However, this capacity can be hindered if the parents themselves are unable to contain or make sense of the emotions due to their own past traumas.

Intertwined with the creation of relationships is separation and loss. Geronimo had not only to separate from his mother (and she from him) but also to recognise and bear the grief and joy this encompassed. For Bion, socialisation and a desire to communicate with others has to do with coming to terms with this separation and loss, which, in turn, allows the child to share the mother and accept the presence of the father in the relationship. The "intentional pointing" that a child learns to make is, according to Burhouse (2001), an indication of the awareness of separation and of trying to feel included in the world of others and their desire for this to happen.

Meltzer (1986) talks about "the theatre of thoughts", in which the child is not able to link what he does with his mouth to his relationship with his parents, from breastfeeding to making sounds for attention, to crying, to smiling. The awareness of others is first located in the mouth before thought processes can develop in the mind.

Geronimo never felt at ease. He was constantly surrounded by sensory overload. The sensation of his own body, an awareness of others, the impact of the environment: it was all too difficult to perceive, as if everything was too confusing, too fast, too noisy, too frightening. He created a world of hallucinatory soothing, in which certain objects—his dummy, teddy, buggy—became his focus and escape. Similarly, he used his parents, demanding all their attention at night. Most of all, he escaped into sleep. It seemed as if the anxiety and discomfort in relation to other people were constant unless he was sleeping or in the dark, stuck as if in the womb. Thus, growth had to start with learning to form relationships.

Rhode (2005) says,

> It seems that the position of the child relative to the mother's internal object is an expression of the Oedipal constellation in relation to eye contact, on a very primitive level that concerns the child's experience of existing . . . [T]hese Oedipal conditions must be in place for developmental imitation and introjection to go ahead. They must also be in place, I believe, to allow for the much more sophisticated shifts in identification and point of view which are implied by Britton's work on the third position (Britton, 1989, 1998) and by Hobson's Relatedness Triangle, which addresses the relationship between the infant's attitude towards the world, the other, and the other's attitude towards the world (Hobson, 2002: 107). (p. 64)

She goes on to say:

> In order for the child to feel supported rather than intruded into by what Grotstein (1981) has called the Background Object of Primary

> Identification—which he conceptualizes as the parents' ancestors stretching back through the generations—the internal object must be felt to be located at the optimal depth in relation to the child. (p. 65)

Informed by such psychoanalytic thinking, the work we undertook with the parents, making them aware of the conflicts in their personal history and the gaps in their own development, was one important strand of the treatment. Another was working with the child on his own, exploring Geronimo's sensibilities and giving him the tools to regulate his emotions, accompanying him all the way in the process. Finally, there was the parent–infant psychotherapy, in which we helped the parents understand and identify the optimal distance from which Geronimo could comprehend them and reach out to them.

The process of Geronimo's treatment was arduous and, at four weeks, longer than many of our other cases. His comforting hallucinations were already taking up a great deal of his waking time, whereas in other cases presented in this book (Nicola, Filippo, and even Joseph) the relationships that need to be worked on are still relatively new and the bad habits not so deeply entrenched, and, therefore, easier to manipulate.

Summary

In this chapter, I have tried to demonstrate the type of treatment we use on children over the age of three who come to us after being diagnosed with autism. I have shown how arduous, painful, and difficult it can be to effect change in behaviour when a child has reached this age, for both the child and the family. However, the everyday intensity of the work allowed us to "break the ice" with Geronimo. We were able to start a process of finding the non-autistic aspects within the child, and to uncover the conflictive experiences in the parents so that new thoughts and ways of exploring could be developed. We offered the family a previously uncontemplated alternative: to challenge their acceptance of autism and to create the type of relationship in which they could accompany Geronimo out of his autistic space. I hoped to show the slow but steady process of forming the basic conditions for experiences to be felt and remembered, for thoughts to be thought, for communication to be necessary and possible.

In Figures 7.5 and 7.6, it is possible to see how, in the summary of the follow-up at the end of the four weeks, the behaviours had moved from severe signs of not being able to react to others, to behaving very

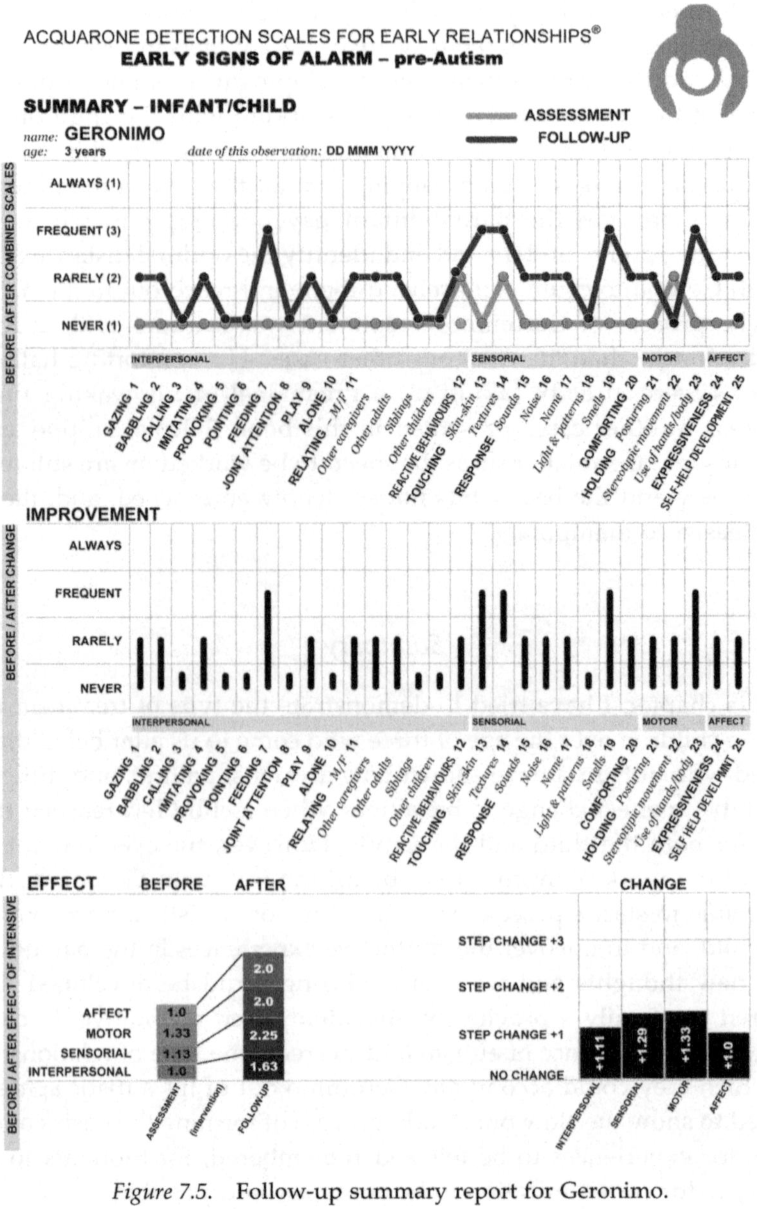

Figure 7.5. Follow-up summary report for Geronimo.

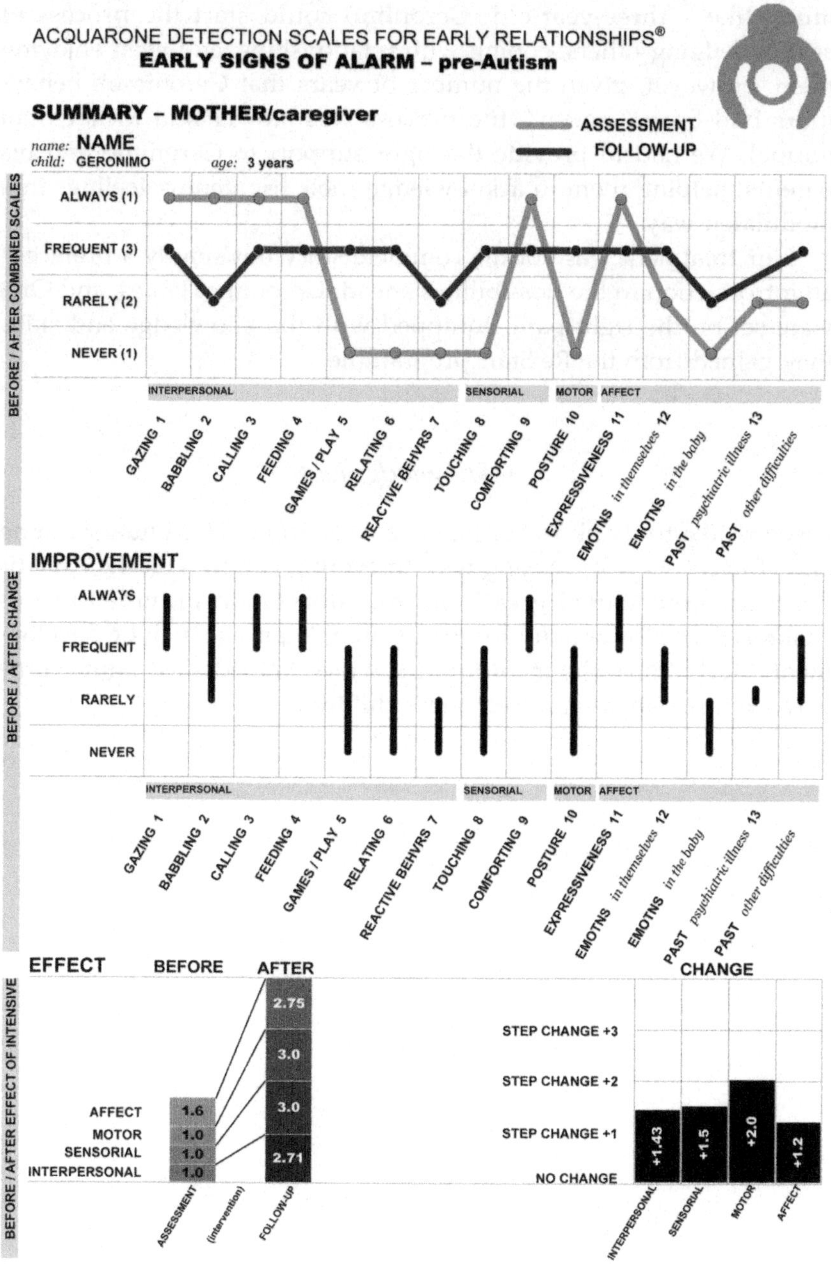

Figure 7.6. Follow-up summary report for Geronimo's mother.

much like a three-year-old. Geronimo could start the process of acknowledging others, coping with relationships, and even enjoying them. However, given the number of years that Geronimo's behaviours had been "frozen", the process was slower and firmer than normal. We had to provide the right support to Geronimo and his parents, helping them to acknowledge their frightening feelings in a modulated way.

Our treatment was not the complete story but simply a preface—an introduction to the possibilities ahead. Geronimo, James, and Orla were set on the right path, equipped with the knowledge and skills they gained from the Re:Start programme.

Acknowledgment

I would like to thank Isabel Jimenez Acquarone. Her understanding and efficient way of working with the young children on the Autistic Spectrum contributed greatly to the information provided in this chapter. I am also grateful for the invaluable psychoanalytic developmental techniques she incorporated, which helped shed light on the way we think about and treat these children.

CHAPTER EIGHT

Filippo (aged eighteen months): a focus on siblings

Stella Acquarone

> "As I came into his house, Filippo looked up at me—intense and serious—then carried on playing with his car on the floor, his eyes fixed on the wheels going round and round. He did not hear his mother calling him, and moved away as I approached. At the sound of food being served, he jumped up and climbed into his high chair, put on his bib, and took up his spoon and fork. He ate quickly, without a smile or glance at his mother, then climbed down from the chair to carry on playing with his car on the floor, not making a sound. His mother remained at the table, her plate untouched, her presence not acknowledged by her son."
>
> (Clinical notes, Stella Acquarone)

Filippo's mother and father, Hisako and Gianni, were thirty-five years old. They had met on a plane from Japan and now lived in England. Hisako was an artist, Gianni a businessman. They had three children, Luca aged five, Mario aged three years and six months, and Filippo aged eighteen months.

Filippo could speak a little of three languages—Italian, Japanese, and English—by the time he was a year old, but was unable to look anyone in the eye and never laughed. He did not want to play or be with people, preferring to be left alone. His mother had realised something was "very strange" with him, but could not put her finger on it. When the family contacted us and requested a home visit due to family circumstances, we agreed.

Our visit entailed both a family meeting and some observation time, and in Filippo we found a strong and bossy character. The boy clearly loved the food his mother expertly cooked for him, and we were interested to see that he ate with great speed, using his cutlery expertly, and that he demanded extra helpings with great impatience. Filippo ate so quickly and demanded so much attention from his mother that she did not have a chance to start on her own plate of food by the time her son got down from his high chair.

Filippo did not wish to keep company with his siblings. Social encounters were non-existent, and he played by himself, becoming annoyed if anybody wished to engage with him. His play was repetitive, and consisted of him forming endless lines of toy blocks or cars. Even though Filippo seemed serious and mature, we could feel in the countertransference a very frightened boy who did not want to experience anything new, any changes to his routine, or to share with others. He made himself understood but did not interact with people other than using them to get what he wanted. As he scored six signs of alarm on the Acquarone scale (Figure 8.1), and because the paediatric assessment carried out prior to our seeing him confirmed that Filippo displayed signs of autistic behaviours, it was decided to undertake a two-week intensive treatment to discover the origins or cause of the child's reluctance to relate and communicate. Figure 8.2 depicts the mother's assessment.

The treatment

Working with the parents

The parents undertook individual and couple therapy to explore both their current and past experiences. It came to light on the third day (after nine hours) that Hisako was still deeply affected by a miscarriage she had had prior to conceiving Filippo. Hisako described how she almost died from a haemorrhage as the "deformed baby came out

ACQUARONE DETECTION SCALES FOR EARLY RELATIONSHIPS®
EARLY SIGNS OF ALARM – pre-Autism

ASSESSMENT – INFANT/CHILD

name: **FILIPPO**
age: **1 year 6 months** *date of this observation:* **DD MMM YYYY**

		NEVER	RARELY	FREQUENT	ALWAYS	OBSERVER REACTIONS
INTERPERSONAL	**1. GAZING** *Eye-to-eye contact within a relationship and the maintenance of this contact*	●				
	2. BABBLING *Making sounds for the benefit of the partner in the parent-infant relationship*				●	
	3. CALLING *– The facial expressions – Noises or gestures that seek to produce an affectionate response from the partner*	●				
	4. IMITATING *– Moving mouth, tongue, etc., in imitation of mother's (or another) – The repetition of a sound or a movement heard or seen by the child*		●			
	5. PROVOKING *Inciting the person into interacting, not just to use as an instrument to do something for him/her*		●			
	6. POINTING *Indicating with index finger to a person about an object of interest*	●				*... object of need*
	7. FEEDING *Child's attitude during the intake of food, including anticipatory behaviour (e.g. head-turning, moving arms the food/breast)*			●		
	8. JOINT ATTENTION *Looking in the same direction*	●				
	9. PLAY *– Capacity to play the same game for more than 5 minutes, and share with another person – Take turns and stay with a person – Children*		●			
	10. ALONE				●	
	11. RELATING *Behaviours indicating the capacity to relate & accept emotional warmth.*					
	– Mother, Father		●			
	– Other caregivers	●				*... adults*
	– Other unfamiliar adults	●				
	– Siblings	●				
	– Other unfamiliar children	●				
	12. REACTIVE BEHAVIOURS *tolerance to frustrations, including: – a) Capacity to accept emotional warmth – b) Capacity to bounce back after stressful event – c) Capacity to adapt to changes...please indicate*	●				
SENSORIAL	**TOUCHING**					
	13. *Skin-to-skin contact initiated by infant for play or affection*				●	
	14. *Does the child touch paint, foam, sand, water, playdoh, plasticine and other messy substances*				●	
	RESPONSE					
	15. *Response to sounds*		●			
	16. *Response to noise*		●			
	17. *Response to name*				●	
	18. *Response to light & patterns*				●	
	19. *Response to smells*				●	
	20. COMFORTING *Child's ability to find relief from distress by themselves (e.g. thumb sucking, touching hands, playing with one car, others)...specify*	●				*... uses mother*
MOTOR	**HOLDING**					
	21. *The posturing of the child when he is supported in the arms of the mother (e.g. floppy, rigid, restless) – General muscle tone when sitting or standing*		●			
	22. *Stereotypic movement of arms, eyes, etc. – Walking: on tiptoes or sluggish*				●	
	23. *Use of hands: for grasping, for helping himself – Use of body: to reach, to climb, to hide, other...*			●		
AFFECT	**24. EXPRESSIVENESS** *The body or facial expression of emotional states (e.g., sad, worried, anxious, bland, happy, or others)...specify*	●				
	25. SELF-HELP DEVELOPMENT *– Ability to cope independently with the environment, (e.g., dress) – Eating – Being careful with him/herself or others*				●	
	ANY OTHER OBSERVATIONS NOT LISTED ABOVE:					

Figure 8.1. Filippo's assessment.

ACQUARONE DETECTION SCALES FOR EARLY RELATIONSHIPS®

EARLY SIGNS OF ALARM – pre-Autism

...affecting the baby or being affected by the baby...

ASSESSMENT – MOTHER/caregiver

name: **NAME**
child: FILIPPO *age:* 1 year 6 months

	Item	NEVER	RARELY	FREQUENT	ALWAYS	OBSERVER REACTIONS
INTERPERSONAL	**1. GAZING** *Eye-to-eye contact with the baby and the maintenance of this contact*				●	*... watchful*
	2. BABBLING *– Making sounds for the benefit of the parent-infant relationship* *– Talking*				●	*... with anxiety*
	3. CALLING *Facial expressions, noises or gestures seeking to produce an affectionate response from the infant*	●				*... liked to have an 'independent' child*
	4. FEEDING *Mother's attitude towards infant's hunger and need to feed:* *– Does she anticipate behaviour and have meal or breast easily available? – Does she pay attention, talk with the baby and enjoy feeding? – Does she interrupt with any excuse (e.g., talks to others and looks away)? – Is she fearful, full of anguish or has she any delusions? – Is she apathetic?*	●				*... over anxious* *... fed baby's 3 course meal at the rhythm imposed by daughter*
	5. GAMES / PLAY *– Playful encounters, including songs and teasing*		●			
	6. RELATING *Behaviours indicating the capacity to relate & accept emotional warmth towards the baby*		●			
	7. REACTIVE BEHAVIOURS *including:* *– Tolerance to frustrations – Capacity to accept emotional warmth – Capacity to bounce back after stressful event – Capacity to adapt to changes*		●			
SENSORIAL	**8. TOUCHING** *– Skin-to-skin contact initiated by infant for play or affection*	●				*... felt rejected*
	9. COMFORTING *– Mother's ability to find relief for the baby's distress*		●			*... felt rejected and not needed*
MOTOR	**10. POSTURE** *The posturing of the mother when the infant is supported in her arms or any other way (e.g., other, rough, balanced precariously)*		●			
AFFECT	**11. EXPRESSIVENESS** *– Expression of emotional state (e.g., sad, worried, anxious, bland, happy, others)...specify*				●	*... anxious*
	12. UNDERSTANDING OF EMOTIONS *– in themselves* *– in the baby*	● ●				*... felt to observer very blocked about understanding*
	13. PAST *– Psychiatric illness* *– Other difficulties*	● ●				

ANY OTHER OBSERVATIONS NOT LISTED ABOVE:

© Acquarone 2013

Figure 8.2. Filippo's mother's assessment.

in pieces". A month later she became pregnant with Filippo, who was born healthy at full term. It seemed as if both the mother and the father were "frozen" with fear and guilt. When pregnant with Filippo, Hisako had been plagued by a constant fear that things might go terribly wrong—that she might miscarry again or that the child would be born with a disability. During their psychotherapy, the mother and father learnt to put words to their grief, and realised that they were projecting on Filippo the ghost of the "monster" baby that had died pre-term. By the time Filippo was conceived, they still had not fully recovered from the loss and trauma of the miscarriage, and it seemed that the sense of terror continued to exercise enormous power in the mind of the mother, and it was this that Filippo was unable to cope with.

Working with Filippo

Filippo continued to play on his own during the sessions, not wanting to include me or share any of the toys—everything was his. I stayed with him and I spoke about the novelty and pain of sharing with another person. I started playing by myself, finding toys similar to the ones he had chosen to play with. When he tried to grab them off me, I simply said something similar to what he would say, such as "Mine!", or "I will protect it". I had the impression that even when we were together he was not going to leave his fantasy of power and protection. I told him that it must be difficult to enter a family that felt such sadness, and at the same time I showed him the "feelings faces" (happy, sad, scared, and angry) we use. The sad face struck a chord with him, and he stared hard before saying "Sad" and then "Angry".

I started playing with a large teddy bear. I took its clothes off and replaced them. We were two people in the same room, exchanging few words as we played side by side. I wanted Filippo to learn to trust me. While sitting with him like this, I was reminded of how, at my parents' farm, the horses that were to be ridden by the children would be broken in more slowly and gently than the others. More time was spent allowing the animals to become accustomed to people, their presence, their smell, and their occasional strokes. These horses became gentle pets who seemed concerned for the children, not just animals over whom others exerted power.

In the same way, we went gently with Filippo, taking slow steps. We spent time with him, talked with him and then, once he was accustomed to us, we "scaffolded" him. This is our term for holding his hands and showing him how to use them: for instance, when using playdough, while "cooking pizza" with the dough, using paint, and playing with pieces of foam. We played together, slowly, allowing the new experiences to gently unfold. If I felt him feeling fear or caution, I talked gently about his emotions, helping Filippo to understand them.

I ventured the possibility that there was fun to be had with play. For example, I mentioned that there was some foam that I was going to use and that it was white and soft. I put it on the table and played with it by myself, enjoying its soft sensation in my hands. I then drove some toy cars into it. Filippo looked sideways and offered no other interaction. The second time I got out the foam, I first explained what I was going to do with it, and then did it. Filippo came near. His hands were trembling and I covered his hands with mine and we touched the foam together. He then retreated and I waited, saying simply, "When you're ready." On the third attempt, Filippo brought a toy car with him—a sign that he wanted to join in.

Filippo began to slowly emerge from his autistic space during his individual therapy. However, in the sessions when his mother was present, his body recoiled and he regressed into his position prior to our new-found relationship. As a result, I spent time explaining to him that mummy could also be with him, and that she wanted to be there. He seemed frightened and he covered himself up with a sheet, his eyes cast down. Hisako, having by this time been made aware of her son's personality and the impact of the miscarriage and her anxiety, spoke softly to Filippo. She told him of her "troubles" before he was born, and that she had lived in constant fear that something bad was going to happen to him. She cried. Filippo looked at her and started crying, too. They seemed to "meet" one another in their sadness, to connect in a way I had not seen or felt before. It was a very moving scene, and revealed previously hidden emotions in both mother and son. Soon they could share not just an ancient grief but a new joy, such as the delight of doing a simple jigsaw puzzle together.

Filippo's father, Gianni, underwent a similar process of awareness of his important input to the family. He learnt to speak about his feelings, rather than ignore them, and to share them with Filippo. Gianni was a farm boy who was used to coping with life's events in a very matter-of-fact way. Even though that did not help the mother on one level, since he was unable to give her the sympathy she needed, he was able to provide support. Through therapy, however, he came to realise that ignoring events and feelings was hurtful to her and that he needed to handle them differently, and so he endeavoured to do so.

Working with the siblings

Luca and Mario entered therapy as part of their brother's treatment. Their parents had no concerns about the brothers' emotional development; however, the psychotherapist's role working with the boys was an interesting one. Luca and Mario were two boys whom family and friends considered to be "well" and not in need of any therapy. Their physical, cognitive, and emotional development was progressing without concern and they would not be in a consultation room were it not for their mother's deep concern about Filippo. They were, in short, "healthy" patients about to enter treatment, but healthy patients who had become part of an unhealthy system. My role as their therapist was to look at the world in which these boys lived: to explore and unpick the impact of having a brother with pre-autistic behaviours, of having a mother whose energy appeared to be deeply focused on her son's needs, and of having a father who was trying to meet the needs of his whole family, both physically and emotionally. I had to look at the impact the two boys had on their brother, whose behaviours needed to change to enable optimum communication and contact between all members of the family.

Theoretical underpinnings

To support the family in the best way possible, the therapists aimed to facilitate, through rehearsal and direction, a new way for the individual members to come together. To do this, we needed a clear picture of their internal worlds, emotional needs, and learnt ways of relating. We also had to try to understand how these individuals came together as a system, and their impact upon one another. In order to deal effectively with the presenting systems, it was necessary to work in an integrative way with an understanding of a range of clinical theories and approaches. Psychodynamic thinking, in particular around sibling rivalry, was the key approach, but work was also informed by relational psychotherapy (DeYoung, 2003; Hughes, 1997, 1998, 2003), attachment theory (Bowlby, 1988; de Zulueta, 1993), and family systems theory (Boscolo et al., 1987; Carr, 2009).

Case background

Prior to the commencement of the programme, the team discussed the presenting needs and issues within the family. Working closely within the team was essential, so that every aspect of the family system could be addressed. With all initial concerns focused on Filippo, I had a very limited developmental history about Luca and Mario at the start of the treatment. It was interesting to consider, in the light of the incomplete story at the outset, whether the boys' needs had been overshadowed by Filippo's. I was, however, aware that Luca and Mario were both born after planned pregnancies and uncomplicated deliveries. They had met routine developmental milestones, had attended nursery school, and the elder, Luca, was now in primary school.

I met the boys when the family arrived on the first day of treatment. Luca and Mario were beautifully dressed, excited, and a little apprehensive. They hovered near their parents in the first family meeting, leaning against their legs for extra support and comfort. Luca took the first steps away from the family, keen to look at the toys that had been set out. Mario followed a few minutes behind his brother. Luca involved me in imaginary role-play about shops and fancy dress. He was a demanding and creative play companion: deciding on the roles and setting out the rules. Mario hovered on the periphery, seemingly wanting to play but accepting a sidelined role, marginalised by a brother who wished to be in the spotlight.

Initial observations

During the period of initial observation of the children, it became apparent that Luca had placed himself in a dominant position within the family. Not only did he dictate his and his brother's actions and opinions, he also dictated his parents' actions: for example, shaping the entire family's sleeping arrangements by demanding a place in bed next to his mother. In their own therapy sessions, Hisako and Gianni admitted that they perceived Luca as the "boss", and that setting and maintaining limits for him was very difficult.

While Luca was overtly confident, opinionated, and demanding, Mario was quiet and withdrawn, and stayed very much in his brother's shadow. This is not to say that Mario did not have strong opinions, he just seemed to find it hard to make himself heard.

Patterns of attachment

Both Luca and Mario were very much attached to their parents, and enjoyed a loving relationship with them. However, the positions they took in the family and the kind of attachments they formed differed greatly between the two. Luca was welcomed (albeit with an increasing lack of enthusiasm) by his mother into her life and her bed. The insecure attachment resulted in a merging between them. As anxious parents, Hisako and Gianni placed Luca at the centre of their world: his needs were met and his demands were catered to. The natural phase for individuation and separation had not been achieved, as Hisako could not support her son through the painful, yet necessary, process of being a person separate from her. Since he was a baby, Luca had slept in his parents' bed, and, by the age of four, had rarely spent a night apart from his mother. His father, relegated to life outside the matrimonial bed, slept in the guest room. Luca's bedroom was never used.

Mario could be seen as ambivalently attached. While enjoying a loving relationship with his parents, it seemed as if he was more self-sufficient and separate. He would go to his parents at times for comfort, but on the occasions when we saw him upset, angry, or even hurt, he appeared to retreat into his own world. Furthermore, when Luca and Mario played imaginary games together, rather than fight over the roles, such as who would "be mum", Mario would give in to his brother's more persistent demands. I wondered if there was space for Mario's parents to notice his needs. As attachment is based on a parent's availability and "sensitivity to the child's signals" (Siegel, 1991, p. 117), if Mario was not fully "seen" by his parents, were his signals not being attended to? I wondered, too, if perhaps Mario felt that Luca had already taken up all the available space in the family and that was why he stayed in his brother's shadow.

Sibling rivalry

A psychoanalytic reading of Freud suggests that the "fantasies and emotions [of] brothers may be even more primitive and violent than those concerning the parental couple" (Houzel, 2001). Tustin's "nest of babies" fantasy explains how infants' awareness of their own identity gives rise to a distinction between themselves and others, as well as the fantasy that there are "special babies" who are given "special food". Tustin illustrates this by describing a scenario in which a patient believes he is in competition with "predatory rivals" who wish "to take away his chance of life and sustenance" (Tustin, 1972, pp. 177–178). Such feelings of rivalry would doubtlessly have been aroused in Luca when Mario was born, just before his second birthday. In addition, Luca and Mario were part of a family who had not only experienced the trauma of miscarriage, but had a young child with heightened sensitivities to cope with. The usual dynamic of sibling rivalry had thus been made additionally complicated by the non-arrival of an infant, followed closely by the arrival of one who appeared to occupy more space in the parents' mind than would be usual. Not only did Luca and Mario have to contend with a new baby brother, they also had to share their food and emotional sustenance with him. Luca, fearing yet more loss, devoured as much sustenance as possible, while Mario appeared to be pushed to the side of the nest, as if unable or unwilling to make himself seen and heard. Mario seemed to have taken on an adaptive role to his brother, which raised additional concerns about his own emotional development (Sunderland, 2006).

Interventions

Work with the boys involved a combination of directive and non-directive play, informed by an understanding of relational child psychotherapy. We employed a range of toys, games, and activities, including dressing up, shops, playhouse, dolls and babies, paints, playdough, drawing materials, bubbles, zoo animals, crafts, and storybooks. Outings were also arranged to see how the children coped in a variety of settings, as well as to provide them with new and stimulating experiences.

We shaped our interventions to facilitate meeting Luca's need for firm boundaries and to show him that he could not always get his way. With Mario, our focus was on encouraging him to express himself and to speak up about his own wants and desires. Behavioural strategies were put in place. These included reinforcing boundaries and "rules", such as turn-taking, apologising when necessary, accepting "that you have to stay here, as mum and dad need to go upstairs", and learning to ask for what they wanted. We also reinforced positive behaviours, such as sharing, kindness, consideration, etc. At the same time, we offered insight and understanding into the boys' emotional worlds, recognising and exploring their individual fears, desires, and needs.

With Luca, we acknowledged his fear of always feeling in control, of acting as the adult rather than as a little boy, the jealousy he felt towards his siblings, how unfair the world seems when it does not go your way, and that it was all right to get angry and upset. We also explored empathy: how other people could understand how he felt and how he could take other people's feelings into consideration.

With Mario, we emphasised the importance of how he, too, had a voice and opinions, and that it was all right for these to be different from his brother's. We worked to identify his needs and desires, and to let them be seen on equal terms to those of his siblings. We addressed Mario's reluctance to seek comfort when he hurt himself, or had a shock, such as falling over unexpectedly. We did this by expressing his feelings for him and continuing to offer comfort from a more comfortable distance.

With both boys, we practised new ways of behaving with Filippo: talking softly, whispering, giving him space, not putting toys too close to his face. We set these in a context of Filippo having his own way of wanting to be part of their family. We supported the parents in ensuring that the boys practised these new behaviours, and assisted Hisako and Gianni in finding ways to parent together and attend to the differing needs of all three children—for example, making Luca wait while Mario played with Filippo.

The parent–child sessions were an opportunity both for the parents to have time to enjoy being with the children individually and for the boys to have an experience of undivided attention. In these sessions, we not only observed their interactions, but also modelled for the parents ways to enhance their emotional contact with the boys. It was during the parent–child sessions that the theme of separation and attachment came alive.

Prominent issues

Obstacles

Throughout the duration of the treatment, I was very much aware of my position within the therapeutic constellation. Just as they had to share their parents, so Mario and Luca had to share a therapist. To be able to differentiate between each child's needs, it was essential that I remain aware of whose needs I was prioritising and to assist each child in developing their own mental capacities to wait for the attention they deserved. As Luca's tendency was to claim all the attention and Mario's was to slip to the side unseen, my role was to try to readjust this balance. To do so, I needed Luca to experience being by himself without constant attention, to have a life outside of centre stage, and to assist Mario in coming out of the wings and asserting his needs.

Boundaries

In working to address the different, and, at times, conflicting, needs of each child, I began to stretch the boundaries of psychotherapy and to place an increased value on behavioural and practical interventions. This stretch was necessary in part because of the lengthy and intense sessions spent together. Our therapy could not be non-directive. We needed an element of structure to assist with managing the session time, managing my mental and emotional space, and managing the differing needs of each boy. Taking turns became not a way in which to "both choose games", but an essential opportunity to "rehearse" different ways of being. For example, Luca had to rehearse not always being the one who gets to choose, while Mario had to be encouraged to stand up for what he wanted.

As well as turn-taking, I created opportunities for the boys to become more self-reliant, to play happily on their own and to play together without the direct attention of an adult. I also worked to acknowledge their feelings, to assist them in knowing that they both had space in my mind, and that while I may be paying attention to one boy, I was also very much aware of the other. Through the therapeutic process, I helped the brothers develop a sense of comfort whenever they were out of the spotlight of an adult's attention.

Attachment, separation, and individuation

Luca struggled with separation from his mother. He became tearful, upset, and angry when his parents left the playroom to attend their sessions. On these occasions, I had to divide my time between attending to Luca, allowing him to express his feelings and helping him to calm down, and acknowledging that Mario was still there, battling at times with his own desire to help his brother feel better and feelings of impotence (illustrated by him trying to cuddle Luca only to be ignored and to then retreat into himself). It was important that I showed Luca that other people around him would not be overwhelmed by his rage (regardless of the emotional turmoil I felt in the transference). At the same time, I acted as an example to Mario that the whole world does not have to bend to the will and whims of his brother, and that it was all right for Mario to keep playing, to hang on to his own wants and feelings without succumbing to his brother's emotional turmoil.

One afternoon it was arranged that Mario would spend time with one parent while Filippo was with the other. Luca remained with me, having lost both parents to his other siblings. Luca's fury at not getting his parents to himself resulted in another hysterical outburst. As a therapist, my job was both to contain Luca in his fury, to recognise and acknowledge his rage, and to not let it overwhelm him or me. It was also necessary for me to support his mother, to help her to leave the room without being completely overwhelmed by her son's rage. She had to maintain the firm boundary that had been set—to leave Luca behind with me. In doing so, I helped her to reclaim the role of "parent" in their relationship, and showed both how to make space for others in the nest, while claiming appropriate space for themselves.

Our work also enabled Luca and Mario to stake individual spaces in their parents' minds, a theme worked on in the individual adult and couple session as well as the joint sessions. One afternoon, Gianni returned from his individual session with pictures he had drawn for the two boys in which he carefully included their personal likes. The joy of the children in receiving not only a gift from their father, but an affirmation that he had kept them in mind was wonderful to witness.

As the treatment progressed, it became apparent that it was increasingly essential for Luca to separate more from his mother, and that having the father reclaim his place in the marital bed would be both a practical and symbolic shift. In order to assist with this move, we provided the boys and their parents with transitional objects, a reminder of the other to work "through the process of holding and being held" (Athern & Madill, 2002, p. 382), and a tool with which to separate.

Gianni's transitional object held a specific role, to sit on the marital bed and show Luca that that space belonged to him, even when he was out working late in the evening.

Transference, countertransference, and mirroring

Transference and countertransference were of vital importance in my learning to distinguish between the needs of each child. I felt exhausted by my time with the boys in the first week, and was particularly overwhelmed by Luca. I reflected on how my exhaustion, and the irritation it triggered in me, might reflect both Luca's fury with Mario for taking the spotlight away from him and his mother's deep tiredness, as though she was being "devoured" by her son. In the early days of treatment, it seemed to me as if much of our team supervision focused on the emerging needs of Filippo and his parents. At times in our discussions, I felt as if the boys' needs were given less time and, therefore, "less value", and I reflected how this could mirror the boys' own experiences at home. It was Luca whom I discussed in most detail with my colleagues after the first week: his demanding, yet engaging behaviour had begun to dominate both our time together and my mind. It was my colleagues' frequent prompting, asking about Mario, that supported me in not allowing Luca to dominate my mind (in much the same way that he dominated his mother's bed) and to make the space for Mario that he deserved.

Mario's need to accept both care and attention stayed strongly with me. I dedicated myself to raising Mario's awareness of his own desires, and working to meet them both practically and emotionally. For example, I saw how Mario would turn his face away from his brother when Luca overrode a clear wish of Mario's. When I pointed this out to them, Mario began to emphasise his point more strongly, by moving to the side of the room and curling up in a ball. While becoming clearer at showing his unmet needs, Mario remained resistant to having them met. He shied away from my attempts to cater to his needs, as if wishing to remain self-sufficient, not wanting to open the gate to the possibility that he might be ignored or let down. As Mario struggled with my direct interventions, I used stories with puppets to externalise his needs, creating a scenario in which a bunny that fell over needed to learn to let a puppy help him. It seemed as if this indirect approach was more bearable to Mario, and I observed him begin to create more opportunities to have his needs met. For example, on a trip to the park, we played a game in which Mario pretended to fall over and I would go to him and check if he had hurt himself, after which he would get up, run, and pretend to fall again.

Working with two children with opposing needs every day was exhausting. I found myself preoccupied with them, thinking of them when I was not at the clinic, and even dreaming about them at night. Group supervision and discussions with colleagues were essential for me to express my sense of feeling overwhelmed. While I had the boys six hours a day, I was not their only therapist, as some days I had other work commitments to attend to. They had to learn to share me and I had to learn to allow the other professionals to work with the boys in their own way, while maintaining a consistent message, much as Hisako had to create the space to allow Gianni his own way of parenting their sons.

Developments after the two-week treatment

Filippo

In the Acquarone scales depicted in Figures 8.3 and 8.4, completed at the end of the intensive programme, two clear signs of development can be seen: first, that Filippo was able to integrate his emotions, and second, with his behaviours now aligned in the Frequently and Rarely columns, it was clear that Filippo was now successfully on the road to being able to trust new experiences, daring to be curious, to share, to explore, and to have fun with his parents and siblings.

Filippo's behaviour at the dinner table also went through a transformation. As Hisako came to verbalise her feelings and begin to understand how Filippo felt, she learnt to make him wait when she served him his food. She also gave herself time to eat with him. As soon as the issues with his mother were brought out into the open and held, Filippo became slower and more attentive. His manners at the table changed. It seemed that it was his fury at his mother for not seeing him for who he was that had shaped his hurried mealtimes. Now there was space for him in his mother's eyes, and within the family as a whole.

The follow-up treatment, weekly meetings with mother and son, sometimes separate and sometimes together, continued for a year and half. These sessions explored in more depth other personal and parenting aspects, as well as Filippo's ability to relate to, and mix with, the children in the nursery.

ACQUARONE DETECTION SCALES FOR EARLY RELATIONSHIPS®

EARLY SIGNS OF ALARM – pre-Autism

FOLLOW-UP – INFANT/CHILD

name: **FILIPPO**

age: **1 year 6 months** *date of this observation:* **DD MMM YYYY**

		NEVER	RARELY	FREQUENT	ALWAYS	OBSERVER REACTIONS
INTERPERSONAL	1. GAZING			●		
	2. BABBLING			●		
	3. CALLING			●		
	4. IMITATING			●		
	5. PROVOKING			●		
	6. POINTING			●		
	7. FEEDING			●		*... allowing time to talk*
	8. JOINT ATTENTION		●			
	9. PLAY			●		
	10. ALONE			●		
	11. RELATING *– to other children*			●		*... not seen*
	– to adults			●		
	12. REACTIVE BEHAVIOURS *capacity to...* *a) accept emotional warmth b) bear stressful event c) adapt to changes*		●			
SENSORIAL	TOUCHING 13. *Skin-to-skin*			●		
	14. *Textures*		●			
	RESPONSE 15. *Sounds*			●		
	16. *Noise*			●		
	17. *Name*			●		
	18. *Light & patterns*		●			
	19. *Smells*			●		
	20. COMFORTING		●			
MOTOR	HOLDING 21. *Posturing*			●		*... not toeing any longer*
	22. *Stereotypic movement*		●			
	23. *Use of hands/Use of body*			●		
AFFECT	24. EXPRESSIVENESS			●		*... mimicking and pretending*
	25. SELF-HELP DEVELOPMENT			●		

ANY OTHER OBSERVATIONS NOT LISTED ABOVE:

General positive movement from never/always to rarely and from rarely to frequent
0/23 Never – always
8/23 Rarely

Figure 8.3. Filippo's follow-up assessment.

ACQUARONE DETECTION SCALES FOR EARLY RELATIONSHIPS®
EARLY SIGNS OF ALARM – pre-Autism
...affecting the baby or being affected by the baby...

FOLLOW-UP – MOTHER/caregiver

name: **NAME**
child: FILIPPO *age:* 1 year 6 months

		NEVER	RARELY	FREQUENT	ALWAYS	OBSERVER REACTIONS
INTERPERSONAL	1. GAZING			●		*... less anxious*
	2. BABBLING			●		*... started to talk slowly*
	3. CALLING		●			
	4. FEEDING			●		*... became attuned*
	5. GAMES / PLAY			●		*... able to coordinate*
	6. RELATING			●		
	7. REACTIVE BEHAVIOURS			●		
SENSORIAL	8. TOUCHING		●			
	9. COMFORTING			●		*... calm about self value*
MOTOR	10. POSTURE			●		
AFFECT	11. EXPRESSIVENESS		●			*... could show happiness*
	12. UNDERSTANDING OF EMOTIONS – *in themselves* – *in the baby*		●			*... able to understand*
	13. PAST – *Psychiatric illness* – *Other difficulties*			● ●		*... allow insights to keep*

ANY OTHER OBSERVATIONS NOT LISTED ABOVE:

Figure 8.4. Filippo's mother's follow-up assessment.

Luca and Mario

By the end of the treatment programme, it appeared to us that Mario was more assertive. He was more able to express his own will and to speak up for what he wanted, whether it be asking for a piece of paper in his favourite colour, or playing a different game to that chosen by his brother. In short, Mario had found his voice.

Luca seemed to be able to overcome the subsequent shock at not being able to persuade Mario to do as he wished all the time, and learnt to act in a gentle and more considerate manner. He also learnt to slow down and to take turns, to allow space for others, and to understand that the word "fair" applied to everyone. Furthermore, Luca was able to deal with potentially overwhelming feelings, such as his anger, in a more contained manner. A key turning point was the change in family bedtime routines. The father reclaimed his place in the parental bed and Luca managed to accept having to sleep apart from his mother.

The boys also became able to cope with being separate from each other, to play different games, or with different people, and to play *with* Filippo, not just *to* him.

Summary

This chapter aimed to illustrate in detail the nature of our work with siblings of children with autism. The family constellation is such that just as a trauma can resonate and have an impact beyond those immediately concerned, so can positive change. Whether the impact is negative or positive, what is helpful is for the family to be given support in realigning itself to best meet the needs of all concerned.

By the end of the treatment, a very positive shift in the siblings could be observed, in both their individual emotional development and their capacity to relate more appropriately to other people, particularly Filippo. Luca was a highly intelligent and socially adept child, whose tendency to use his skills to rule those around him could be kept in check by consistent, appropriate limits. It was suggested that he might benefit from ongoing therapeutic support in the future should his underlying insecurities and need to dominate disrupt family life and relationships. Mario was a bright and sensitive child whose tendency to retreat inwardly when he felt he was not being heard could be overruled by reassurance that he had his own space in the family. Mario needed support from his parents in seeking and accepting comfort from other people.

As can be seen from Figures 8.5 and 8.6, Filippo and his mother improved in the regulation of Filippo's behaviours and the appearance of warmth and enjoyment in both their lives. The graphics show at a glance the rate of improvement. Normal behaviours would be 2 or 3; however, Filippo's behaviours were often measured as 1 and 4, and for his mother, too. By treating their underlying experiences,

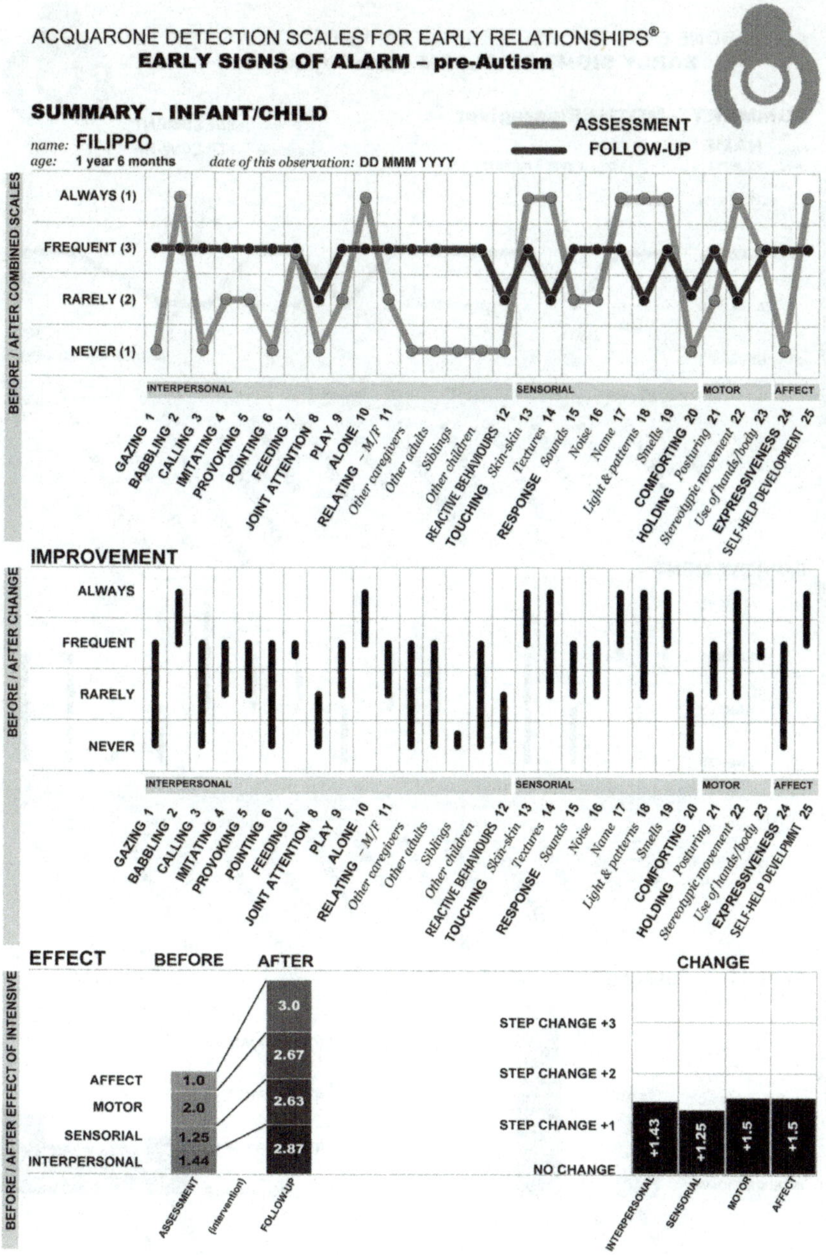

Figure 8.5. Follow-up summary report for Filippo.

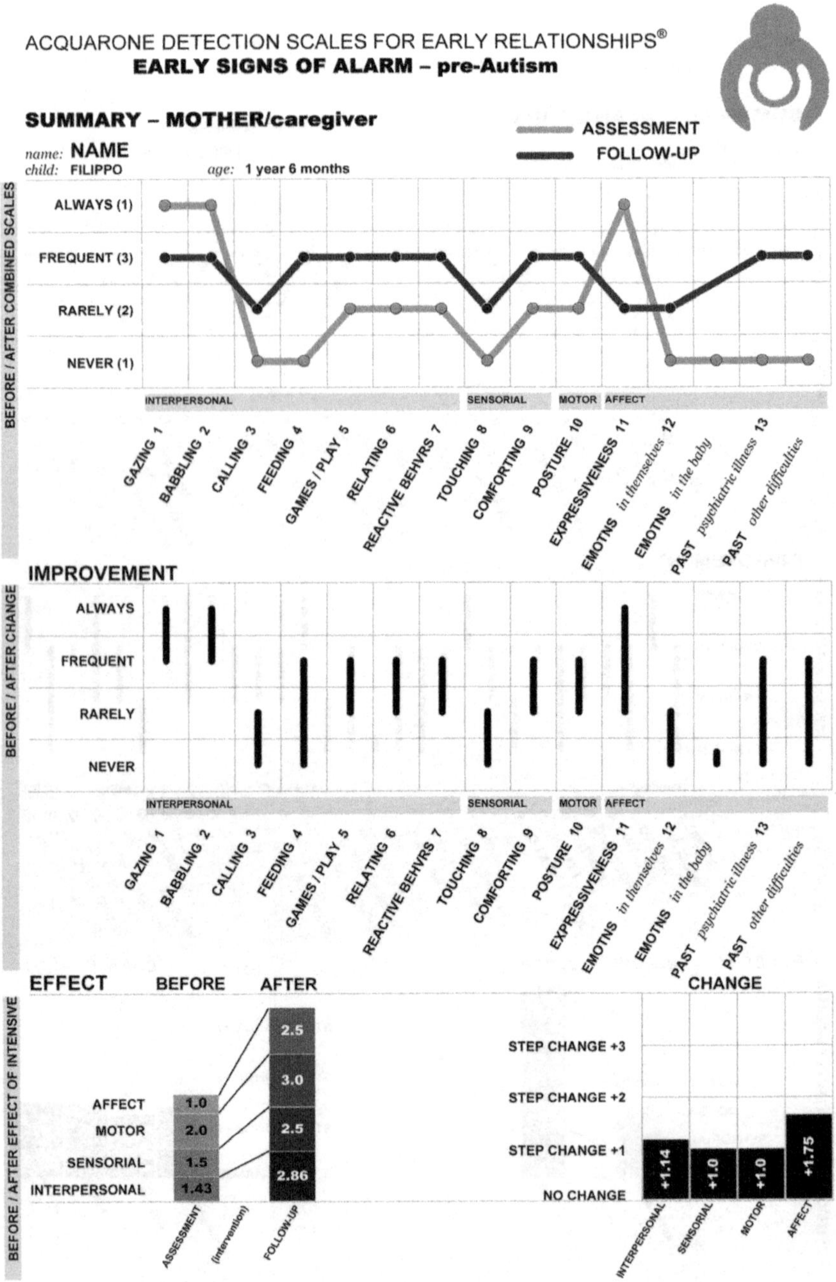

Figure 8.6. Follow-up summary report for Filippo's mother.

anxieties, and emotions, on both a conscious and unconscious level, their individual and reciprocal relationships improved by becoming more flexible and adaptive, and with a new-found sense of fun and enjoyment.

We do not measure the siblings' developments here, but Luca and Mario clearly benefited from their own therapy sessions. They were helped to come to terms with their feelings and those of their brother, and learnt to play with him in a way that Filippo could understand and enjoy.

Acknowledgement

I would like to thank Dominique Hawksley for her contribution to the writing of the siblings clinical material in this chapter.

CHAPTER NINE

Nicola: an intensive treatment with an eight-month-old

Stella Acquarone

> "Nicola would look down, serious and avoidant in her mother's arms, or in the grandmother's lap, or father's attempted cuddle. Down and serious as if the world were a nightmare to be blocked out. Her body was curved tightly inwards like a snail and her face wore a constant frown. With her hands clasped rigidly in front of her, Nicola sucked anxiously on her right hand, or left—the self-calming action creating further distancing from the body that held her."
>
> (Clinical notes, Stella Acquarone)

It was via the Internet that Nicola's parents, Hanna and Aleksi, first contacted us with concerns about their youngest child. They described feeling as if their six-month-old daughter, Nicola, did not know who they were. The mother spoke of "desperately" wanting "to connect with Nicola".

They sent us video footage, at our request, to enable us to make an initial evaluation of possible signs of autism. (We offer this service to families who live abroad, asking them to send video clips of their infant in different situations, such as feeding, playing, alone and with siblings, and bedtime routines.) Nicola was their fourth child and the mother knew that her behaviour was very different to her three brothers, and felt that something was wrong. Nicola did not seem interested in her mother or other people. In fact, if Hanna, Aleksi, or anyone else came close, Nicola would cry, and she would continue to do so until they moved away and no longer looked at her. We agreed, after having watched the videos, that the family was right to feel concerned. As they lived in Finland, we set up a conversation with the mother and undertook some further observations of Nicola.

The video analysis

The video footage showed a girl that was floppy, with seemingly little muscle tone, and with her hands constantly clasped near her mouth. Nicola was clearly disturbed if people came too close to her, screaming, turning away, withdrawing into herself. She had been breastfed since birth, but had established a very uncomfortable-looking position when feeding, arching her body backwards, her eyes either closed or looking away from the mother. Nicola was not interested in being held by any member of the family, immediately protesting by turning rigid and arching her back, whether being picked up to be put to bed, or cuddled, or carried. Her energetic, noisy brothers were not interested in her. Her grandmother opted to hold Nicola at arm's length, looking away from her so that Nicola did not cry. The only time the child seemed relaxed was when an adult flicked through the pages of a book. It was then that she came alive, seemingly delighted by the movement of the pages rather than by the pictures, or the company. Most of the time, Nicola was content to stare into space, or at a hanging mobile, or at the leaves blowing in the breeze in the garden. In all the footage, the mother's concern and anxiety could be clearly detected in her voice whenever she addressed her daughter.

Our interventions over Skype consisted of listening to the mother's worries and offering her new ways of relating to, and behaving with, Nicola so that we could identify the child's sensitivities. These trial behaviours included suggesting that Hanna talk to Nicola from a distance, rather than up close, playing different kinds of music and observing her daughter's reactions, and spending time with her in a calm space away from the siblings. We asked Hanna to tell us about her daily observations of Nicola and to report any "positive" behaviours. Hanna asked her mother to help look after the three other children so that she could spend the extra time with Nicola.

After four weeks of support via Skype, Hanna requested to come to London to receive direct help for Nicola, as her behaviours had not improved. Her husband, Aleksi, was willing to pay for the treatment but was reluctant to accompany her. He was sceptical about the programme and first wanted to speak to several families who had already undergone the Re:Start treatment process. Worried about his daughter, aware of our emphasis on full family participation, reassured by discussions with families who had received our help, and convinced by his wife's concerns about Nicola's deteriorating behaviour, the father finally agreed to attend. The family came to London and were put up in an apartment across the road from the clinic. Aleksi, aware of the financial impact of being away from his own business, still had some reservations, which he shared with us, but only on the first day.

Family history

The family consisted of Nicola and her three older brothers: Oskar, aged nine, Samuel, aged seven, and Daniel, aged five. The boys were in school and were well behaved. The parents had waited a few years to have the fourth child, and had hoped for a girl. They, and the whole family, were delighted by her arrival. Both Hanna and Aleksi were around forty years old and had a good relationship. Hanna was a teacher, but had not worked since having her first child. She was happy at home and there was no financial need for her to return to work.

Assessment

During the assessment, the parents talked about how happy they had been when Nicola was born—the girl they had always wanted. She was a good baby from the start, sleeping well by the second month and rarely crying for attention. However, Hanna soon realised that Nicola avoided eye contact, even when she spoke or sang to her. Nicola did not touch her when breastfed, but leaned outwards to avoid all skin contact. She did not snuggle up to her parents, or allow herself to fall asleep in her mother's arms. Nicola vehemently disliked being picked up, either becoming "floppy" in their arms or arching backwards in anger. At first, Hanna thought this was simply because girls are different to boys, since none of her sons had behaved this way as babies. However, when she discussed Nicola's behaviour with friends and observed other baby girls with their mothers, Hanna quickly realised her daughter had a deep reluctance to be with people, preferring to be with objects or completely on her own.

As part of the assessment, we needed to observe how Nicola managed her senses, to discover when and why her fears, anxieties, and other overwhelming feelings manifested themselves, and in what way. We saw that with the family group Nicola showed no inclination to engage with any of her siblings; however, she seemed to like the voice of her father and to profoundly dislike the voice of her mother. We noted that the mother spoke in high-pitched tone, and that there was no intonation resembling "motherese"—the soft, slow, and repetitive child-directed speech typically used by carers. During the initial assessment period, we realised that Nicola found it hard to look at or even recognise her parents. It was as if she needed more time to capture and piece together the separate features of their faces. It seemed as if her visual processing was impaired and was not allowing the baby girl to find recognition and peace in her mother's face, hands, or body. Nicola also demonstrated a very high reactivity to stimuli, and was in a state of constant startle (as if hyper-vigilant).

On the Acquarone scale, Nicola scored thirteen signs of alarm (Figure 9.1). These did not improve after Hanna trialled the new behaviour patterns that we had instructed her to try when we were Skyping.

The mother's results on the Acquarone scale (Figure 9.2) revealed the negative impact Nicola was having on her; Hanna was anxious and fearful of the daughter who could not relate to her and who found the external world unbearable.

Intervention

Work with Nicola

Once the assessment was complete, we started our work with Nicola and her parents. We wanted to assist her in forming relationships with

ACQUARONE DETECTION SCALES FOR EARLY RELATIONSHIPS®
EARLY SIGNS OF ALARM – pre-Autism

ASSESSMENT – INFANT/CHILD

name: **NICOLA**
age: **8 months** *date of this observation:* **DD MMM YYYY**

		NEVER	RARELY	FREQUENT	ALWAYS	OBSERVER REACTIONS
INTERPERSONAL	**1. GAZING** *Eye-to-eye contact within a relationship and the maintenance of this contact*	●				
	2. BABBLING *Making sounds for the benefit of the partner in the parent-infant relationship*		●			
	3. CALLING *– The facial expressions – Noises or gestures that seek to produce an affectionate response from the partner*		●			
	4. IMITATING *– Moving mouth, tongue, etc., in imitation of mother's (or another) – The repetition of a sound or a movement heard or seen by the child*	●				
	5. PROVOKING *Inciting the person into interacting, not just to use as an instrument to do something for him/her*	●				
	6. POINTING *Indicating with index finger to a person about an object of interest*					
	7. FEEDING *Child's attitude during the intake of food, including anticipatory behaviour (e.g. head-turning, moving arms the food/breast)*				●	*... fast anxious*
	8. JOINT ATTENTION *Looking in the same direction*	●				
	9. PLAY *– Capacity to play the same game for more than 5 minutes, and share with another person – Take turns and stay with a person – Children*		●			
	10. ALONE				●	
	11. RELATING *Behaviours indicating the capacity to relate & accept emotional warmth.*					
	– Mother, Father		●			
	– Other caregivers		●			
	– Other unfamiliar adults		●			
	– Siblings		●			
	– Other unfamiliar children		●			
	12. REACTIVE BEHAVIOURS *tolerance to frustrations, including:* *– a) Capacity to accept emotional warmth – b) Capacity to bounce back after stressful event – c) Capacity to adapt to changes...please indicate*	●				
SENSORIAL	**TOUCHING**					
	13. *Skin-to-skin contact initiated by infant for play or affection*	●				
	14. *Does the child touch paint, foam, sand, water, playdoh, plasticine and other messy substances*	●				
	RESPONSE					
	15. *Response to sounds*	●				
	16. *Response to noise*	●				
	17. *Response to name*	●				
	18. *Response to light & patterns*	●				
	19. *Response to smells*	●				
	20. COMFORTING *Child's ability to find relief from distress by themselves (e.g. thumb sucking, touching hands, playing with one car, others)...specify*			●		
MOTOR	**HOLDING**					
	21. *The posturing of the child when he is supported in the arms of the mother (e.g. floppy, rigid, restless) – General muscle tone when sitting or standing*		●			
	22. *Stereotypic movement of arms, eyes, etc.* *– Walking: on tiptoes or sluggish*		●			
	23. *Use of hands: for grasping, for helping himself* *– Use of body: to reach, to climb, to hide, other...*		●			
AFFECT	**24. EXPRESSIVENESS** *The body or facial expression of emotional states (e.g., sad, worried, anxious, bland, happy, or others)...specify*		●			*... looked away, cut off*
	25. SELF HELP DEVELOPMENT *– Ability to cope independently with the environment, (e.g., dress) – Eating – Being careful with him/herself or others*	●				

ANY OTHER OBSERVATIONS NOT LISTED ABOVE:

Figure 9.1. Nicola's assessment.

ACQUARONE DETECTION SCALES FOR EARLY RELATIONSHIPS®

EARLY SIGNS OF ALARM – pre-Autism

...affecting the baby or being affected by the baby...

ASSESSMENT – MOTHER/caregiver

name: **NAME**
child: **NICOLA** *age:* **8 months**

	Item	NEVER	RARELY	FREQUENT	ALWAYS	OBSERVER REACTIONS
INTERPERSONAL	**1. GAZING** *Eye-to-eye contact with the baby and the maintenance of this contact*				●	*... mothers anxiety transmitted*
	2. BABBLING *– Making sounds for the benefit of the parent-infant relationship – Talking*				●	*... high pitch tone, persistent and repetitive*
	3. CALLING *Facial expressions, noises or gestures seeking to produce an affectionate response from the infant*				●	*... Mother looked frightened*
	4. FEEDING *Mother's attitude towards infant's hunger and need to feed: – Does she anticipate behavior and have meal or breast easily available? – Does she pay attention, talk with the baby and enjoy feeding? – Does she interrupt with any excuse (e.g., talks to others and looks away)? – Is she fearful, full of anguish or has she any delusions? – Is she apathetic?*			●		*... mother breastfeeding ... mother talked a while ... in spite of baby's posture ... being outward*
	5. GAMES / PLAY *– Playful encounters, including songs and teasing*	●				
	6. RELATING *Behaviours indicating the capacity to relate & accept emotional warmth towards the baby*			●		*... fast anxious*
	7. REACTIVE BEHAVIOURS *including: – Tolerance to frustrations – Capacity to accept emotional warmth – Capacity to bounce back after stressful event – Capacity to adapt to changes*			●		
SENSORIAL	**8. TOUCHING** *– Skin-to-skin contact initiated by infant for play or affection*				●	*... little contact*
	9. COMFORTING *– Mother's ability to find relief for the baby's distress*				●	*... constant*
MOTOR	**10. POSTURE** *The posturing of the mother when the infant is supported in her arms or any other way (e.g., other, rough, balanced precariously)*			●		*... good and welcoming*
AFFECT	**11. EXPRESSIVENESS** *– Expression of emotional state (e.g., sad, worried, anxious, bland, happy, others)...specify*			●		*... very clear anxious, worried and sad*
	12. UNDERSTANDING OF EMOTIONS *– in themselves*			●		*... wanted to know about baby internal world*
	– in the baby	●				
	13. PAST *– Psychiatric illness*	●				*... sleeping with her children rather than husband*
	– Other difficulties	●				

ANY OTHER OBSERVATIONS NOT LISTED ABOVE:

Preoccupied since Nicola 4th month about not being able to understand and have a relationship with her

© Acquarone 2013

Figure 9.2. Nicola's mother's assessment.

her parents and with us. We began Nicola's treatment in a quiet room with the curtains drawn, the semi-darkness intended to take Nicola back to her time in the womb, when she felt protected and calm. We also wanted to find out whether the child's visual processing might be affected by too much light. At eight months old, Nicola was not yet sitting up, but also did not like being on her tummy. As a result, we placed her either in a baby seat or on her back, on a soft, plain blanket. We would sit in front of her for a while, keeping very still. We would place a small coloured ball in front of us, or reach out and gently touch her hands, feet, or legs. We spoke in short sentences, our tone soft. We tried very slowly to give her some sense of being there, of being present inside a body that had boundaries, a skin, and ears to hear one or two words only, not a string of words. We encouraged Nicola to touch us, to feel our skin. We used very slow, simple experiences for her to be able to perceive us and to then take pleasure in her perceptions. And so the rhythms of trust and safety began.

After a few sessions, it was decided to see how Nicola would react to more light, and so we gradually emerged from the semi-darkness by opening the curtains very slowly. We asked one of the parents to place themselves in front of the baby. They had to be still, so that Nicola had time to process their face, to put all the pieces together. At one point, when Hanna was talking, Aleksi started playing a silent game of peek-a-boo with Nicola, hiding his face behind his hands and then reappearing. After a while, Hanna began to breastfeed the baby, who remained looking calmly at her father. Gradually, Nicola wanted more contact with her parents—her father primarily, whom she looked at for longer, and whom she began looking for if he was not directly in front of her.

Concerned about Nicola's apparent dislike of her mother's voice, we asked Hanna to try speaking more slowly to her daughter, and to modify her rather squeaky tone. At first Hanna found this request upsetting, as if she were doing something "wrong", but after discussing these feelings in her own therapy sessions, she was able to keep the focus on Nicola and worked hard to lower and soften her tone. We requested that the parents speak softly to each other, or to Nicola, to avoid confusing her with too many conversations in the room. This gradual approach enabled Nicola to start to take in and process information coming from the different senses, organs, and emotions aroused by the sounds and experiences.

By the middle of the second week, we were able to add to the complexity of Nicola's interactions: we began using three different coloured balls for her to look at, as opposed to just one, we brought in more elaborate toys and musical instruments for her to look at, touch, and play with, and we moved on to include her siblings in our work. One brother at a time was asked to come into the room. Each one had to learn to be still, quiet, and to observe their sister. We asked them to tell us where Nicola was looking, what she was doing, what she might be thinking. While they learnt about her, Nicola could take them in, and learn about them. By the end of the third week, the three brothers could all be in the room at the same time, sitting quietly and still, so that Nicola could see them and take in their differences. Talking in turns, they realised that Nicola was looking at them, seriously at first and then with a shy smile. This was a big breakthrough for the family, who suddenly felt that Nicola was not only allowing them to be with her but also wanted to be with them. It was as if the "slow-motion" interactions (being with Nicola in a slow, calm, respectful way) allowed Nicola to experience and enjoy her family, whom she had previously only experienced in "fast-forward" mode, unable to distinguish their characters, behaviours, or intentions.

Work with the parents

The parents underwent both individual and couple therapy. In the first week, Hanna and Aleksi talked about their happy childhoods, their likes and dislikes. Perhaps because she felt more at ease with us after the online interventions, it was not long before Hanna began voicing her frustrations about Aleksi never having enough time to spend with Nicola, as though it were the mother's job. Understandably, Aleksi was at first very uncomfortable with this; however, over the following sessions it became clear just how much he enjoyed being with his daughter and wife.

Hanna was the eldest of three, and had two brothers who were six and eight years younger than her. Being so much older, she had helped her mother look after the boys and had enjoyed taking on the task. Deep down, she fantasised that they were her own children—something not uncommon among teenage girls. What she did not discover until late in her twenties was that she had been adopted from birth and that her two brothers had been conceived naturally. Hanna explored her feelings about this fact through expressive paintings. Her therapist hypothesised that perhaps Hanna felt cheated by her adoptive mother, who had brought her up lovingly but who had not passed on her DNA. Perhaps, too, the birth of a girl who did not look at her might have reminded Hanna of her birth mother, who had chosen to give her away rather than look after her. Hanna continually expressed her anxiety about her precious baby girl's inability to look at her. These feelings seemed to contain both a real grief about having a daughter who did not "smile at, look at, or want to be with" her and deeper historical feelings of rejection.

A lot more material surfaced as a consequence of Hanna's feelings of rejection and fear; these were explored and expressed from different perspectives. It became apparent that the "squeaky" voice that Hanna used with Nicola held within it some of the stress and anxiety of trying to reach her. However, by trying so hard, it was almost as if she was pushing her daughter further away. As signs of connection grew between mother and daughter, Hanna found it easier to soften the tone of her voice.

Aleksi worked long hours and had been on the periphery of bringing up the children. He had grown up with a brother with special needs. It seemed that he had always been frightened that one of his children would be born with a disability, and the fact that Nicola behaved so oddly reminded him of his brother. He started to escape the family by working even longer hours.

The individual sessions were helpful in making Aleksi feel that there was a way to get through to Nicola, that his unconscious conflicts could be faced, and that they were separate from what he was projecting to Nicola. He came to realise that they all had to make a special effort when around Nicola, for the time being at least, until she could catch up and her brain was able to process faces, colours, and joyful experiences.

The parents continued with the couple and individual therapy sessions for a year after the intensive programme.

Work with the siblings

The three boys spent time with the therapists together, but were also given individual sessions. The therapists worked to help them find ways in which they could think about Nicola, her arrival in the family, and how they felt about her. The brothers spoke about how confused they were by their sister's behaviour, not understanding why she screamed, cried, or could be so silent. They were worried about how worried the parents were. As well as spending time in the playroom, the brothers, who were clearly able to follow instructions and stick to boundaries, were also taken to the zoo and on other outings, including horse riding. These trips often engendered further disclosure about the difficult feelings Nicola brought out in them. The boys were able to express their uncertainty about what was happening with their baby sister, asking many different questions, such as: Was she disabled? Did she have cerebral palsy, like the sister of one of their friends? Why was she different? And many similar questions.

It became apparent that each boy had a very different, personal response to Nicola. The eldest, Oskar, had felt displaced when the second boy was born. He thought that maybe he was not good enough, and that was why his parents had had a second child. But by the time the third child, Daniel, was born, he realised that his parents simply wanted a big family, and it did not have anything to do with him. Similarly, the news about another pregnancy had brought up more feelings about being "one of many". He was worried, though, that Nicola was not responsive and did not smile. The second boy, Samuel, spoke of feeling "sad that she doesn't like me", while the youngest revealed guiltily that he did not like his baby sister at all, especially as she was taking up all his mother's attention. We admired his honesty and helped him explore further the complex feelings of being part of a big family. As well as exploring and expressing their feelings, we also spent time developing the boys' observation skills: for example, closely watching how ants behaved in the garden, and looking carefully at the variety of animals in the zoo. We wanted to improve the boys' observation skills so that they could apply them to their baby sister and learn how to understand her better.

Progress

At the end of the intensive three weeks, the Acquarone Scale was filled in again for both Nicola and her mother (Figures 9.3 and 9.4). Nicola's results show a girl who had progressed from being avoidant in her behaviours to being delighted when around other people, provided they were respectful of her sensitivities and difficulties. However, these difficulties were understood and worked through far quicker than in older children, and Nicola's recovery was complete. In a similar case presentation, where there was no intervention, the child was diagnosed as being on the autistic spectrum three years later.

We also focused on sensorimotor issues that were clearly impinging on the child's capacity to relate, such as the tone of her mother's

ACQUARONE DETECTION SCALES FOR EARLY RELATIONSHIPS®

EARLY SIGNS OF ALARM – pre-Autism

FOLLOW-UP – INFANT/CHILD

name: **NICOLA**

age: **8 months** *date of this observation:* **DD MMM YYYY**

		NEVER	RARELY	FREQUENT	ALWAYS	OBSERVER REACTIONS
INTERPERSONAL	**1. GAZING**			●		
	2. BABBLING			●		
	3. CALLING			●		
	4. IMITATING			●		
	5. PROVOKING			●		
	6. POINTING			●		
	7. FEEDING			●		
	8. JOINT ATTENTION			●		
	9. PLAY			●		
	10. ALONE			●		
	11. RELATING – *to other children*			●		
	– *to adults*			●		
	12. REACTIVE BEHAVIOURS *capacity to... a) accept emotional warmth b) bear stressful event c) adapt to changes*			●		
SENSORIAL	**TOUCHING** 13. *Skin-to-skin*			●		
	14. *Textures*					
	RESPONSE 15. *Sounds*			●		
	16. *Noise*					
	17. *Name*			●		
	18. *Light & patterns*					
	19. *Smells*					
	20. COMFORTING			●		
MOTOR	**HOLDING** 21. *Posturing*			●		
	22. *Stereotypic movement*			●		
	23. *Use of hands/Use of body*			●		
AFFECT	**24. EXPRESSIVENESS**			●		
	25. SELF HELP DEVELOPMENT			●		

ANY OTHER OBSERVATIONS NOT LISTED ABOVE:

Figure 9.3. Nicola's follow-up assessment.

ACQUARONE DETECTION SCALES FOR EARLY RELATIONSHIPS®
EARLY SIGNS OF ALARM – pre-Autism
...affecting the baby or being affected by the baby...

FOLLOW-UP – MOTHER/caregiver

name: **NAME**
child: NICOLA *age:* 8 months

		NEVER	RARELY	FREQUENT	ALWAYS	OBSERVER REACTIONS
INTERPERSONAL	1. GAZING			●		*... with joy*
	2. BABBLING			●		*... nicely in a glare tone*
	3. CALLING			●		*... learn to wait and see*
	4. FEEDING			●		*... nicely resting*
	5. GAMES / PLAY		●			*... learn the signs to start game*
	6. RELATING			●		
	7. REACTIVE BEHAVIOURS			●		
SENSORIAL	8. TOUCHING			●		*... carefully*
	9. COMFORTING			●		*... when necessary*
MOTOR	10. POSTURE			●		*... calm, nice and firm*
AFFECT	11. EXPRESSIVENESS			●		*... Continue to be able to show and talk. And feelings now*
	12. UNDERSTANDING OF EMOTIONS					*... constant*
	– *in themselves*			●		
	– *in the baby*			●		
	13. PAST					*... understanding family dynamic*
	– *Psychiatric illness*			●		
	– *Other difficulties*			●		

ANY OTHER OBSERVATIONS NOT LISTED ABOVE:

Figure 9.4. Nicola's mother's follow-up assessment.

voice, and her extreme sensitivity to noises on the periphery that seemed to mask the messages and sounds directed at her.

Looking at the mother's results after the three-week programme, it is clear to see just how much of a change had taken place with Hanna. She started feeling connected, was more able to understand her daughter, and realised the importance of each parent's individuality, as well as the couple issues that she and her husband had to work through.

It was noticeable how quickly the changes occurred in the mother and father's understanding of their daughter. It is possible to think that, by reacting early to the difficulties they had in reaching and relating to their daughter, the parents were forced to seek help more quickly, which in turn prevented Nicola's behaviours, as well as their own, from becoming too entrenched and so harder to work with.

Discussion

What we saw in this case was how the nascent brain difficulty in processing perceptions can generate an aversion to looking and being looked at. We could see the impact of this brain perturbation in Nicola's inability to recognise and form relationships with her mother, father, and siblings.

Alvarez (1994) considers the mother's most important function is to sensitively coax the child into a more alert state. "Reclamation" is crucial for helping the mother (and father and siblings) to stop vicious cycles occurring. Based on observations of what ordinary mothers of ordinary babies do when their baby is going through a phase of being withdrawn or having temporarily lost interest in the goings-on around them, the mother must provide a "live company" to coax her baby back into being interested in the world. However, with Nicola, we had to take into consideration the fact that the child was not able to perceive the mother properly. The more the mother tried to "re-claim" the child by seeking contact, the more stimuli the child had to struggle with, and as a consequence the more overwhelmed, fearful, and withdrawn Nicola became. We had to help the mother "re-claim" Nicola in a more subdued, but more effective, manner.

Alvarez (2012) says that a first stage of relating might be "vitalizing" emotional encounters. Nicola needed help in coping with these encounters before she could be helped to bear their emotional content.

Ratey (2001) says,

> . . . autistic children often shun many kinds of physical contact. Part of the reason is that sensory information coming to them from the outside world comes too fast for their brains to process and they are simply overwhelmed by the stimuli around them. A typical example is to shut down or attempt to get away from the stimuli. This is compounded by an inability to pay attention, because the information that comes to them comes in fragment or pieces. For example, a healthy baby can shift his attention from the eyes to the nose to the

> mouth of his mother within fractions of a second. But an autistic baby takes five to six seconds just to process the nose. Because of the delay, the infant cannot take in a whole face at once, just parts. Missing a social cue such as a smile or a frown is easy. The result is that the baby receives only partial information about the world, and the information he does receive is often confusing. (p. 78)

Nicola had to be approached slowly and in a steady way at the beginning. We sat motionless in front of her to give her time to "take in" and process our faces. We placed just one item in front of her, then two. We gave her time to take in the stimuli surrounding her and to begin to catch the various parts—voice, face, and touch—which she could then slowly integrate into a whole: the mummy or daddy.

Sometimes, we do not realise that our faces are complicated to take in, that the breast does not look the same every time, that the milk does not flow in the same manner, and that our emotions are not there in the same way. Sometimes, we do not realise that to a very sensitive child the world is an extremely confused, threatening place, one to be avoided in order to preserve some sense of inner calm. Yet, this insular retreat can itself be frighteningly lonely, as the autistic space may have within it a dangerous emptiness.

Life brings constant novelty and newness for the baby: in the nappy changes, at bathtime, in everyday encounters. For the oversensitive child, however, every new sensation brings with it a sense of danger. The child wants to survive each encounter but, overwhelmed by their difficulty in processing the stimuli, retreats. The baby seeks instead stimuli that can be coped with: for example, the movement of the air, their fingers, the pages of a book, the pitch of their cry, or a calmness within. With Nicola, we began the treatment by reducing the stimuli and slowly finding a way in which she would allow her parents and us to help her cope with, process, and understand her terror.

Summary

By recognising the signs early and seeking help quickly, Nicola's parents gave her the best opportunity to address her pre-autistic behaviours. Almost every baby cries if picked up too suddenly, but Nicola found every experience "too sudden". By understanding

Nicola's perception of the world, her parents learnt to provide her with a "slow-motion" experience of them to enable her to process and integrate their actions. Every successful integration brought about a greater capacity to process and integrate.

In Figures 9.5 and 9.6, it is possible to visualise Nicola's fear of the external world when she first came to us. For her, people were to be

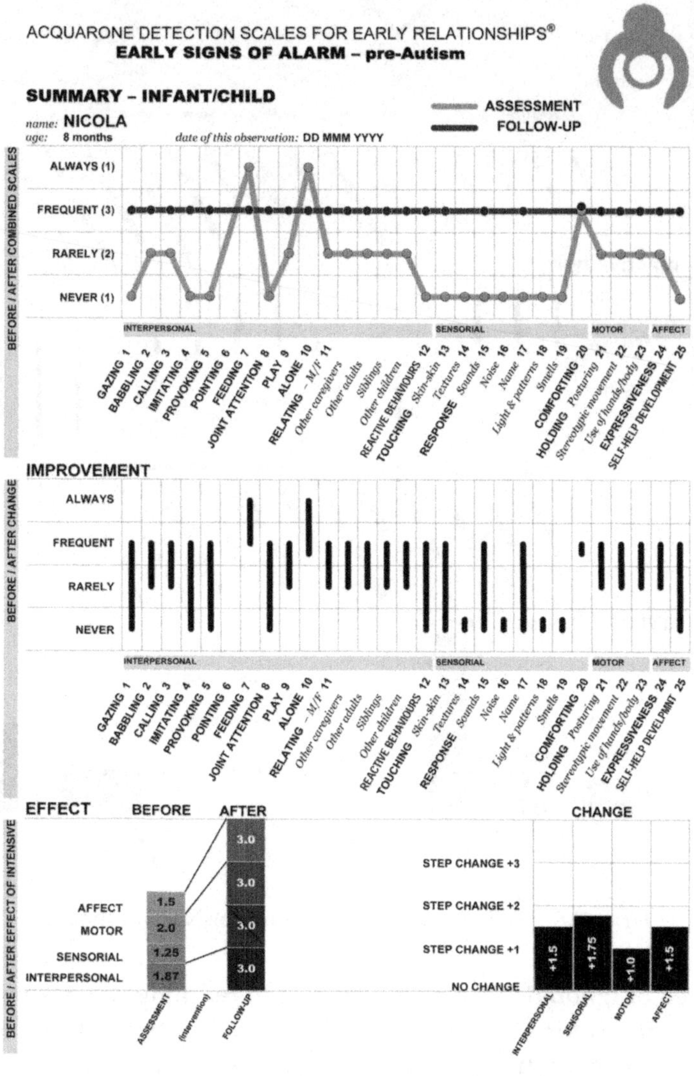

Figure 9.5. Follow-up summary report for Nicola.

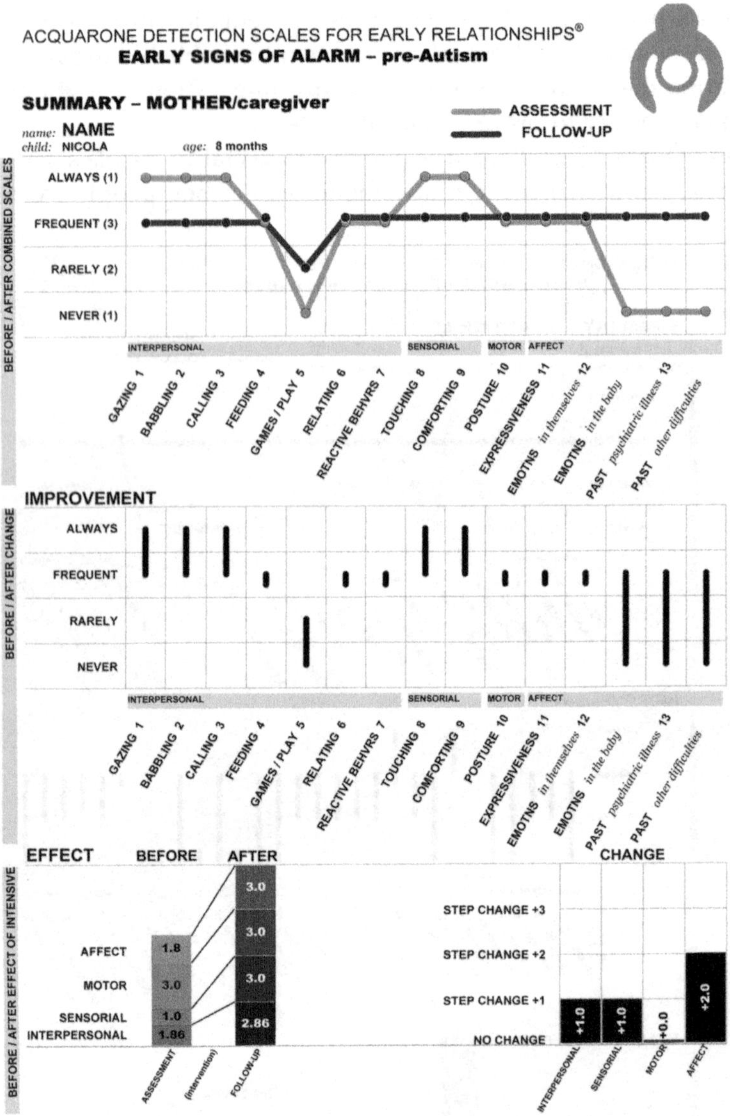

Figure 9.6. Follow-up summary report for Nicola's mother.

endured or ignored. Nicola was delayed in reaching the developmental milestones for her age, and had no wish to be with, imitate, or demand company from her family. Likewise, the graphics show how the mother retreated after her attempts to connect with her daughter were met with rejection. Yet after the intensive Re:Start treatment, we saw, and could measure, the pleasure and enjoyment both mother and daughter were able to experience once the "gates" to forming interpersonal relationships were "unlocked" for Nicola. From this point onwards, there was an enormous jump in the quality of Nicola's interactions with others, as well as an increase in her motivation to join in and play with family members, through the imitation and growth of affection, expressiveness, and fun.

Nicola is now twelve years of age and a successful member of the class in an all-girls school. She plays the violin, excels in sports, and has many friends.

Acknowledgment

I would like to thank Isabel Jimenez Acquarone, for her collaboration in the treatment of the infant and the parent.

CHAPTER TEN

The parents

Geoff Ferguson

Introduction

The Re:Start programme is a treatment programme that involves the whole family, as each member of the family will have adapted in response to the child who is showing autistic behaviours. Our programme helps each member of the family to change, so that they are better able to support the autistic child in changing.

Like all parents, the parents of an autistic child experience a mixture of feelings about their child. They may feel joy, pride, and love; they may also, depending upon the nature of the child's needs, have realistic concerns and fears about what the future holds for the child and for the family. However, they might also have more ambivalent thoughts about their child, some of which will be unconscious. This chapter is about the ways in which the parents' unconscious processes can affect the outcome of the child's treatment.

Thinking about the parents in this way is not to imply a simplistic view that a lack of parental warmth is the main cause of a child's autism. The "refrigerator parent" theory was prevalent as an explanation of autism from the 1950s onwards, but is a theory that is now no longer widely held. We still lack an explanation for autism, but it does seem that there is a significant but complex genetic susceptibility to the condition. However, environmental factors after birth probably play a part in lessening or increasing its severity. One of these environmental factors will be the parents' way of relating to their child. We should keep in mind, though, that in some cases parents' problematic way of relating to their child might be a response to their child's communication difficulties, rather than an initial cause.

Parental responses

In many cases, the parents, or more usually the mother, will realise that there is something wrong from almost the very beginning. What follows is usually a long process, sometimes lasting several months or years, of trying to have these concerns confirmed by a diagnosis and to seek support for the child and the family. Sometimes partners, other family members, and professionals will downplay the problem or dismiss the mother's concerns. The case of Joseph illustrates the way in which a mother's concerns about her child can be dismissed as arising from her "anxiety".

In some cases, the child will appear to be developing normally and then start to regress, perhaps around the age of two. Language and social skills that had appeared to be developing well start to be lost. This is very distressing for the parents. One mother who brought her daughter to the clinic for treatment recounted how proud she was that her child was more advanced than her sister's child, who was about the same age. It was, therefore, extremely distressing for her to come to terms with her envy when her daughter started to regress and fall far behind her cousin. This parent experienced a grief that had become stuck, a grieving process seen in many parents who use the clinic.

Along with a parent's conscious thoughts and feelings, there may be more difficult reactions that are harder to accept and to think about. Most parents-to-be want their child to have a happy childhood and to grow up to be a self-confident and successful adult. In fact, parents often consciously want their child to have a happier and more successful life than their own. A new child represents the possibility of a kind of perfection that the parents might not have been able to achieve themselves; it is as if the birth of a new child offers a new beginning.

To understand these more difficult reactions, it is useful to use the psychoanalytic concepts of an unconscious inner world and projection.

Inner worlds

The concept of an inner world describes the way in which, from our earliest moments, our sense impressions, internal drives, and fantasies gradually coalesce to become unconscious groups of associated impressions. Some groups of impressions form around pleasant experiences and desires, and we experience these as "good"; while others may group together around frightening or painful experiences and desires, and they will be "bad".

Psychoanalysts describe these groupings of good and bad impressions as internal objects. They provide a way for us to organise our external and internal experiences; by maintaining a split between good and bad objects, they also allow us to protect what is good and to disown what is bad.

We use these internal objects as templates to organise our experience of the world. In doing so, we tend to read the world in terms of these objects; especially at times of stress, our world might seem to us to be split between thoroughly good people, experiences, and thoughts, and thoroughly bad ones. In other words, we project these inner templates on the world.

This process of projection happens all the time: it is how we make sense of the world. Our expectations of a benign or malign world are based upon the relative strength of these internal good and bad objects. This is a dynamic process in which our experience of the external world is mediated by these internal objects while the internal objects, in turn, are modified by our further experience of the external world.

Projection is also dynamic in that it can be used to regulate our internal world. Bad thoughts and feelings can be a threat to the stability or even existence of our inner world. By projecting these bad objects outwards, seeing them as being in the external world, we can protect ourselves from their threat. Projection is a common defence; we seek the reassurance of seeing bad qualities in others and in this way remove those threats from ourselves.

The parents' projections

Given that we constantly use our internal objects to make sense of the world, it is inevitable that parents start to use these templates to imagine their child even before it is born. This is more than just having expectations or wishes for their unborn child; it is the beginning of a firm belief of what their child, or the parent–child relationship, actually is or will be. These beliefs could distort reality or even contradict it.

These projections can be used as a defence. For example, parents' idealisation of their unborn child can be seen as the projection to their child of their own internal image of perfection. This image, this good object, is identified with their child, and in this way is kept safely away from their own disappointments, their own ambivalence, their own internal bad objects.

Joseph's parents, for example, felt blessed by the "perfect" baby who was no trouble. As well as idealising her young son, Joseph's mother, Louise, also initially described her own childhood as being a very happy one. It was only later in the treatment that she was able to explore her early experience of having a manic-depressive mother and of being bullied by her older sisters. In seeing her own young family as perfect, Louise was able to identify with this current ideal as part of her way of denying the past. Coming to terms with Joseph's difficulties was then extremely distressing.

Alternatively, a parent might keep their good and bad objects safely apart by projecting to their child their own unconscious negative forces that are so threatening. The stronger or more disturbed these bad objects are within the parent, the more likely the parent is to fear giving birth to a damaged or damaging infant. Many parents-to-be have a fantasy that the unborn child is dangerous; the dangerous child is a common theme in literature and film, from John Wyndham's science-fiction novel, *The Midwich Cuckoos,* to the 1973 horror film, *The Exorcist.*

Filippo was conceived shortly after his mother, Hisako, had experienced a very traumatic miscarriage, nearly dying as the "deformed baby came out in pieces". During her pregnancy with Filippo, Hisako was tormented with a fear that this child, too, would miscarry or be born with a disability. This experience had left Hisako with a guilt and terror that interfered with her ability to respond to Filippo. The chapter about Filippo includes a very moving description of the way in which Hisako and Filippo were finally able to connect once Hisako had recognised the power of her projections.

A child with a special need, such as autism, can present a serious psychological problem for the parent. The infant can represent a narcissistic blow, a realisation that this potentially perfect extension of the parent's self is flawed. Alternatively, the "damaged" infant can appear as a confirmation of the parent's own internal badness and destructiveness. The parent's reactions to these challenges can include anger and rejection towards the child, as well as guilt at what they imagine to have been their own destructiveness in causing the child's difficulties. These are very difficult feelings that are often repressed.

Of course, alongside these more difficult emotions might also be feelings of love, compassion, and loyalty. The parents' challenge is to accept the more negative thoughts and feelings as natural and realise that these negative reactions can exist alongside more positive ones. How the parents manage these ambivalent feelings will have a significant effect upon their emotional availability for their child and, consequently, upon the child's emotional development.

Parents may deal with this ambivalence in a number of ways, but the most common are denial, guilt, merger, and projective identification. These are described in more detail below.

Denial

Denial is a common defence that is used to deal with distressing thoughts. As mentioned above, one form of denial involves the unborn child in carrying the parents' projection of perfection; a "split-off" good object that denies the possibility of any badness. In some cases, the force of this projection and denial is so great that the parents struggle to recognise or accept any of their child's difficulties.

This form of denial is more likely to occur where the child's difficulty is more subtle or develops gradually. In the case of autism, the early signs might appear only gradually and might be hard to detect initially. The parents might go through a long period of uncertainty, of feeling that something is wrong but unable to name the problem. This period of uncertainty is not helped when professionals minimise the problem or are unable to give an early diagnosis. Some parents report a great feeling of relief when a diagnosis is finally given, bringing to an end the terrible uncertainty.

Given the subtlety of the early signs of autism, it is usually the main carer who is more likely to have the first concerns about the child. In the Re:Start programme, the mother is often the first to have noticed that something is wrong and is the driving force behind the family seeking help. As was the case with Nicola, the father might well be reluctant to seek treatment.

Where one parent denies that there is a problem, quite often the parent in denial projects to the concerned parent all their own doubts, fears, and guilt. So, for example, we find that it is not uncommon for the father's denial to take the form of an accusation: "There is nothing wrong with our child; if there is a problem, it is in your capacity as a mother." Family members or even professionals might describe the mother as being too depressed to bond with her child, or so neurotic that she imagines difficulties that do not exist.

Of course, the reality could be quite complex; the mother might well have an underlying depression or anxiety, or those conditions could have been triggered perinatally. However, it is also possible that the mother's perception is accurate, that she knows her child best, and that the child is not responding as she might expect.

An implied or explicit criticism within her partner's denial can be devastating for the mother, especially when combined with professionals who are reluctant to make an early diagnosis of developmental problems. Not only does the mother have to carry her concerns alone, she finds that, for other people, it is she who has become the problem.

Managing guilt

When we are faced with a painful situation, a common reaction is to seek someone or something to blame, which often results in feelings of guilt. This is partly an attempt to make sense of the inexplicable. A world of arbitrarily painful experiences is a very frightening place that might invoke the terror of childhood when we might have felt surrounded by threatening bad objects. We try to find the cause for the situation, for someone or something to blame, even if it is ourselves.

Parental guilt is present in several ways. Overwhelmingly, parents believe that they are the cause of their child's difficulties. Did they do, or fail to do, something during the pregnancy or after to cause the problem? All parents are prone to guilt, but in conditions such as autism, where the aetiology is uncertain, there is even greater scope for parental guilt. Some unsubstantiated theories of causation increase the likelihood that the parent will feel guilty, one example being the unproved link with vaccinations.

Within our programme, it is common to find that one or both parents harbour secret theories about the cause of their child's autism. For example, one mother eventually disclosed her belief that the autism was caused by a blazing row she and her husband had had in front of their child when he was only a few days old. She blamed her husband for the row and so, indirectly, for the child's autism. This was one of many grievances that she held against her husband and that prevented them from adopting a unified and productive approach to the child's treatment.

As well as perhaps tapping into other long-standing sources of guilt, a parent's unfounded guilt at having caused the child's autism can be a reaction to ambivalent feelings towards that child. All parents experience some negative feelings towards their children. As mentioned above, parents can project bad internal objects to their children, seeing them as damaged or damaging. The autistic child's apparent refusal to respond fully to the parent can feel to the parent like an intensely painful rejection and can give rise to feelings of frustration and anger, such as that felt by Joseph's mother. These negative feelings can, in turn, lead to more guilt.

It is important for guilt to be expressed and explored, so that parents can come to a more realistic understanding of the child's difficulties and of what causes them. Where the cause is unknown, as in autism, the parent has to come to terms with the arbitrariness of life. If the negative feelings and guilt are not consciously accessible, then these feelings might be expressed indirectly: for example, in the inability to tolerate the child feeling any distress. This can present a considerable obstacle to a successful treatment, in which the child might need to feel a healthy level of frustration.

Merger

Another form of unconscious negativity may be seen in the way in which a parent unconsciously acts to hold back the child's development, keeping the child in a state of merger with them. For example, the tendency to keep their child as an infant can be seen in the reaction of parents when they watch via CCTV as the therapist begins to work with their child. The intensive treatment programme usually starts with the parents observing sessions in this way, watching the therapist giving the child simple tasks to perform. A typical task would be to sort objects into groups according to their colour. The parents are invariably surprised at what their child can do, and very often at the degree to which the child understands and follows the therapist's instructions.

In a way, this reaction of the parents is not surprising, as many would have been warned to expect their child to have a slower developmental path. None the less, the parents' surprise does show that they have not seen their child's developmental age. In some cases, this seems to be more than just an underestimation of potential. With some families, there appears to be an unconscious wish for their child not to grow up, to remain dependent, even merged. This can be seen most clearly in those families where the parents seem to sabotage the course of the treatment: for example, by not following recommendations, or by leaving the programme early.

This way of treating the child as a merged, younger infant can be seen in the case of Geronimo. As a child herself, Geronimo's mother, Orla, had no experience of a safe, containing mother. The lack of a secure internalised mother left her unable to fully separate from Geronimo, a situation that was exacerbated by a difficult pregnancy. Consequently, she felt fused with Geronimo and unable to provide him with the secure parenting that would enable him to develop. By working through some of these dynamics, Orla was able to feel more separate and to allow her son to gain some independence.

There are many reasons for parents to not want their child to grow up. In a very real sense, each developmental step that a child makes takes them further away from dependency upon their parents. For some parents, this process of separation is unbearable. The parent who has not sufficiently resolved his or her own dependency needs will find the child's growing independence difficult to accept. A merger with the child might also be an expression of a parent's unconscious need to control or punish the child.

In the Re:Start programme, we often help parents work through this process of letting go and of allowing the child to grow up. This can take the form of encouraging parents to let the child leave the parental bed and to sleep by themselves, or of weaning the child from the breast or bottle to solids. Sometimes, these are changes that are strongly resisted by the parents.

Sleeping alone and weaning are important positive steps towards independence for any child. For the autistic child, they are further encouragement to engage with the external world. However, there are some parents who find these changes hard to cope with. For them, such developments are a series of painful losses that have to be faced and mourned. In some cases, too, the demanding child has served as a welcome buffer between the parents, and by allowing the child to become less dependent, parents are forced to re-engage with one another.

Projective identification

Closely allied to the concept of merger is that of projective identification. This concept, first described by Melanie Klein (1946), is a more interactive form of projection in that a person doing the projecting subtly influences another person so that they start to act or think according to the content of the projection.

Used as a defence, projective identification allows difficult feelings to be provoked in another, freeing the initial person of them. Parents can sometimes use this defence by provoking feelings in their children that they themselves find difficult. It is common for child or family therapists to find that the problem or misbehaving child is acting out some difficulty between the parental couple. Unconsciously, the parents are provoking bad behaviour in their child, who then becomes the focus of attention by being the problem. It sometimes seems to us in the clinic that it is the child who is bringing their parents to the clinic for treatment, rather than the other way round.

For example, one couple brought in their child who spent most of his waking hours crying or complaining. He did show some early signs of autism, but it was striking how his demanding behaviour became much, much less when he was comforted by clinic staff. He obviously felt more secure when his anxieties were contained by being held by experienced and confident staff rather than his inexperienced and anxious parents. However, beyond that, there was a way in which the parents' deep-rooted anger with each other was being expressed by this child's constant demands. It was as if their diffidence in holding their child was related to their fury with each other. Some confirmation of this came during the treatment: an improvement in the child's behaviour took place alongside the parents' growing ability to discuss the difficulties in their relationship.

In all of the cases described in this book there is a powerful connection between the emotional environment created by the parents and their relationship to each other and the child's developmental path. This parental environment is partly a response to their child's difficulty in relating, but also reflects the parents' own histories and dynamics. In this interplay of unconscious influences, projective identification plays a central role. The descriptions given of the Re:Start treatment also illustrate how an understanding of projective identification helps the therapists to reflect upon their own feelings and fantasies in response to the child, and to see in these the reflections of the child's inner worlds.

Resilience

As well as helping parents to resolve difficulties, the Re:Start programme shows parents how to build on their strengths, including their resilience. Interest in resilience has grown out of the observation that while certain life stressors increase an individual's likelihood of difficulties, none the less there is a group of individuals who seem to survive these experiences relatively unharmed. They seem more resilient.

In its simplest formulation, resilience is the ability of an individual to survive adversity or trauma, to bounce back. Thought of in a more positive way, resilience is the individual's ability to learn from challenges and to find ways to incorporate that experience in their future life. From a psychoanalytic perspective, the degree of an individual's resilience is related to how securely he or she has established internal good objects.

Resilience itself has not figured greatly as an explicit concept in psychoanalytic theory, but similar ideas can be seen in comments such as Melanie Klein's: ". . . hope and trust in the existence of goodness, as can be observed in everyday life, helps people through great adversity, and effectively counteracts persecution" (Klein, 1957). That seems to be a pretty good definition of resilience.

As well as being a quality of individuals, resilience has also been studied within families. Resilience in families seems to be more than the sum of individual resilience, but is a resilience that is found within the family unit as a whole. Again, this is more than just the basic ability to deal with adversity; rather, it is the way in which the family learns from adversity and incorporates that learning into the family structure.

Having a child with autism can place strains upon a family, although that experience will vary greatly, according to factors such as the severity of the autism and the economic position of the family. As an example of one indicator of this strain, a 2010 study (Hartley et al.) showed that the rate of divorce among couples who had an autistic child was almost twice that of a matched comparison group (23.5% *vs.* 13.8%).

Families with an autistic child were the subject of a study on resilience by Bayat published in 2007. It found that forty per cent of the 174 participants reported that the family felt stronger as a result of the experience of having an autistic child. These families showed a resilience that enabled them to learn from their experience.

Four key themes related to family resilience emerged from Bayat's study; the families that felt stronger by the experience tended to report:

1. An increase in a sense of pulling together and of sharing resources.
2. That tackling adversity gave the family a sense of a shared meaning.
3. An affirmation of the family members' feelings of strength, compassion, and patience.
4. A shared spiritual experience or the strengthening of a belief system.

Fundamental to these themes is an ability for members of the family to communicate effectively and to create shared goals. The issues considered earlier in this chapter—denial, guilt, projection, and an inability to allow the child to separate—are factors that undermine a family's resilience. They allow anger, blame, and resentment to go unresolved. Ultimately, they limit the family's ability to help the autistic child reach his full potential.

Thus, effective treatment for the child needs to include measures to help the parents and siblings to explore and resolve these issues. Individual, couple, and family therapy should be aimed at resolving grief, reducing denial, persecutory guilt, and projections, and helping the parents to recognise and modify the narrative that they have constructed around their child's condition.

Conclusion

This brief description of some of the issues that parents have brought to the Re:Start programme highlights the key importance of involving parents and other family members in treatment.

A child with special needs can present his parents with many challenges. Along with their love and the discovery of their child's unique qualities, parents might also experience more negative feelings. These feelings often include grief, disappointment, anger, and guilt. Sometimes, these feelings are coloured by the parents' projections before and after the birth. There might be disappointment that an ideal of perfection has not been realised or a feeling that the child embodies the parents' badness.

While perfectly natural, these negative feelings are difficult to accept and, in being defended against, distort the parents' ability to nurture their child. However, there is the possibility for the parents to work through denial, projection, and other defences, and to come to know their child for who she or he is. They can then find joy in their child's unique qualities and potential for growth.

CHAPTER ELEVEN

Working with the children in their context: home visits and follow-up

Stella Acquarone and Isabel Jimenez Acquarone

While the chapters have so far focused on our intensive clinic-based treatment, we must stress the broader scope of the interventions that combine to create the complete Re:Start programme. Just as we involve the whole family in each treatment, so we must consider and integrate all aspects of the child's life. As part of our programme, we observe the child (and family) in their own environment: in the home, going about their daily routine, and at nursery, preschool, or school. We watch how the child behaves with the people most important to them outside their immediate family—the grandparents, nursery workers, nannies, child-minders, and teachers. Just as we work with parents to reach their child, so we wish to collaborate with and support other key people in the child's life. We not only try to rule out possible organic factors that may be influencing the child's behaviour, but also any possible environmental factors.

Home visits

Essential to the Re:Start programme are our home visits. During the intensive treatment, we undertake a weekly home visit when a member of our team spends hours with the family at home, usually at the weekend. The role is to be in the background: not to actively participate but to observe the interactions, behaviours, and events that occur in the family setting. The therapist tries to be as unobtrusive as possible. They watch the family at home, shadowing them as they go about their daily routine, and accompanying them if they go out. The visits, which last around a few hours each, enable us to learn how the family functions outside of the unique setting of the clinic to ensure that we fully understand the everyday reality of life for the pre-autistic child, and so that we can tailor our programme to best suit the needs of the child and family.

The observations are videoed so that they can be later viewed by all the professionals involved; as a group, the therapists can discuss and reflect on what the family members are going through and how they are coping. During the subsequent observations, at the end of the second and third weeks, we might step forward to make helpful suggestions regarding the child and their toys, or on the relationship with a sibling, comment on the family's activities, or offer advice on trying out new behaviours. Yet, we do this without becoming involved with the events around us. It is necessary to note that while we aim to be unobtrusive, our presence will, of course, have an impact on the family. This impact does not affect the value of the observation and lessens as the family gets used to the therapist being in their home.

Sleeping and playing

We consider it important to understand the family dynamics—how they communicate and interact with each other in the home. At the same time, we focus on the practical. We like to see where the child with the autistic behaviours sleeps, and it is not unusual for us to discover that their bedroom is on the floor above or below where the parents sleep. Sleeping arrangements can often be an indicator of how far the family has tried to adapt itself to accommodate their sensitive child. If bedtimes are a particular issue for the family, then we might arrange for an additional home visit to be made in the evening, in order to get a better understanding of the dynamics and issues at play. We also look at the toys, as well as the set-up the family has for playing, if, indeed, there is one. We observe how "child friendly" the home is, and whether there are any tensions in this area (for example, if a parent is worried about staining white carpets in rented accommodation, or if a child is exposed to an overwhelming cacophony of noisy electronic toys and devices). When appropriate, we help the family consider ideas and resources to enhance imaginative play, for all of them to enjoy.

Mealtimes

We observe how the family plans and prepares the family meals and how they eat. We see if the child is involved in meal preparation, if he eats at the table, if the family eats together or separately, and how the child behaves when eating. For those families who travel from overseas for treatment, and who might be living in temporary accommodation, we undertake the observations in the apartment where they are staying, but often observe family mealtimes in local restaurants.

At mealtimes, any ritualistic or strange behaviour is observed. It is not unusual for us to discover that there is a perception by one or both parents that the infant will only eat certain foods, and if these foods are not served the child would starve. Observers are particularly aware of any transferential issues at mealtimes. It is common for parents to feel enslaved by their child's demands when it comes to food; many go to great lengths to accommodate their child's wishes and yet still feel rejected or not good enough. Our observations and insight enable us to note the issues that need particular attention. As treatment progresses and tensions around food and mealtimes are discussed, parents learn to recover their usual selves and become separate from the child. Indicators of progress during treatment can often be observed during mealtimes.

Toilet training

This is a particular issue for those children who come to us between the ages of three and five. We work on toilet training from a number of different fronts: from physical awareness to emotional understanding.

We talk about the struggle each child faces in having to relinquish the "baby" within, where mummy has to clean and change him (just the two of them). In this way, he learns to come to terms with and fully embrace his new "big" child, able to take responsibility for himself. We consider that some children resist taking control of their bladder and bowels in order to keep control of others around them and avoid growing up. To succeed in this area, the child needs to loosen his grip on his parents and focus instead on his own body. He needs to be aware of himself as fully separate in order to become fully independent.

Psychoanalytic concepts useful to the home visitor

Bick's method of infant observation

All our therapists undertake Esther Bick's method of observing the infant in his home environment, from birth to aged two. The object of this analytic training is to witness the development of the family relationship and of the emotions involved. When we visit the home of a family with a pre-autistic child, we apply the same thinking. We do not question or talk, but observe how the family members behave with each other in the home, to see what they do in their space, and how they organise themselves so that we can capture the nature of the difficulties involved.

Early home visits are especially useful for fully comprehending the impact that the child's behaviours and sensitivities are having on the family, and vice versa. Observing how the family behaves in the home has an additional role later on in the treatment, and helps us to see the families "as they really are" and to aside put our clinical theories and judgements. We watch with fresh, non-judgemental eyes while remaining fully aware of our own shortcomings and possible feelings of frustration at not completely understanding the situation. Whatever our reaction to what we see, we keep our focus firmly on the family and their problems.

By observing other people's ways of being, and being "in it" together, a mental space of curiosity and imagination opens up, in which we are actively trying to make sense of what we see, allowing the experience to take place, and leading to active problem-solving.

Bion's theories: learning from experience and the "container–contained"

According to Wilfred Bion, "learning from experience" is the most important way of learning (1962). Learning from experience, with an emotional understanding, enables us to bear the frustrations of what we do not know. In order to learn in this way, the experience needs to be encountered without prejudices, theories, or desires. Yet, in everyday life, this is not easy to do, as the levels of frustration make people impatient for the required outcome. This can lead to us lying to ourselves, but this is not conducive to the development of thoughts.

> If frustration can be tolerated, the mating of conception and realizations whether negative or positive initiates procedures necessary to learning by experience. If intolerance of frustration is not so great as to activate the mechanisms of evasion and yet is too great to bear dominance of the reality principle, the personality develops omnipotence as a substitute for the mating of the pre-conception, or conception, with the negative realization. This involves the assumption of omniscience as a substitute for learning from experience by aid of thoughts and thinking. There is therefore no psychic activity to discriminate between true and false. (Bion, 1962, pp. 307–308)

We struggle to find our truth.

> Truth is always food for the mind – lies are poison but truth is also explosive, as it can be felt as catastrophic if we cannot integrate it quickly enough . . . We accept that life is mysterious, and that discovery deepens mystery, rather than solves it. The human mind is unfathomable. What we find is mystery and awe at the immense beauty of the world. (Bion, 1962, p. 98)

Another important concept of Bion's is that of the "container–contained". This refers to the mother's capacity to take on all the primitive emotions, fears, and unbearable feelings from the infant and transform them into bearable ones. For example, the child with colic will scream in terror at the pain. In response, the mother holds the baby and comforts him, saying, "There, there, mummy is here. It's not so bad, you'll see. Just relax and the pain will go away." Thus, the mother contains the baby's raw or primitive feelings and transforms them.

However, when this does not happen, either because the mother cannot "contain" or the infant will not allow himself to be "contained", the therapist can offer containment to both mother and baby. The therapist models the action, which the mother can later practise herself when she is alone with her baby. This is manifested in listening and feeling heard, noticing and feeling noticed, and understanding and feeling understood.

Thinking, according to Bion, is the result of a positive emotional experience and, in this sense, relies on encouraging emotionally informed, "feelingful" observation by the therapist. By working this way, the therapist is able to hold the family's mental pain of not knowing, puzzlement, and not understanding. Furthermore, by getting the family to talk about their traumas, the therapist helps them to interpret, process, and tolerate what is felt to be dangerous or unbearable.

How do we apply these concepts to the home visits? By being humble in the family's presence, by finding out how they want us to help, by understanding the truth from the family setting, and by learning from their difficulties how they might adjust their behaviour. The process becomes mysterious and interesting and needs to be contained and loved. The truth appears in the insights gained from the experience into the causes to any unhappiness or the barriers to a happy life. A great deal of tolerance to frustrating realities has to be developed, to create space for thoughts to be born or restructured in a way that is possible to think and talk about, thereby making the emotional experience a truly valuable one.

Transference–countertransference and projection

We observe the family with an awareness of emotional states and means of communication: whether conscious or unconscious. In our observation work, we use the concepts outlined in Chapter Two. These include:

- transference: the transferring of feelings about one person (usually linked to their first experiences with their parents) to another;
- countertransference: the impact the patient has on the therapist's feelings that can guide the therapist into the deeper, unconscious feelings troubling the family;

- projection: when feelings are too unbearable to own, and so are expelled and placed on other people as a form of defence (Freud);
- projective identification: an unconscious process that makes person B act in a way that person A falsely believes to be true (Klein).

We are aware that the relationship we create with the family, whether in the clinic or at home, is a working (conscious) relationship with transference aspects (unconscious). We aim to bring an awareness to the unconscious transference, which, once elucidated, combines with our conscious knowledge to make the therapeutic impact.

Attachment theory

Bowlby's attachment theory provides the understanding that the type of security we experience with primary carers in infancy determines the type of relationships we have in later life. Attachment patterns can be reshaped later in life, but not as easily as in early childhood. We are able to observe in the home the lived enactments of attachment, such as reliability, flexibility, and boundary setting/keeping. We can apply our knowledge of this so as to further deepen the parents' awareness of the type of attachments that are formed within the family.

We carry out home visits before, during, and after the treatment, to understand the ordinary everyday life of the family and we need such theories and concepts to help us maintain a neutral yet informed attitude to what we see before us. By so doing, we can emulate change and creativity in handling different situations and promote both curiosity in the parents and imitation, attention, and concentration in the child with autistic behaviours.

Follow-up

Consolidating progress

We consider that the enormous changes that take place over the three- or four-week intensive programme need to be followed up with at least a year of weekly meetings with the family.

As we mentioned in earlier chapters, the purpose of the Re:Start programme is to break the thick "crust of ice" in order to reach the "core" where the water of life flows. In other words, we try to find new ways for the child to "be" with his family, without resorting to repetitive actions, self-comforting behaviours, or a retreat into isolation. Our follow-up sessions aim to:

- consolidate the positive changes made during the treatment in the life of the family, and the child in particular;
- further develop potential, but ensuring reflection on emotions and verbalisation of emotional states;
- steer the family through inevitable periods of regression;
- support the child to think about and find ways to manage the new experiences and situations he will encounter as he gets older;
- reinforce the child and parents' new-found awareness of "avoidance mechanisms";
- consolidate progress with helpful techniques and tips;
- continue the building of self-awareness in the child, siblings if there are any, and the parents.

Re:Start aims to help pre-autistic children rebuild their minds with their parents' help. We consider that our work in the clinic barely touches on the process of recognising the emotional states and structuring the mind, but we are able to lay the foundations upon which the family can work to help the child be able to attend, concentrate, vary their behaviours, and develop representative play. The child becomes aware of his autistic tendencies but is no longer controlled by them, while the parents learn to understand that their child's autistic behaviours are often a means of defence and protection.

Some parents decide to carry on with the individual psychotherapy and couple therapy after the intensive treatment. They do this not only to continue on their path of self-discovery, but also to find additional resources that allow them to be more creative and enthusiastic about recovering their child from the extreme fear and anxiety by which they are governed.

After the tremendous change that takes place, it is not uncommon for parents to suddenly become "stuck". They might no longer see any signs of progress, or find it too difficult to continue with the structured play and unstructured way of being with their child. At the same time, the child might feel that their parents have become tired, and so could be discouraged to develop new skills, as if making progress is too hard and too slow in materialising.

Once the intensive treatment is over, we trust that the family can manage by themselves with a gradual lessening of our help. Ongoing sessions allow us to reaffirm our faith in their abilities. They are a time for the family to share their successes, to start consolidating what they have learnt, and to develop their own style based on the principles that they have explored with the professionals in the clinic.

An example

Eight-month-old Nicola and her family lived in Finland. While setting up the treatment in the UK, I also contacted several psychotherapists in Finland to explain our work and our aims. At the end of the infant–family treatment, I travelled to Finland and established a team to support the family. This consisted of a clinical psychologist and psychotherapist and child therapists. The team undertook weekly therapy with Nicola, couple meetings with the parents, and occasional whole-family sessions. This team was supervised in Finland by the lead psychologist, who received regular contact and consultation from myself.

Liaising with schools

Some parents need or want more than a year's ongoing support, and some children need more than a year to get better, particularly those about to start primary school. We have found that children who have undergone the Re:Start programme manage well in mainstream school if provided with one-to-one support in the classroom. On occasion, when we treat four-year-olds already at school, we ask the school to come to the Parent Infant Clinic in the last days of the programme to see what the child is capable of achieving and understanding. We work with the teaching assistant (TA) and the Special Educational Needs Co-ordinator (SENCO) to integrate what is "possible" within the child's educational capacity, rather than limit expectations to the boundaries of the autistic "label". We attend regular meetings with the school and answer any queries relating to the child.

What is essential is that the follow-up is individually tailored to the needs of each child. Three-year-old Geronimo, for example, continued individual sessions for three years, three times a week, and we regularly attended meetings at his school for several years. Eighteen-month-old Filippo, on the other hand, only attended follow-up for a year. We had no direct contact with his primary school when he started there, but learnt that he settled well and was given TA support in class when required.

As well as liaising with the school, we also try to work closely with other involved professionals, such as speech and language therapists, occupational therapists, sensory therapists, music therapists, and other colleagues in related fields.

The programme for integrating the child in school is explained further in Chapter Twelve.

Conclusion

In this chapter, we have illustrated the necessary scope of the programme to ensure that we work with each child in their context. By fully understanding the home dynamics, we are in the best possible position to be able to support the parents in making any necessary long-lasting changes. By including not only the parents, but also the extended family, we are best able to support the parents in helping the child while also ensuring that they themselves receive support from the wider family.

By engaging with schools, we are able to ensure that the wider system has a firm grasp of the child's needs, that there is a complete understanding of their way of being, and that their education and learning is unhampered by their condition.

We work with the child at home, in the nursery, and in school to provide them with the necessary understanding and support so as to minimise the impact of their autistic tendencies and create the best opportunity for them to flourish in every environment.

CHAPTER TWELVE

Integration into mainstream education following the Re:Start intensive family treatment programme

Isabel Jimenez Acquarone

Bearing in mind both the intensive intervention and the neurobiological differences present in infants with pre-autistic behaviours, I have found the following three-step method to be the most effective when working with children in the nursery and home environment. Each step follows on from the next, and can be returned to if necessary in order to effectively tackle issues that arise as the child becomes more connected and independent.

I shall briefly outline each step and then move on to give a more detailed explanation of the basis of the approach and the reasoning behind it.

Initially, my work in the nursery is a continuation of the treatment programme carried out in the clinic, with the focus still on restructuring the child's mind so that they are able to hold thoughts and organise them. This first step has a behavioural–neuroregulatory emphasis, where I look at what is involved for neurobiological behaviour connection to occur, aiding the child physically in order for him to restructure himself and his movements, and increasing his ability to follow his peers and teachers. This step revolves around establishing an initial connection with the child through understanding his level of sensitivities and his experienced threshold of the wider world.

Once this first connection is made, I move on to the associative stage, where the aim is to enrich the child by putting names, words, sounds, and feelings to pictures, surrounding objects, and their lived experiences.

The final stage is the therapeutic approach. By building on the associations and the behavioural foundations provided in the first two steps, logical reasoning is used to teach the child how to understand, accept, and deal with their own emotions in the nursery setting. This eventually leads to an ability to relate to others, through interaction, communication, and affection.

Step 1: Behavioural–neuroregulatory approach

This step incorporates the following techniques.

- Giving gentle praise and encouragement, rather than overwhelming the child with too much exuberance, and with use of varied words and phrases—not just "good boy/girl", which is repetitive. Using the thumbs-up sign is also a clear way of showing that the child has done well without over-empowering them in having completed a certain task.
- Reward of using visual cues of "high fives", incorporating chance as to the placement of the support worker's hand in order that the child has to look closely in order to see where they should place their hand. Again, such rewards should be measured, as "whooping" sounds and over-excitement from the support worker can overwhelm the child into never repeating the experience.
- Negative reinforcement through ignoring bad behaviour (as long as the behaviour does not involve aggression, since this is immediately stopped if the child or anyone else is under threat of harm). If the child acts out through direct provocative stereotypes (repetitive, purposeless behaviour), this should be ignored. For example, Johnny walks over and looks directly at you, sticking his finger up his nose. You have previously corrected him about this, but he continues to look directly at you, gauging your reaction and testing whether he will get your attention. If you rise to such behaviour, the child learns that he has your attention through a negative action, rather than calling your name or

through proactive behaviour. In these situations, it is vital to move on without even addressing the bad behaviour. It is important to reinforce positive behaviour so that they can replace other behaviours the child has adopted in order to attraction attention.

Such methods of praise, reward, and negative reinforcement through ignoring bad behaviour are all based on establishing certain neurobiological circuits; however, when adopting such techniques it is important to take into account and initially assess the individual's set of sensitivities and threshold (in all of their senses) regarding the nursery environment.

What is important is to ensure that certain behaviours occur that are the norm in the nursery setting: for example, "circle time", sitting down on a chair at a table, touching new objects, and experiencing new sensations, etc. Through encouraging the child to incorporate these activities in their behaviour, they will be able to observe others and join in. Initially, this might be a struggle, as many children are often labelled the "poor so-and-so" and are left to their own devices by the staff, who do not want to upset them or others. When these children start nursery, it is difficult for them, as indeed it is for many children when faced with new challenges; however, with cues from the support worker and nursery leader, children with pre-autistic behaviours can learn to follow the group, listen, and experiment.

Alongside this is a controversial standpoint taken by some professionals and parents that the child needs to "zone out" and disengage, and that this is his safe space. They believe that encouraging him, or "finding" him and bringing him back, is abusive, in the sense that the child undergoes a certain degree of discomfort being in the present. I agree that finding the child might cause initial anger and resentment on his part, but by finding him and bringing him back while explaining what is happening, the action is less traumatic and becomes a regular habit and part of his normal behaviour. Each time he goes, you fetch him back with your voice, so that eventually "zoning out" becomes harder for him than staying in the here and now. By being present, he will understand, if he is able to understand and follow, that he has a better chance of making sense of the world, his peers, and his lived experience.

The support worker "scaffolds" the child physically in order to structure movements, encourage actions, and aid task completion, while describing what is happening and what they are doing. Scaffolding while explaining sends a clear message that the child can do the task, and is able to start and finish it. Task completion then becomes a habit that later aids him in school and at home to stay focused on an activity or experience. With reward at the end of the task, the child feels a sense of achievement, which encourages him to repeat the action. Moving from 100% scaffolding to total independence is a slow process, but with continued support, is extremely successful.

Once one task is completed or one goal attained, it can be incorporated into a string of goals. These often include feeding, getting dressed (putting on clothes and shoes), educational tasks (sitting in circle at story time), and paying attention when another person is speaking. Support workers have a set dialogue and a logbook to record progress. Communication is fluid and clear, and by using the same repertoire it is more likely for the same response to occur in the child both at home and at nursery. There is no room for confusion or for work to be undone.

Employing verbal cues with signs can be especially useful when the room is overcrowded and noisy or when the child is outside and further away. It is important not to rely just on using signs, as the child might resort to this easier option and not use verbal communication to convey his needs. Verbal cues paired with signs should also be few and far between. Songs, and words to help guide the child from one activity to another, can be more successful in encouraging speech and verbal interaction. Pointing, combined with verbal cues, is one of the few signs that I would readily encourage ("Look, I want you to see this", or "Look at this"), as it provokes joint attention, vital for learning and social referencing.

Step 2: The associative path

The child has now established a basic relationship and connection with the support worker. At this point, the support worker's role is to label the world around the child, initially in a singular manner by the use of simple names: animals, animal noises, colours, shapes, noises, smells, foods, and numbers, incorporating two or three aspects together once one is grasped. For example, duck, the duck says

"quack", the yellow duck, the yellow duck says "quack", two yellow ducks, etc. Associations should also be made through drawing animals and objects, using actual objects, and employing pictures, photographs, and books. The child is able to take the information on board and starts to put together his new world, gradually feeling more settled and secure with the information he is taking on board.

The associative process fills and enriches the child's internal database and has to be done in a manner and at a pace in which the child is able to grasp and use the information adequately. Initially, the child might not feel confident enough to verbally relay the new information, but might, through pointing, express that he has understood and incorporated his new knowledge. For example, responding to the following requests: "point to the colour blue"; "point to the blue triangle"; "point to the big blue triangle", etc.

Step 3: Therapeutic work

Once the associative process has been mastered, the child now has the vocabulary to understand the nursery environment and all it involves. Through the use of these new words and associations, the support worker can relate to situations and incorporate feelings. I always, and strongly, suggest starting with the four basic feelings: happiness, sadness, fear, and anger. These feelings need to be incorporated not only verbally, but with exaggerated facial expressions that leave no doubt in the child's mind which emotion the support worker is conveying. The use of feelings should be extended and readily used. They can be quickly and simply drawn, like the examples in Figure 12.1, whenever required, so that the child can point to how they are feeling.

Blank faces can be placed in front of the child so that he can draw the emotion in question; eventually, the child can make the expressions himself to convey his own inner emotions. The support worker can also point out other children's and co-workers' feelings in this way.

Pinning the drawings on everything will allow feelings to become familiar and easily recognisable to the child, as well as less daunting or overwhelming. While pointing out these feelings, it is important also to discuss why the individual might feel one way or another in order for the child to make sense of what they see, or what they might

Figure 12.1. Drawings of the four basic emotions.

feel inside. Discussion should be communicative and complete, to give the child reasoning and thought behind the emotion.

Goals

The support worker's role in the nursery is to assist in monitoring the child's progress towards achieving their goals. The support worker has to assess whether they are getting the best out of the child or whether they need to revise their approach for each goal to be attained.

The initial goal is the starting point and a place to work from. It should be a short-term goal, such as getting the child to sit on a seat, first for five minutes, then ten, then fifteen, etc. Or the goal could be about entering a new place, such as a toilet cubicle, or putting a piece of fruit that he has never tried before in his mouth, even if it pops out.

After successfully mastering the short-term goal, and repeating the action several times, then the mid-term goal can be attempted. This goal should incorporate the short-term goal already learnt. For example, the child sits on the chair and does the task in front of him, or is able to go to the toilet unassisted, or begins to eat the piece of fruit, one bite at a time, then two, etc.

Longer-term goals include meeting the general expectations or desires of the parents, such as seeing their child happily integrated in, and attentive at, nursery (as mentioned, this must include where the parents see the child and their desire and dreams for their child).

Parents and homework

Parents are also included in the follow-up care we provide. They are given homework, which incorporates and includes them in the work done in the nursery. It also prepares the child for what will be done the following week and helps them revise what they learnt the previous week. This reinforces experiences lived and those that they will face. If a child zones out a lot and yet has some grasp of the material learnt (because the parents spoke about the subject the weekend before), he will be able to pick up where he left off and be able to follow new instructions more easily, rather than feel lost and disconnected by what is being said. What is familiar to the child is safe ground, and if it is safe ground he is more likely to feel relaxed enough to learn and interact.

Involving the parents also allows them to feel included in the process. They can see where their child is going, how he is progressing, and the steps taken by the nursery staff.

Issues

Some of the early issues that arise in the nursery setting usually include the child's movements around the classroom. Sometimes, they are not used to following others—they have only known being followed or have been allowed to run around freely. Tantrums occur, however, when the child realises that the situation has changed and that he must incorporate himself into the nursery routines. If the teachers and staff are able to bear the tantrums, they will occur less often and not last as long. Taking a strong stance against bad behaviour is vital for the child to realise that he achieves nothing through acting out. Tantrums would not be tolerated from other children and there should be no separate rule or standard that sidelines autistic children who are able to play on staff. They understand what is expected of them, and their ability should not be underestimated.

In many cases, the child is not used to following instructions, hence the vital use of scaffolding, which, as mentioned above, is an initially 100% aid but which reduces over time as the child is able to complete tasks independently. Scaffolding should be as if the support worker were the "puppeteer", guiding the child's actions through manipulating their arms and hands, feeling how much the child can take on board; once they feel more action and co-ordination on the part of the child, the support worker can step back and allow independence to take hold.

Sometimes, there is an issue regarding certain items of clothing, or changing from the PE kit into school uniform and *vice versa*. The best way to address this is through role-play, or dramatisation. Usually, this involves taking a doll or teddy and acting out how the child is behaving with his clothes, repeating the role-play several times and in a dramatic manner to highlight the problem area. Then the dramatisation should move on to how or what should happen. Again, it is important to incorporate the feelings of the child in the play, not using the child's name but using the teddy or doll as a third person to catch the child's attention. At times, clothes can be used for sensation-seeking purposes and it is important to look closely at what is causing the problem: sometimes, tags on the back of clothes are genuinely itchy, or woollen jumpers are irritable to sensitive skin. The support worker must always remain open-minded and try to see the whole picture.

Toilet training can be a problem area for some children, causing a great deal of anxiety to a child who wants to remain a baby, who does not want to let go of their pee or poo, or is worried when sitting on, or standing next to, the toilet. There should not be a song and dance over using the toilet (which can make the whole ordeal scarier). It should be as matter of fact as possible, with a quick pat on the back when things go well before returning to the class or playroom. Sometimes, pictures and photos on the toilet wall can make the space less daunting for the child, and just going there for hand washing can create a familiar safe space where they will feel at ease and relaxed enough to use the toilet appropriately. It is better not to make a bigger thing of it than it already is in the child's mind, but to point out the other children who come and go from the toilet area in a relaxed manner. When accidents occur, there should not be a big fuss made. Instead, the support worker should simply point out what has happened so that the child has a body awareness of the accident without any feelings of shame.

Snack and mealtimes that include fruit and vegetables can also cause issues. It is always best to try to incorporate fruit that can be readily chewed (e.g., bananas), as well as less popular vegetables (e.g., carrots) that can be mashed into those that are liked (e.g., potatoes).

Once the carrots are being regularly incorporated, one then switches the amounts: for example, less potato and more carrot. Eventually, less mashing will be required in order for the transition not to be so obvious and a shock to the child.

Hiding certain vegetables in mouthfuls of food that the child likes also works well, as does making up a story about vegetables or fruit using teddies or dolls, and pointing out other children who are eating well. These measures can all help to reinforce the idea of the fruit or vegetable being eaten and enjoyed. Parents should also use the same strategy at home, rather than allowing their child to reject certain foods or rigidly sticking to one food type. After a time, the child will accept the new tastes, savouring the flavours of the fruit or vegetables, and will be able to eat independently, without scaffolding or shadowing (hanging over them), and enjoying the experience of tasting new foods.

"No"

Saying "No" is the usual, normal, and safe answer for the autistic child to give. As individuals who are easily overwhelmed, "No" is the safer option when being asked whether they want something or should try something. It is important that you show you acknowledge this. Tell them that you understand how difficult it is for them and how daunting trying something new can be. However, you are also there to help them experience the world, and although they have said "No", you are saying "Yes" and will support them through the experience.

Pitfalls

Sometimes, there are pitfalls; an unexpected bad experience can occur at home or in the nursery setting, away from or with the family. In these cases, the ongoing dialogue between home and nursery proves vital, as, through communicating and verbally processing the experience, the child will be far more likely to process what has happened, come to terms with it, and quickly move on.

Sometimes, a string of good days can be followed by one bad day. This can be caused by an overload of information processing, by the child testing the waters to see if he can regress to his former state, or by a sudden fear that comes over him as he becomes aware of the new world into which he is emerging. When this happens, it is best to continue moving forward and to not lose track of where the child was before this point. Bad days are inevitable, as the energy required to be constantly attentive and aware is exhausting for the child, while the former state of being disengaged can be a far easier option.

There are times when new issues arise because the child has a new-found confidence in his ability to verbalise and talk about old issues. When this happens, it is important to listen and help the child process these, acknowledging the issues, and the child's capacity to communicate them. Yet, at the same time, the child will need help understanding them, how to resolve them, and how to move on. This can all be done with fun games using the three steps described above: through the behavioural and neuroregulatory approach, the associative process, and therapeutically.

Techniques

It is important for support workers, nursery staff, and parents to use a variety of techniques and not to get stuck on just using one or another. These techniques include:

- dramatisation;
- storytelling (asking the child to point out different characters), change the name of characters and the story using the same book;
- drawing (using the feelings faces for people, animals, and even objects: for example, the star in the nursery rhyme "Twinkle Twinkle Little Star" can be given a happy or sad face);
- songs (with actions and facial expressions);
- play (in the nursery "home corner", using different types of objects with a variety of sensations, etc.).

Choose your words with care!

Although it might appear that the child's attention is elsewhere, he is absorbing and relating to the information you are relaying and will process it over a period of time. He also incorporates the terms used around him and any expressions that he hears, even from a third person across the room. The child should never be spoken of as if he does not exist or is not there. Conversations about the day should be done to one side with the parent and not in front of the child.

Praise and time out

How much praise or time out should be given? Enough for them to know that they have done something correctly but not so much that you might scare them—for example, by "whooping"—or overly empower them into feeling omnipotent when they do not complete a task. Also, vary your words. Too much talking and the children can switch off or feel overwhelmed, so always be measured and creative with words and expressions without boring them or overly praising them. It is important that the praise be enough to engage, but not empower.

Clear boundaries must be set, and if these are crossed in a purposeful, directed, and deliberate manner (usually with some aggression) then the time-out policy needs to be incorporated. The child needs an explanation of what he has done, and why he has to sit out and think about it. It has to be for a short period of time, and once he has had his time out, he then should continue with the activity he was doing. If he is using time out as a means of getting out of an activity, then he must complete the activity regardless, if possible. Time out should be used to defuse a situation and to send a clear message that a boundary has been crossed.

There should not be a specific "naughty" chair, but a general symbol or place for time out that can be used anywhere. Parents also need to use time out and to stick to the boundaries that they set their child. During time out, the child should not be left alone, but supervised so as to come to understand and come to terms with what he has done, and aided in his understanding if necessary.

Games, fun, and expressions

There must be clear and consistent behaviour on behalf of the support worker, visual clarity of expression of feelings, and a general acceptance of moving the child towards complete independence. It is important to avoid using too many cues or involving too many individuals, as the child who is easily distracted will have trouble focusing and concentrating on new tasks and is, therefore, more likely to withdraw further. As the child develops, more co-workers can be taken on board, but the child's threshold of distractions must be carefully monitored before involving more people.

Use others (nursery staff, pupils, parents, siblings) to dramatise feelings or act out for you to show how they are feeling. Feelings can be given to almost anything, from a bird flying overhead, to a bee buzzing close by, to characters in a story. The more familiar feelings become, the less likely the child will fear them and will realise that others feel the same way and that he is not alone.

Break it down

Break down the child's world as simply as you can, his basic sensations and senses. How is he seeing, hearing, smelling, etc.? Through observation of behaviour and being attuned, it is easier to get a feeling of where the child is. Make associations of those senses and the links between them. If the links and associations are not working well, if they are broken or have been linked up inappropriately, they might have to be remade, broken down, and reconstructed correctly. This can be done through patterns and new associations, which can be established with new feelings and behaviours.

Grey areas and loopholes

Sometimes, the child may resort to repetitive behaviour. This can be because he is bored, he wishes to test the adult, or he is scared of what he is encountering. If a child becomes locked into performing repetitive actions, there are several ways of helping him. For example:

- change your tone of voice;
- ask the child to stop;
- ignore the behaviour and try to distract him ("Look at that!");

- do something physical with him: go for a walk (outside or simply up and down the stairs); try squatting down, standing on tiptoes, or balancing on one leg, so as to focus his attention on the physical activity.

If the child still does not stop, then a short time out with an explanation will help him understand where the limits are and that a boundary has been crossed; this especially applies if the child is looking directly at you while continuing with the unwanted behaviour. Explain why you have moved him to area, step, or chair. When he stops, praise him immediately in a measured way, and move on to a new activity.

The path to integration and independence

Always bear all three techniques in mind when aiming to achieve new goals or change existing patterns of behaviour. In general, the most important point of the process is to ensure that, for the child, disengagement is more of an effort than engagement, that the child stays present, focused, and connected. As he advances, the child must be constantly reviewed with the parents to ensure the path towards integration is taking shape. However, integration requires independence, and so it is the support worker's role to slowly create a distance between themselves and the child, so as to promote independent behaviour. There should be a gradual move from scaffolding the child to becoming a shadow on the wall, still present and supportive, but no longer physically, thus allowing the child to develop his own way, make his own friends, and form a distinct personality.

With all this body of knowledge, the support worker is equipped to assess the nursery environment and educator from the young child's perspective, by:

- seeing through their eyes;
- hearing through their ears;
- feeling their emotions.

In this way, the support worker can effectively intervene when necessary; by entering the child's world she will be able to know how to lead him out of it into the wider world of the nursery environment. It is through this awareness, this attunement with the child, that the support worker understands the best way to lead him forward—to excel and reach his full potential.

PART III

PARENTS' FEEDBACK AND AUTHORS' CONCLUSION

CHAPTER THIRTEEN

Testimonials: feedback from four families who have undergone the Re:Start programme

Valentino

I first heard about Dr Stella Acquarone and her clinic in 2002 after my son, Valentino, was diagnosed with autism. At the time, I was completely in the dark about what the diagnosis meant, as the spectrum is so vast.

I was extremely anxious about the future for my son and that of the rest of my family, and at a complete loss as to what to do.

Entering into Dr Stella's treatment was a massive leap of faith alongside an understanding of the therapy we would undertake. Each child and family is treated individually, and the therapy for all of us was "intense". It was a real eye-opener as to the mechanics of the family and how we contributed to Valentino's experience and behaviour.

During the weeks of the treatment, Valentino began to "emerge" and had the space to start communicating. His speech, having been virtually nothing, started to come thick and fast.

The team are very supportive but firm. You definitely need to be of a strong constitution to do as they say, but equally, when you start seeing the results, you can dig deep. And the results speak for themselves, literally.

Valentino is now nine years old in a state school with "statemented" support. He is able to communicate and learn, and is always a work in progress—as are all children.

I will forever fly the flag for Stella and her team. They brought my little boy back to me and I highly recommend their treatment to anyone who discovers their child has autism.

(Melanie Sykes, television presenter and benefactor of the International pre-Autistic Network (ipAn)

Thomas

My son was eight months when we determined that he was not developing as we expected. We worked out for ourselves that it was probably autism, although too early to formally label. He had typical traits such as lack of eye contact, pointing, ordering objects, etc. He was not comforted by me and this was heart-breaking. He had stopped talking and was making various sounds; he could not make decisions like choosing drinks, and lots of other traits. He was also beginning to get angry because he could not express himself. As I understand it, at this age (two to three) key language skills are laid down and will be difficult to pick up later if they have been delayed. My belief is that the earlier that you support and the more that you can do, the better the outcome.

We went to our health authority and had very good support, but it was limited as to what they could provide. We found out about the Parent Infant Clinic intensive infant–family programme and had an assessment. It was very clear that this assessment was to determine if the traits of autism were really present and if they felt that they could actually help. In our case, they felt that they could. I had just lost my office job, but luckily ipAn [the International pre-Autistic Network] supported the treatment by providing the money for the therapy services. We contributed what we could afford.

We had the intensive infant–family programme over three weeks, during which time Thomas started talking. Before and after the programme, therapists came to our son's nursery for an hour once or twice a week, or to our house. They continued to provide support for the next two years.

The outcome for my son is that instead of going to a special needs school, he is now mainstreamed. He is statemented and still needs support, but the outlook is so much more positive then we could have hoped for. The approach also looks at the family, not just the child, and that was very supportive in helping us to support our son. I learnt to understand why our son was disengaging and how to re-engage with him.

It is four years since we received help and we have seen huge progress and continue to do so. Thomas progresses in school and out, and is in the normal school year for his age. It is difficult to describe what it is that demonstrates why things are so positive, but, as social communication is one of the most difficult areas for children with autism, and as Thomas now has quite a few friends in his class, there is no doubt he has progressed in this area. His classmates like him and he likes them and they ask to go to each other's houses, parties, etc. None of them knows that he is on the spectrum. Some of the autism traits seem to have gone or are greatly reduced, such as aligning objects, eye contact, lying on the floor watching wheels spin. He needs speech therapy as his language skills still need help, but it is not holding him back at school or with friends. I suspect he will continue to need additional support, but, based on where he is today, I'm hopeful he will continue to progress and develop well.

(Mary and Peter)

Celine

The Parent Infant Clinic has been a good support for our family. We first approached them when our child was thirteen months. I was having concerns about our child's lack of smiling and happiness, eye contact, and unusual shyness with strangers. I approached the local authorities for various tests, but they all came back stating no problems. I was still not satisfied about our child's detachment from us, her lack of joy and fear when meeting new people, so I started to research using the Internet to find a sanctuary for help. I knew that these issues we were facing could be turned around but I could not do it on my own. I needed someone who had seen these issues before and had knowledge of what I was saying.

I finally found the Parent Infant Clinic and their motto of early intervention, which, if done at the right time, can change everything. This really hit home for me, so, with my husband's support, I decided to ask for help. We did, and the support was good. It helped me that people saw the same little things I saw in my child. For the first time since my child was born, I felt I was doing something to help instead of just hoping it would go away, and because our child was so young this gave me more strength as I knew connections in the brain were still forming and could be altered for the better. So, after a few discussions with the Centre, we decided to undertake a two-week intensive family course. We would meet every day from 9 a.m. until 4 p.m. The day would consist of different session for all members of the family and joint sessions were also commonplace. A lot of talking took place and feelings were brought to the table.

The counselling sessions for our child were the most beneficial, because it was at these sessions that we were able to see the improvements being made. The counsellor would work one-to-one with our child, learning about her personality and observing. Obviously, the two-week course was no miracle, but with weekly one-hour sessions with a counsellor until she was three years old, big improvements were seen. Eye contact became better, and interactions between myself and my child became better. Smiling and happiness was something I would say my child started to do more of. Things improved certainly for the better.

Now, at three years and eight months, Celine is doing well at nursery. Her teacher tells me she is one of the brightest in the class: she only needs to be told once and she gets it. Her handwriting is very good and she can write and count in twenties; she excels in PE and ballet, often getting the PE star. In the most recent report, her teacher stated that Celine was popular among her peers and teachers. However, she can be very bossy and intimidating to other strong characters in her class. She is very strong-minded and this sometimes cannot be turned. The nursery also reports that she is a popular, talkative, and happy child. However, for me, she is still reserved with new people.

I'm glad I undertook the intensive course and the continued counselling sessions for our child—it was definitely of benefit to Celine and our family.

(Charles and Brigitte)

Gabriel

We met Stella after our two-and-a-half-year-old son was diagnosed with mild autism and hypersensitivity. At that time, he hardly spoke, avoided interactive play with other children, struggled with transitions, and wanted to wear only blue. Stella's approach is holistic. She assembled a team that worked with the entire family: multiple speech, psychoanalytic, and occupational therapists for our son and individual and marriage therapists for my husband and me. Two years later, and our son didn't test on the autistic spectrum; eight years later, and he's thriving in a normal school with friends and a swimming team. We are relieved and thankful to have met Stella and started our son's treatment from a very young age.

(Jane and Edward)

Conclusion

Stella Acquarone and Isabel Jimenez Acquarone

This book has shown how we work with the families of children like Joseph, Geronimo, Filippo, and Nicola—families who try so hard to reach their autistic children only to see them retreat even further. We at the Parent Infant Centre work with many families who know the worry and panic evoked by having a hard-to-reach child. It is a state of concern amplified by not knowing where to turn, what to do, or what the long-term prognosis might be. In this book, I have put forward a method to identify the early signs of alarm. These signs are the markers that some parents are right to feel worried about. They are also a tool for those professionals who come into contact with babies and young children, as they offer a concrete measurement that the child's development has deviated from the "normal" path. They confirm, in the light of the ever-expanding knowledge of relational neurodevelopment, that "wait and see" is not a valid professional response, since the window of greatest neuroplasticity is now. They also offer a sense of hope: once a cause for concern has been clearly identified something really can be done about it.

These days, it is quite common to read about early signs of alarm that have been tested and proved to be prodromal signs of severe later mental health disturbances. In 1984, Massie and Rosenthal drew up a list of these warning signs based on the retrospective study of forty autistic children (Massie & Rosenthal, 1984). Since then, their hypotheses and findings have been proved right by others in the field. For example,

- posture and head lag (Baranek, 1999; Baranek et al., 1997, 2005; Flanagan et al., 2012);
- a preference for objects rather than faces (Maestro et al., 2005; Muratori et al., 2014);
- impact on the parents or carer: the infant shows some fault in regulation of the fundamental motives for engagement with the parents, making parents change the rhythm and phrasing of their speech, play, and relate quality when they are with their child (St Claire, et al., 2007);
- difference in the quality of the speech and communication of the parent towards their child who displays avoidant or disengaged behaviours, such as lack of eye contact, and difficulty on the part of the baby to relax in the mother's arms (Danon-Boileau, 2007);
- slow brain processing (Ratey, 2001).

The identification and full understanding of the interplay between specific genes (not all yet discovered) and the environment will perhaps never be fully established. However, certain genetic mutations explaining abnormal neurobiological functioning may have recognisable features at birth or soon after, and it could well be that the transformations visible later (such as larger brain size or amygdala) are a consequence of having to accommodate intermittent brain connectivity, mysterious sensibilities, or slower ways of brain processing, all of which need better understanding and attention.

In 2010, the National Scientific Council on the Developing Child, Center on the Developing Child, Harvard University, published a report entitled, *Early Experiences Can Alter Gene Expression and Affect Long-Term Development* (Working Paper No. 10). It explained how new research had revealed that "environmental influences can actually affect whether and how genes are expressed". Thus, the old ideas that genes are "set in stone" or that they alone determine development have been disproved. Following this, in 2013, Neelroop Parikshak and colleagues from UCLA were the first to map autism-risk genes by function and uncover how mutations in the genes disrupt foetal brain development.

Identifying signs of alarm might be the first step in validating or assuaging a parent's concerns but it is not, on its own, enough. If we are alarmed, we need to act. Because of this, we have developed an intensive psychoanalytic–neuro-psychological family treatment programme that aims to greatly reduce the child's need to escape into and rely on his autistic behaviours. Our method has been distilled after many years of offering different approaches to treating autistic children (as well as those presenting autistic behaviours), from short-term intensives to one or more hours a week over many years. We call the programme Re:Start as it offers an opportunity for families to establish their relationships afresh. We try to strip everything back and return to the basic relationships to explore what is not working properly. We look at what it is possible to develop, why there is no attunement, and how we can achieve a secure attachment between parent and infant.

While underpinned by psychoanalytic thinking and led by parent–infant, adult, and child psychotherapists (adding speech and language, music, and other therapies as necessary), our team is truly multi-disciplinary, as, in our experience, this is the most effective way to work. By bringing together a team of psychotherapists with colleagues from a range of related disciplines (music, art, speech and language therapies, physiotherapy, and neuro-developmental), we are able to consider fully the ways in which the child relates to the world and, from there, begin to expand his potential. By involving a range of disciplines, we can consider possibilities beyond our own expertise.

A multi-disciplinary team of this kind has to meet regularly for planning, discussion, and evaluation in order to achieve a more integrated outcome. With support from the team, parents find the skill and motivation to continue the work both within the clinic and at home. The child, too, develops his own motivation to relate: to his parents and not just to his therapist. His experience of encountering, coping, and even enjoying being with other people during the sessions creates a template from which he can learn to communicate and relate to other children and adults in real-life settings, such as nursery and school.

The Re:Start programme demands three intensive weeks (up to thirty hours a week) from the whole family. This might be a lot for many families to cope with or accommodate, and we understand the huge commitment it takes to sign up to the programme. However, bearing in mind the long-term impact of an unknown disorder that can be severe, such as autism (which is a childhood psychosis), it is a wise investment. According to an estimate by Knapp and colleagues (2007), the UK government's expenditure of

> £4.6 million for the lifetime cost of someone with low-functioning ASD is higher than previously estimated by Järbrink and Knapp (2001), partly because we have used a more recent price base but mainly because we have been able to be more comprehensive in our measurement of the various economic impacts . . . we have also identified costs to families. A high proportion of the overall costs of ASD falls to families, whether in terms of out-of-pocket expenses, lost employment opportunities and income or (although not costed here) time spent providing informal care, commonly with considerable psychological impacts. (p. 1)

They go on to state that

> . . . early intervention pays off. The high costs associated with supporting adults with ASD warrant attention because there ought, potentially, to be some scope for reducing them by making more widely available those early interventions that have been shown to alter patterns of behaviour. Those interventions could divert many people from care pathways that are expensive . . . and improve the quality of life of those individuals and their families. (pp. 23–24)

Our approach is rooted in our understanding of neurobiology and the essential link between an early loving relationship and the development of the mind, the emotions, and behaviours. We consider the emotional and psychological dynamics created within the family and help bring about change that best suits the needs of the child and the family as whole.

We work to help the parents develop an understanding of their child's sensitivities, so that they can find new ways of relating to and reaching their child. Often, it is all too easy for parents of autistic children to become self-critical, and to feel upset because they do not enjoy their child or feel that they are failing, bad parents, sometimes resulting in them distancing themselves emotionally from their child. Similarly, it is not unusual for parents to begin to distance themselves from the child because they feel it is impossible to know him or to relate to him because of the strange way the child perceives and feels. Conversely, some parents try so hard to reach their retreating, sensitive child that the child feels intruded upon and simply retreats further, resulting in the parents suffering painful rejection.

This vicious circle of thwarted attempts to reach and get to know their child is one that we wish to help break. Once parents' early concerns are shared and acknowledged, help is already on the way: their self-esteem becomes activated and they can reflect with the professionals that respect them and are able to discover with them the child's real personality, as distinct from their "ideal" child, or from the product of their unconscious feelings and unresolved conflicts that are projected on the child as a result of fear or frustration.

From all the children and families we help, a new hope emerges. Parents who come to us extremely worried about their child's autistic behaviours find, during the course of the intensive Re:Start programme, that change is possible. They quickly become very knowledgeable about their child and themselves. It is having this knowledge that helps parents to understand their child's perception of the world and to present to them a new experience of the world, one that the child can understand and cope with.

In most cases, the children we see go on to successfully integrate into their everyday life at home and in the nursery or school. Parents find that the three or four weeks of hard work is worth it. They are extremely happy with the immense progress that takes place, and that continues to happen over the following years. Parents find they are wiser and happier about their child and family. They understand their child better, are more attuned to their feelings, and more able to manage their child's behaviours. Parents of slightly older, or harder to reach, children are sometimes frustrated or impatient that their child is "more difficult" or "more complex" than the younger children; yet, as they persist in the treatment, they learn to overcome their frustrations and continue the work to support their child.

We continue to consolidate progress made during the treatment over the following year with regular contact and therapy for those family members who need it. For children aged two and older, it is likely that follow-up will need to be more frequent and longer term, especially for those who are more severely autistic or whose family circumstances or physical problems present additional hurdles. For those children who need continuous weekly psychotherapy for many years, we regularly visit the school to help staff understand the child's internal world of perceptions and feelings. Teachers and assistants obtain an insight into how we work and learn how to best support the child as a sensitive individual, rather than simply prescribing a typical behavioural programme for autistic pupils.

Early detection means that parents' concerns are understood; early intervention means that they are acted upon. This quick response gives the parents every opportunity to establish a reciprocal, loving, and joy-filled relationship with their child. It ensures that parents can trust their instinct of knowing "what is best" for their child and build upon their knowledge of "why". It ensures that parents are supported in trying new ways to reach the child they fear is becoming unreachable. Early detection and intervention also play an important role in improving communication, strengthening family relationships, and minimising the risk of a family breakdown. "One purpose of the drive for earlier identification is that treatments delivered at very young ages, when the brain is most plastic, may ultimately lessen or prevent the lifelong challenges related to autism" (Yirmiya & Ozonoff, 2007).

Early intervention enables a child to develop his non-autistic potential and create a mind that can be reflective and considerate of others as well as of himself. This means that such children become able to value the importance and richness of relationships and experience and share positive emotions, such as happiness and joy. These children are able to access mainstream education and create fulfilling, independent social and working lives.

We think that it would be helpful to expand the boundaries of early health checks so that when a mother or parent raises a concern, even though the child appears in good health, that those from whom they seek advice are knowledgeable about the early signs of autism. Parents hold the key to discover the early misattunement in the relationship, as they are best placed to know when something is "not quite right". The earlier this is discovered and discussed with the parents, the better for the family dynamic and for realigning the child's development and brain connectivity.

Of course, we do not discriminate, and do not deny the potential advantages of treatment to families with slightly older children, up to the age of five years. All who want it can receive help if they are prepared to invest in the intensity of the programme and involve the whole family. It is perhaps important to note that, at the same time, we do not discriminate on financial grounds. While such an intensive, highly staffed programme is costly, we do all we can to assist those without personal funds or health insurance to access the treatment, with the help of contributions from the International pre-Autistic Network (ipAn; www.preautism.org).

Our methods are reinforced by the 2003 National Autism Plan for Children, produced by NIASA (National Initiative for Autism Screening and Assessment), which states that

> There is some indication . . . to suggest that very brief treatments are ineffective, and that programmes involving 20 or so hours per week are likely to result in more enduring gains (Rogers, 1998). The involvement of families in therapy also seems to be crucial for generalization and maintenance (Howlin and Rutter, 1987). For this reason current intervention programmes have begun to focus specifically on helping parents to foster communicative interactions with their child in the months following diagnosis. (Shields, 2000; Sowter et al., 2000; Sussman, 1999)

Furthermore, the NICE (National Institute for Health and Care Excellence) guidelines, *Autism: The Management and Support of Children and Young People on the Autism Spectrum* (August 2013), state that "there are interventions that can help some of the core features of autism, some of the symptoms, behaviours and problems commonly associated with autism, and support families and carers".

The Re:Start programme works, and we at the Parent Infant Centre shall continue exploring what the best methods are to:

- reach those children who retreat into the autistic space;
- free them from the constraints of their self-comforting behaviours and fear of relating to others;
- enable them to experience all their feelings;
- facilitate communication and improve relationships between them and their families.

Re:Start improves the quality of the encounters between parents and child. It is a programme based on better relationships. "Effective psychodynamic mother–infant psychotherapy during critical periods of right brain plasticity allows for the expansion of the human unconscious not only in infancy, but over the course of a life span" (Schore,

2013, p. 167). If the skeptic suggests that the child was not going to be autistic anyway, or that early intervention is an alarmist reaction, we would answer that better relationships can only be beneficial, and certainly never harmful.

Over the years, we have travelled through the lives of many little children with their parents and families and observed that the younger they are at the start of treatment, the easier they are to help, and the more completely they relinquish their autistic behaviours. Early intervention, skilfully done, can not only save vast sums of money, but also, and more importantly, avoid the agony that so many families are forced to endure. As the motto of the International pre-Autistic Network states, "It can be too late but never too early".

APPENDIX I

Scales and graphs: measuring the effect of the intensive intervention (the "numbers" and how they are calculated)

The following charts summarise the improvement, effect, and change in the infant and the mother (or primary carer) in thirty cases of an intensive infant–family intervention. The first two charts show the averages of all thirty cases. The subsequent charts show the average outcomes for babies displaying early signs of autism in different age ranges: 0–1 year old, 1–2 years old, and 2–4 years old. Improvement, effect, and change are shown in the interpersonal, sensorial, motor, and affect areas for both the infant and the mother (or primary carer).

Using these summary scales, it is possible to make comparisons of the intensive treatment outcomes between the different age groups. In the final chart on page 246, I compare and measure the changes and improvements for each age range.

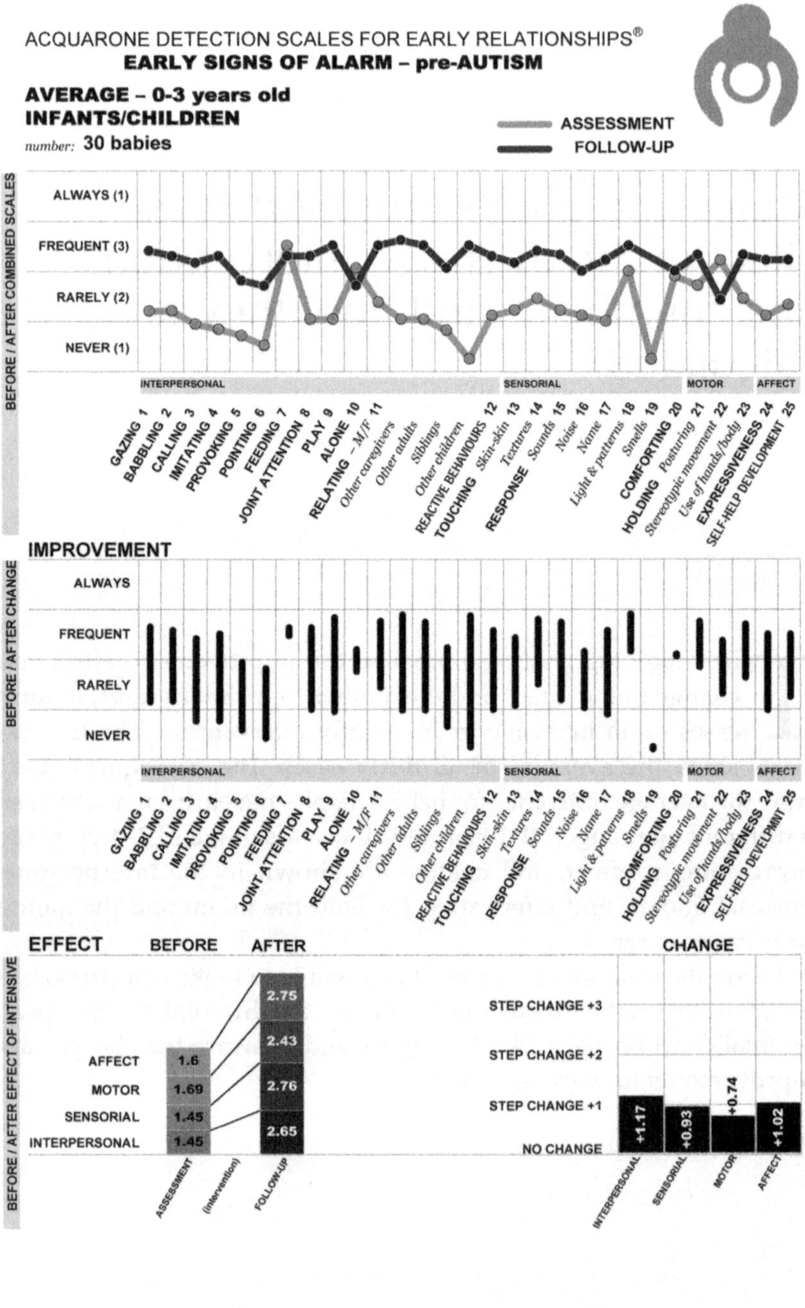
ACQUARONE DETECTION SCALES FOR EARLY RELATIONSHIPS®
EARLY SIGNS OF ALARM – pre-AUTISM
AVERAGE – 0-3 years old
INFANTS/CHILDREN
number: 30 babies
ASSESSMENT
FOLLOW-UP
BEFORE / AFTER COMBINED SCALES
ALWAYS (1)
FREQUENT (3)
RARELY (2)
NEVER (1)
INTERPERSONAL
SENSORIAL
MOTOR
AFFECT
GAZING 1
BABBLING 2
CALLING 3
IMITATING 4
PROVOKING 5
POINTING 6
FEEDING 7
JOINT ATTENTION 8
PLAY 9
ALONE 10
RELATING – M/F 11
Other caregivers
Other adults
Siblings
Other children
REACTIVE BEHAVIOURS 12
TOUCHING Skin-skin 13
Textures 14
RESPONSE Sounds 15
Noise 16
Name 17
Light & patterns 18
Smells 19
COMFORTING 20
HOLDING Posturing 21
Stereotypic movement 22
Use of hands/body 23
EXPRESSIVENESS 24
SELF-HELP DEVELOPMENT 25
IMPROVEMENT
BEFORE / AFTER CHANGE
ALWAYS
FREQUENT
RARELY
NEVER
EFFECT
BEFORE
AFTER
BEFORE / AFTER EFFECT OF INTENSIVE
AFFECT 1.6
MOTOR 1.69
SENSORIAL 1.45
INTERPERSONAL 1.45
2.75
2.43
2.76
2.65
ASSESSMENT
(intervention)
FOLLOW-UP
CHANGE
STEP CHANGE +3
STEP CHANGE +2
STEP CHANGE +1
NO CHANGE
+1.17
+0.93
+0.74
+1.02

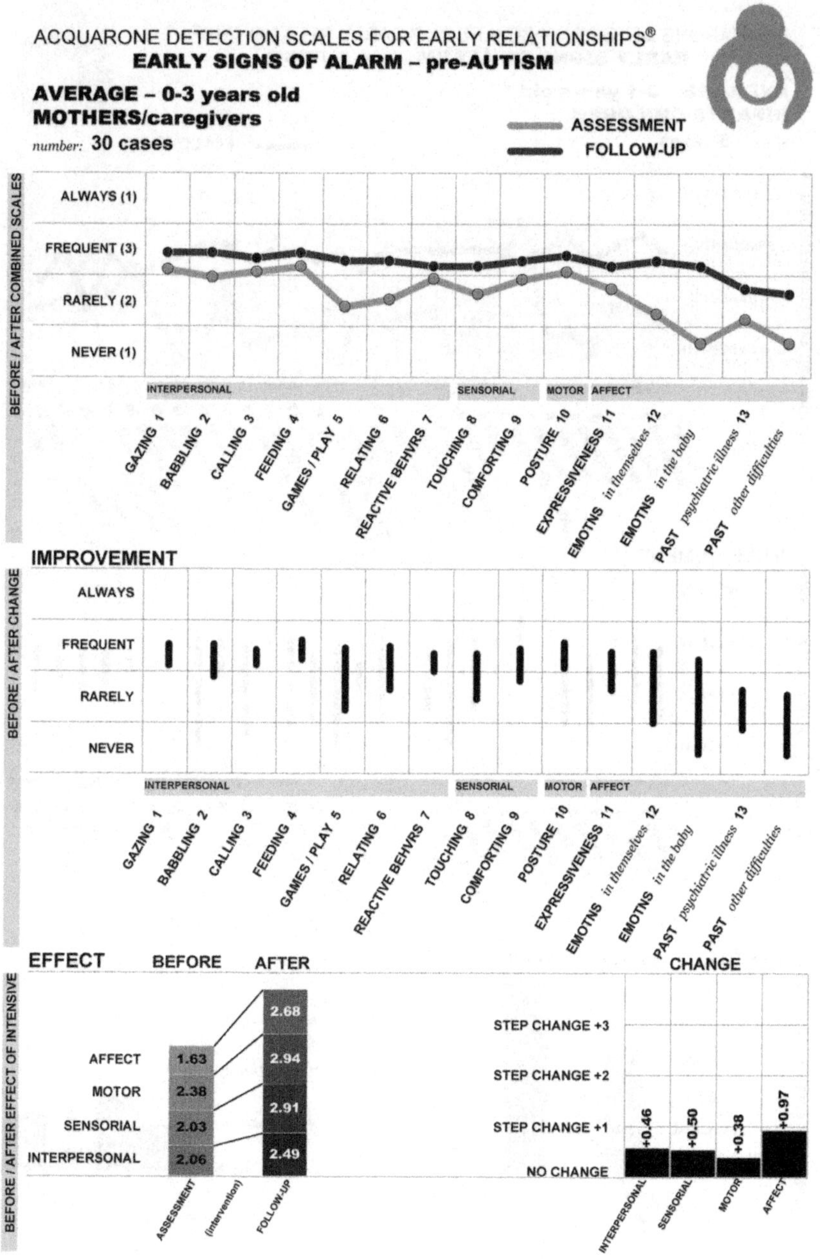
ACQUARONE DETECTION SCALES FOR EARLY RELATIONSHIPS®
EARLY SIGNS OF ALARM – pre-AUTISM
AVERAGE – 0-3 years old
MOTHERS/caregivers
number: 30 cases
ASSESSMENT
FOLLOW-UP
BEFORE / AFTER COMBINED SCALES
ALWAYS (1)
FREQUENT (3)
RARELY (2)
NEVER (1)
INTERPERSONAL
SENSORIAL
MOTOR
AFFECT
GAZING 1
BABBLING 2
CALLING 3
FEEDING 4
GAMES / PLAY 5
RELATING 6
REACTIVE BEHVRS 7
TOUCHING 8
COMFORTING 9
POSTURE 10
EXPRESSIVENESS 11
EMOTNS in themselves 12
EMOTNS in the baby
PAST psychiatric illness 13
PAST other difficulties
IMPROVEMENT
BEFORE / AFTER CHANGE
ALWAYS
FREQUENT
RARELY
NEVER
INTERPERSONAL
SENSORIAL
MOTOR
AFFECT
GAZING 1
BABBLING 2
CALLING 3
FEEDING 4
GAMES / PLAY 5
RELATING 6
REACTIVE BEHVRS 7
TOUCHING 8
COMFORTING 9
POSTURE 10
EXPRESSIVENESS 11
EMOTNS in themselves 12
EMOTNS in the baby
PAST psychiatric illness 13
PAST other difficulties
EFFECT
BEFORE
AFTER
BEFORE / AFTER EFFECT OF INTENSIVE
AFFECT
MOTOR
SENSORIAL
INTERPERSONAL
1.63
2.38
2.03
2.06
2.68
2.94
2.91
2.49
ASSESSMENT
(intervention)
FOLLOW-UP
CHANGE
STEP CHANGE +3
STEP CHANGE +2
STEP CHANGE +1
NO CHANGE
+0.46
+0.50
+0.38
+0.97
INTERPERSONAL
SENSORIAL
MOTOR
AFFECT

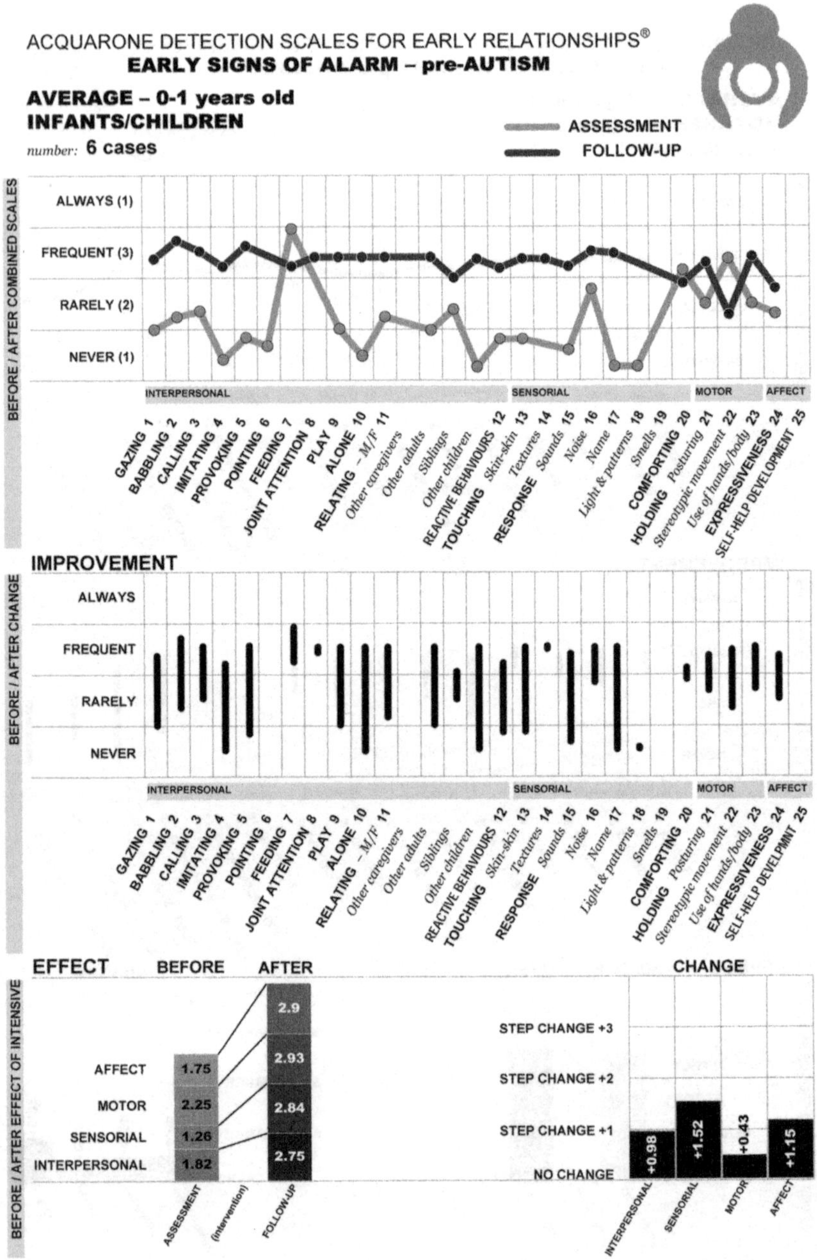
ACQUARONE DETECTION SCALES FOR EARLY RELATIONSHIPS®
EARLY SIGNS OF ALARM – pre-AUTISM
AVERAGE – 0-1 years old
INFANTS/CHILDREN
number: 6 cases
ASSESSMENT
FOLLOW-UP
BEFORE / AFTER COMBINED SCALES
ALWAYS (1)
FREQUENT (3)
RARELY (2)
NEVER (1)
INTERPERSONAL
SENSORIAL
MOTOR
AFFECT
GAZING 1
BABBLING 2
CALLING 3
IMITATING 4
PROVOKING 5
POINTING 6
FEEDING 7
JOINT ATTENTION 8
PLAY 9
ALONE 10
RELATING – M/F 11
Other caregivers
Other adults
Siblings
Other children
REACTIVE BEHAVIOURS 12
TOUCHING Skin-skin 13
Textures 14
RESPONSE Sounds 15
Noise 16
Name 17
Light & patterns 18
Smells 19
COMFORTING 20
HOLDING Posturing 21
Stereotypic movement 22
Use of hands/body 23
EXPRESSIVENESS 24
SELF-HELP DEVELOPMENT 25
IMPROVEMENT
BEFORE / AFTER CHANGE
ALWAYS
FREQUENT
RARELY
NEVER
INTERPERSONAL
SENSORIAL
MOTOR
AFFECT
SELF-HELP DEVELPMNT 25
EFFECT
BEFORE
AFTER
BEFORE / AFTER EFFECT OF INTENSIVE
AFFECT
MOTOR
SENSORIAL
INTERPERSONAL
1.75
2.25
1.26
1.82
2.9
2.93
2.84
2.75
ASSESSMENT
(intervention)
FOLLOW-UP
CHANGE
STEP CHANGE +3
STEP CHANGE +2
STEP CHANGE +1
NO CHANGE
+0.98
+1.52
+0.43
+1.15
INTERPERSONAL
SENSORIAL
MOTOR
AFFECT

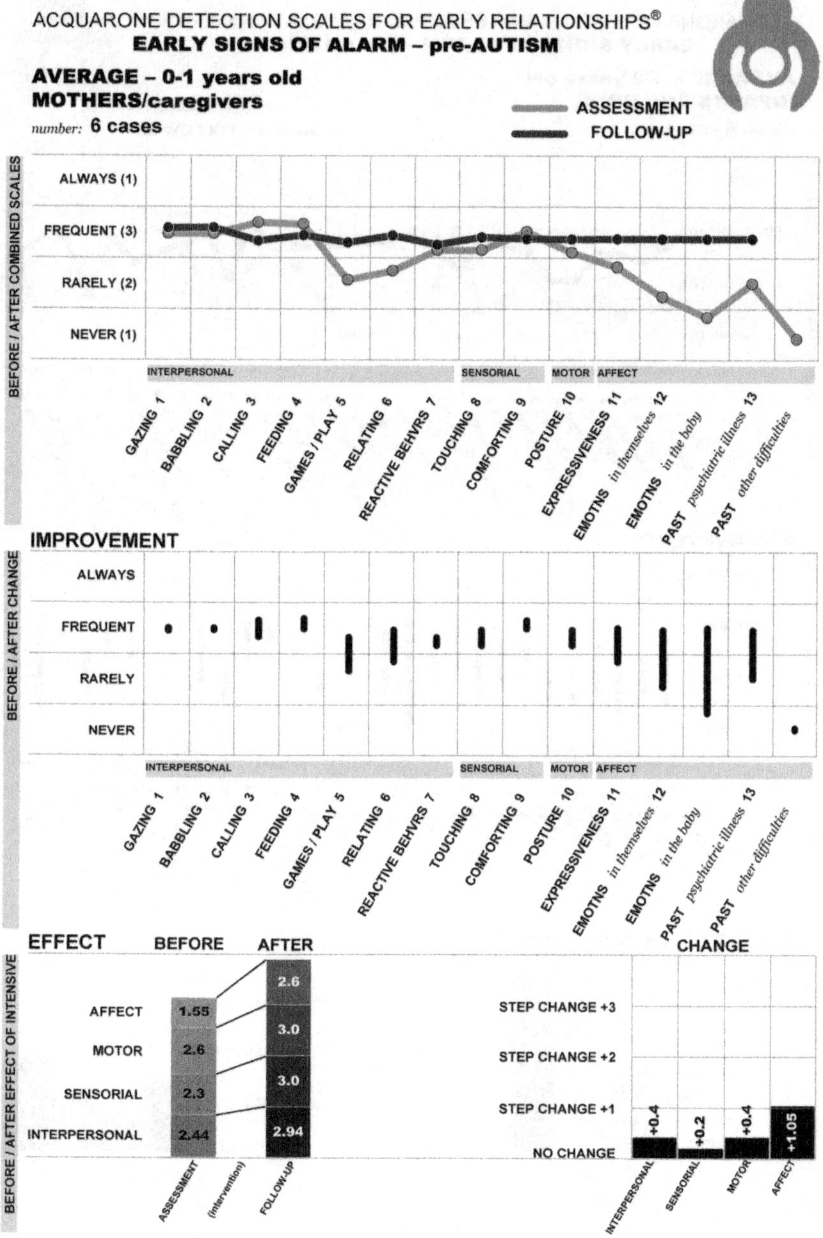
ACQUARONE DETECTION SCALES FOR EARLY RELATIONSHIPS®
EARLY SIGNS OF ALARM – pre-AUTISM
AVERAGE – 0-1 years old
MOTHERS/caregivers
number: 6 cases
ASSESSMENT
FOLLOW-UP
BEFORE / AFTER COMBINED SCALES
ALWAYS (1)
FREQUENT (3)
RARELY (2)
NEVER (1)
INTERPERSONAL
SENSORIAL
MOTOR
AFFECT
GAZING 1
BABBLING 2
CALLING 3
FEEDING 4
GAMES / PLAY 5
RELATING 6
REACTIVE BEHVRS 7
TOUCHING 8
COMFORTING 9
POSTURE 10
EXPRESSIVENESS 11
EMOTNS in themselves 12
EMOTNS in the baby
PAST psychiatric illness 13
PAST other difficulties
IMPROVEMENT
BEFORE / AFTER CHANGE
ALWAYS
FREQUENT
RARELY
NEVER
INTERPERSONAL
SENSORIAL
MOTOR
AFFECT
GAZING 1
BABBLING 2
CALLING 3
FEEDING 4
GAMES / PLAY 5
RELATING 6
REACTIVE BEHVRS 7
TOUCHING 8
COMFORTING 9
POSTURE 10
EXPRESSIVENESS 11
EMOTNS in themselves 12
EMOTNS in the baby
PAST psychiatric illness 13
PAST other difficulties
BEFORE / AFTER EFFECT OF INTENSIVE
EFFECT
BEFORE
AFTER
AFFECT
MOTOR
SENSORIAL
INTERPERSONAL
1.55
2.6
2.3
2.44
2.6
3.0
3.0
2.94
ASSESSMENT
(intervention)
FOLLOW-UP
CHANGE
STEP CHANGE +3
STEP CHANGE +2
STEP CHANGE +1
NO CHANGE
+0.4
+0.2
+0.4
+1.05
INTERPERSONAL
SENSORIAL
MOTOR
AFFECT

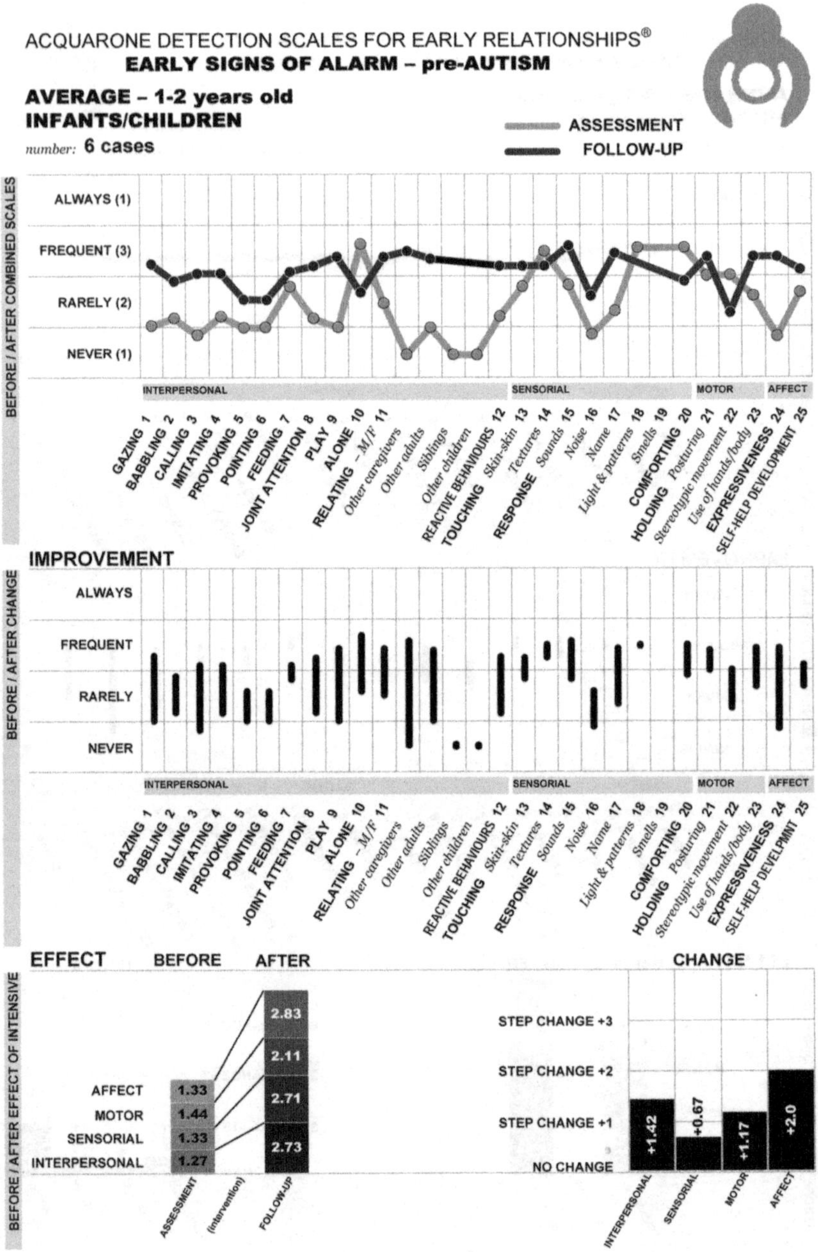
ACQUARONE DETECTION SCALES FOR EARLY RELATIONSHIPS®
EARLY SIGNS OF ALARM – pre-AUTISM
AVERAGE – 1-2 years old
INFANTS/CHILDREN
number: 6 cases
ASSESSMENT
FOLLOW-UP
BEFORE / AFTER COMBINED SCALES
ALWAYS (1)
FREQUENT (3)
RARELY (2)
NEVER (1)
INTERPERSONAL
SENSORIAL
MOTOR
AFFECT
GAZING 1
BABBLING 2
CALLING 3
IMITATING 4
PROVOKING 5
POINTING 6
FEEDING 7
JOINT ATTENTION 8
PLAY 9
ALONE 10
RELATING – M/F 11
Other caregivers
Other adults
Siblings
Other children
REACTIVE BEHAVIOURS 12
TOUCHING Skin-skin 13
Textures 14
RESPONSE Sounds 15
Noise 16
Name 17
Light & patterns 18
Smells 19
COMFORTING 20
HOLDING Posturing 21
Stereotypic movement 22
Use of hands/body 23
EXPRESSIVENESS 24
SELF-HELP DEVELOPMENT 25
IMPROVEMENT
BEFORE / AFTER CHANGE
ALWAYS
FREQUENT
RARELY
NEVER
SELF-HELP DEVELPMNT 25
EFFECT
BEFORE
AFTER
BEFORE / AFTER EFFECT OF INTENSIVE
AFFECT
MOTOR
SENSORIAL
INTERPERSONAL
1.33
1.44
1.33
1.27
2.83
2.11
2.71
2.73
ASSESSMENT
(intervention)
FOLLOW-UP
CHANGE
STEP CHANGE +3
STEP CHANGE +2
STEP CHANGE +1
NO CHANGE
+1.42
+0.67
+1.17
+2.0
INTERPERSONAL
SENSORIAL
MOTOR
AFFECT

ACQUARONE DETECTION SCALES FOR EARLY RELATIONSHIPS®

EARLY SIGNS OF ALARM – pre-AUTISM

AVERAGE – 1-2 years old
MOTHERS/caregivers
number: **6 cases**

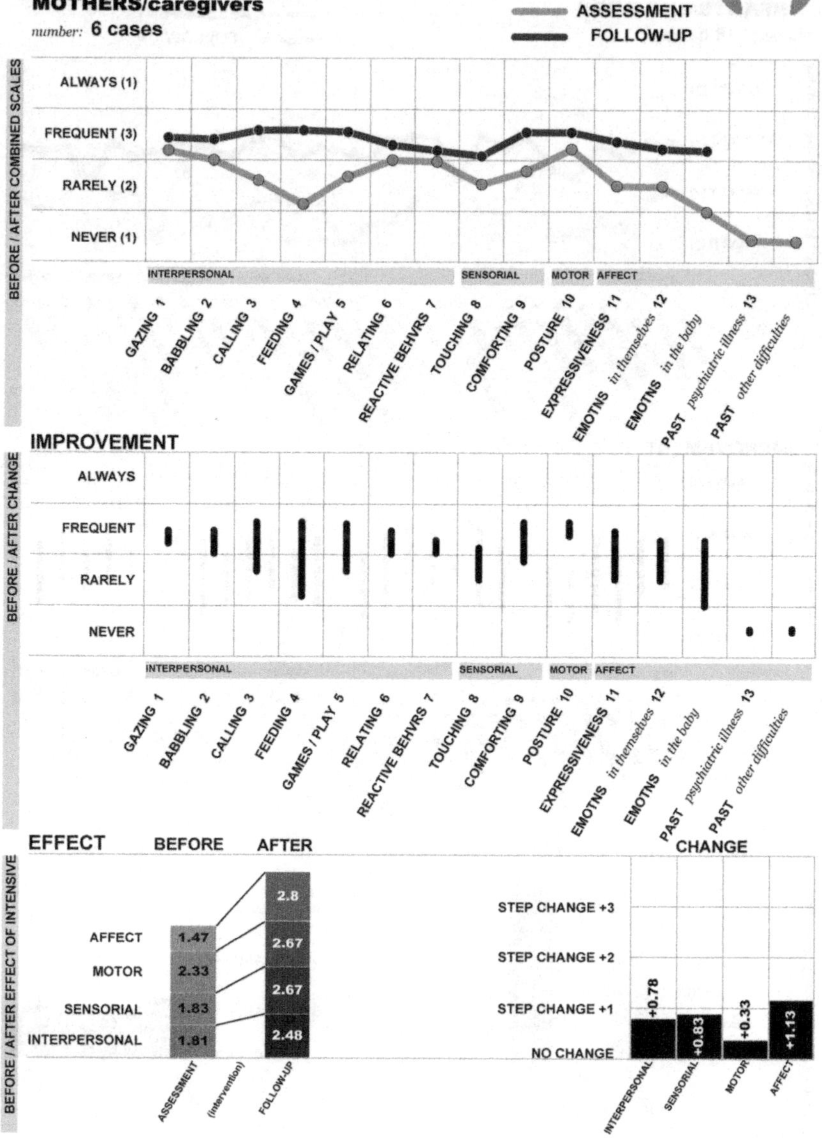

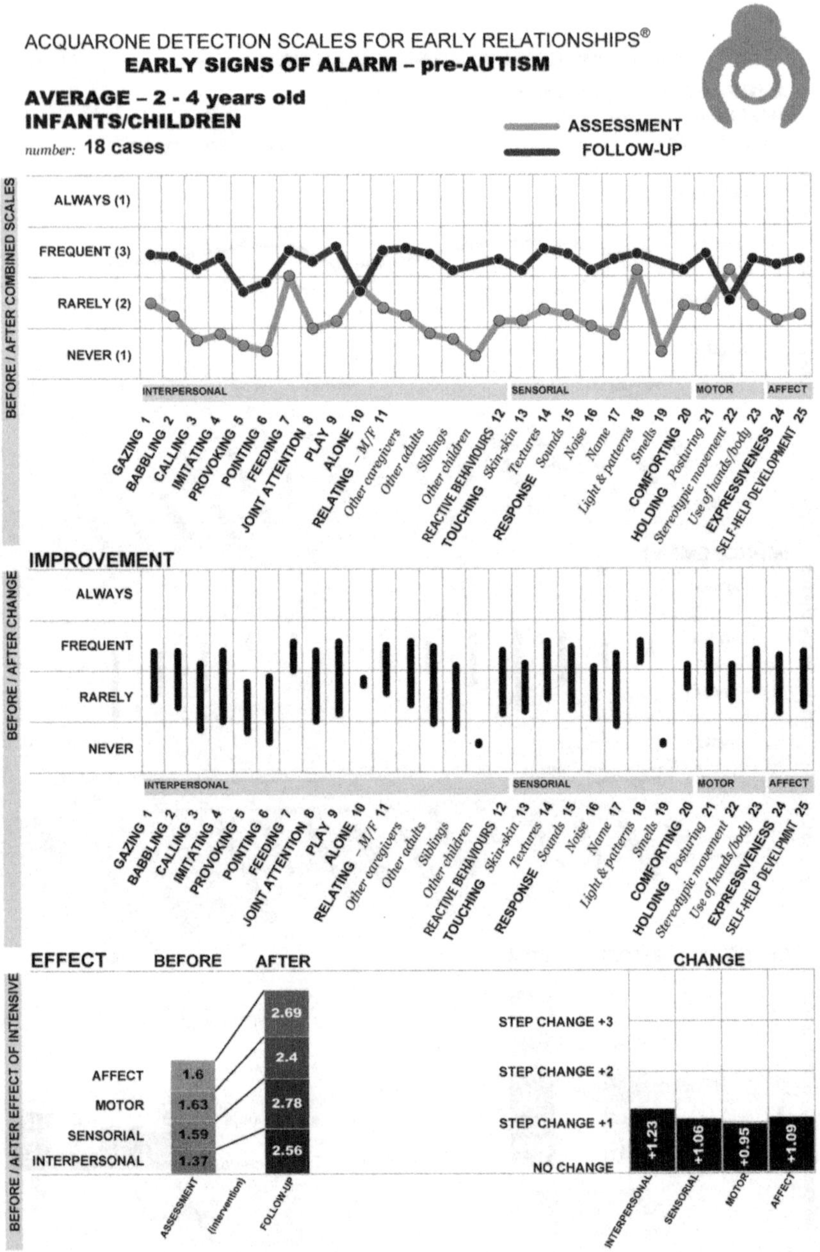
ACQUARONE DETECTION SCALES FOR EARLY RELATIONSHIPS®
EARLY SIGNS OF ALARM – pre-AUTISM
AVERAGE – 2 - 4 years old
INFANTS/CHILDREN
number: 18 cases
ASSESSMENT
FOLLOW-UP
BEFORE / AFTER COMBINED SCALES
ALWAYS (1)
FREQUENT (3)
RARELY (2)
NEVER (1)
INTERPERSONAL
SENSORIAL
MOTOR
AFFECT
GAZING 1
BABBLING 2
CALLING 3
IMITATING 4
PROVOKING 5
POINTING 6
FEEDING 7
JOINT ATTENTION 8
PLAY 9
ALONE 10
RELATING – M/F 11
Other caregivers
Other adults
Siblings
Other children
REACTIVE BEHAVIOURS 12
TOUCHING Skin-skin 13
Textures 14
RESPONSE Sounds 15
Noise 16
Name 17
Light & patterns 18
Smells 19
COMFORTING 20
HOLDING Posturing 21
Stereotypic movement 22
Use of hands/body 23
EXPRESSIVENESS 24
SELF-HELP DEVELOPMENT 25
IMPROVEMENT
BEFORE / AFTER CHANGE
ALWAYS
FREQUENT
RARELY
NEVER
INTERPERSONAL
SENSORIAL
MOTOR
AFFECT
SELF-HELP DEVELPMNT 25
EFFECT
BEFORE
AFTER
CHANGE
BEFORE / AFTER EFFECT OF INTENSIVE
AFFECT 1.6
MOTOR 1.63
SENSORIAL 1.59
INTERPERSONAL 1.37
2.69
2.4
2.78
2.56
ASSESSMENT
(intervention)
FOLLOW-UP
STEP CHANGE +3
STEP CHANGE +2
STEP CHANGE +1
NO CHANGE
+1.23
+1.06
+0.95
+1.09
INTERPERSONAL
SENSORIAL
MOTOR
AFFECT

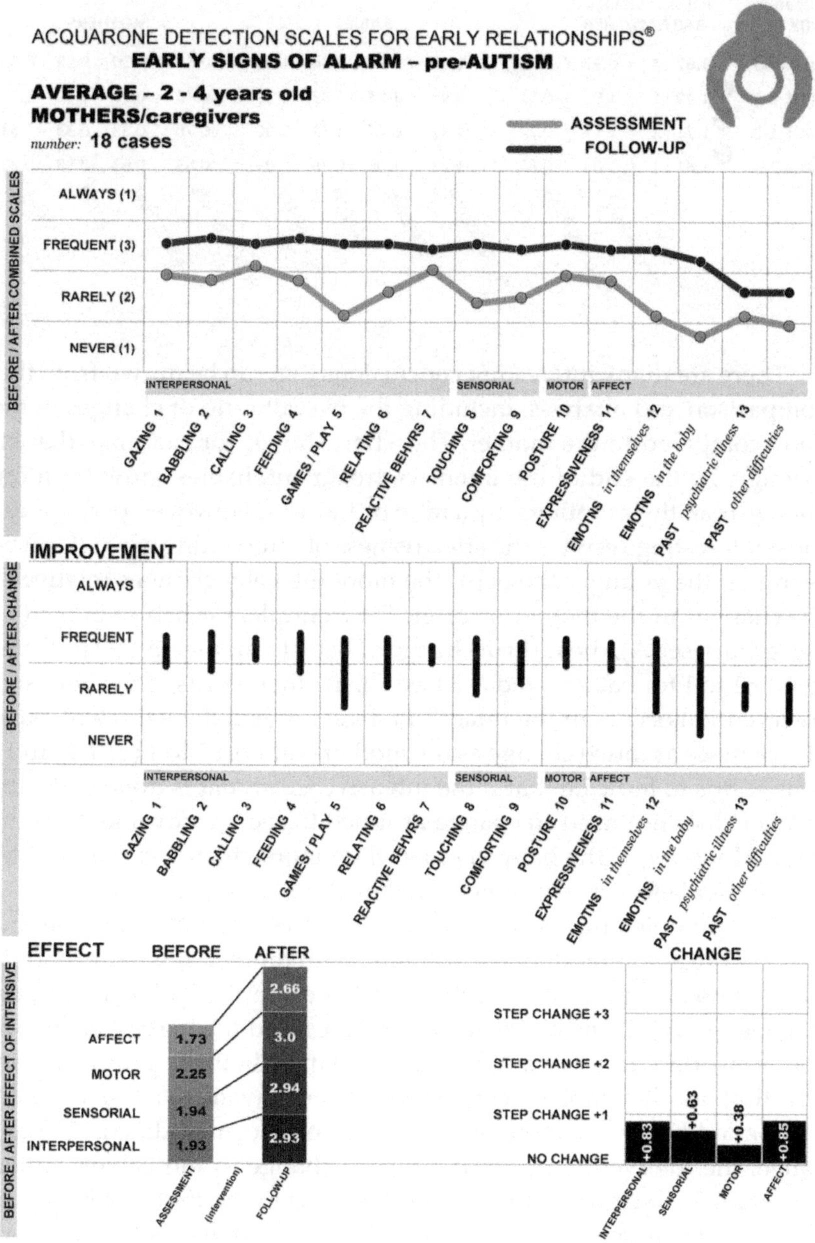
ACQUARONE DETECTION SCALES FOR EARLY RELATIONSHIPS®
EARLY SIGNS OF ALARM – pre-AUTISM
AVERAGE – 2 - 4 years old
MOTHERS/caregivers
number: 18 cases
ASSESSMENT
FOLLOW-UP
BEFORE / AFTER COMBINED SCALES
ALWAYS (1)
FREQUENT (3)
RARELY (2)
NEVER (1)
INTERPERSONAL
SENSORIAL
MOTOR
AFFECT
GAZING 1
BABBLING 2
CALLING 3
FEEDING 4
GAMES / PLAY 5
RELATING 6
REACTIVE BEHVRS 7
TOUCHING 8
COMFORTING 9
POSTURE 10
EXPRESSIVENESS 11
EMOTNS in themselves 12
EMOTNS in the baby
PAST psychiatric illness 13
PAST other difficulties
IMPROVEMENT
BEFORE / AFTER CHANGE
ALWAYS
FREQUENT
RARELY
NEVER
EFFECT
BEFORE
AFTER
BEFORE / AFTER EFFECT OF INTENSIVE
AFFECT
MOTOR
SENSORIAL
INTERPERSONAL
1.73
2.25
1.94
1.93
2.66
3.0
2.94
2.93
ASSESSMENT
(intervention)
FOLLOW-UP
CHANGE
STEP CHANGE +3
STEP CHANGE +2
STEP CHANGE +1
NO CHANGE
+0.83
+0.63
+0.38
+0.85

Changes BY AGE	Ratio of Changes BABY:MOTHER	average BABIES	average MOTHERS	BABIES INTERPERSONAL	BABIES SENSORIAL	BABIES MOTOR	BABIES AFFECT	MOTHERS INTERPERSONAL	MOTHERS SENSORIAL	MOTHERS MOTOR	MOTHERS AFFECT
All Babies	**1.67 : 1** =	0.97 /	0.58	1.17	0.93	0.74	1.02	0.46	0.50	0.38	0.97
AGE 0-1	(A) **1.99 : 1** =	1.02 /	0.51	0.98	1.52	0.43	1.15	0.40	0.20	0.40	1.05
AGE 1-2	(B) **1.71 : 1** =	1.31 /	0.77	1.42	0.67	1.17	2.00	0.78	0.83	0.33	1.33
AGE 2-3	(C) **1.61 : 1** =	1.08 /	0.67	1.23	1.06	0.96	1.09	0.83	0.63	0.38	0.85

There are many interesting conclusions that can be drawn from this comparison and analysis, including the overall ratio of changes in the baby compared to the mother. This chart shows, for example, that on average, by the end of the intensive treatment, babies show far more change than their mothers, by a ratio of 1.67 to 1. However, perhaps the most interesting result is the effectiveness of intervening early. It can be seen that the younger the baby, the more the baby changes relative to the changes in the mother or carer. For example, for babies in the 0–1 age group (see A), the ratio of change of baby to mother is 1.99 to 1, and just 1.61 to 1 for babies aged 2–3 (see C). In other words, if the intensive intervention occurs in the infant's first year of life, the baby will experience twice as much change as the mother—almost 2 to 1 (or 1.99 to 1). This seems to indicate that if the intensive treatment is done early, the mother does not need to change as much to see improvements in the baby. However, if the baby is older, then more change is required by the mother before improvements in her child are seen.

This diminishing ratio of change as babies age might be due to a process of "accommodation", whereby both mother and baby learn to accommodate, or adapt to, each other. For example, with babies in the 0–1 age group, the intensive intervention caused the biggest change in the "sensorial" area but mothers changed most in their "affect", meaning that as the babies responded better physically, the mothers responded better emotionally. In the more "accommodated" 2–3 age range, the intervention caused a bigger change in the babies' "interpersonal" behaviour, but in the mothers—as in the mothers in all age groups—the intensive intervention caused them to feel better emotionally towards their babies.

APPENDIX II

A glimpse inside the mind of a therapist working with children with autistic behaviours

Isabel Jimenez Acquarone

The battle

I am in a world I see but not understand, hear but do not comprehend, feel but do not acknowledge. My world is full of senses yet it is senseless to me. I have no use of words; they are sounds with no meaning. I have a world full of noises that I cannot integrate into sounds around me, they are me, they work their way through me and I switch off. I am in a world where it is all too much, so much that I could not bear be part or inside this. I choose to leave, to go far far away almost dancing on the moon or with the speck of sunlight. I can sway and fly with the wind and am gone. In my world I drown out the noises, the sounds around me merge, in my world I am at peace with myself. If I look to my world your world fades away, simply goes and disappears not being there at all, you all left, all the things that stuck and prodded and pained me I push away. I can push away sensations, I can run and bump into things and not feel them because I feel beyond the realm of real, already feeling raw so another bump or knock is nothing to me.

If I stayed in your world it is painful, to collate it all, the noise, the sound, the voice, the meaning, the expectation which you pull from me – the feelings which hit me like a wave without you knowing. You pull me in again and again and my cries should keep you out. You find my eyes and my soul and connect when I try to leave you find me again and again. There is no peace, I am losing my speck of light, where is my moon? I want to dance alone. You pull me back and call me to follow your voice, your words, your meaning. You find my eyes, I see you see inside of me. What promises can you make me? Don't you understand that I leave because I have no guidance, because it is too much for me and I cannot and will not understand, I shut you out. Leave me alone, the pain is unbearable, your voice begins to make sense, it relays the same message to me and tries to encourage me.

I am not used to following but being followed, you don't let me go, you lead me forward and wait, and wait and wait. You come back for me and wait and wait, you don't let me get by you, you don't give up, you are tired and I am tired and yet you still try to find me. Why? I am looking at you, I am confused. You know when I am gone, when I cry for the baby I want to be, why don't you fall for this? Why don't you stop? I am just being, I want to be left in my space, I am changing now getting angry. I cry and still you pull me forward with your soul not leaving mine. Now I roar at you, I am angrier because you don't flinch; you accept my anger without leaving me behind. I have never felt this before, don't you understand leave me alone I always win, I get my way, I am omnipotent, I am, I am everything. Why don't you see that, if I roar you don't flinch, why? Who are you to bring me back to ask me to stay?

I still roar and you look still into me. I still cry and you still find me. I still bawl and you still stay. I now am looking and seeing who you are. Who are you? Who are you? You are leading me out of my world and into this new one. You explain, you hold onto me, you lead me, you structure me, and you pull me into shape of something I left behind. You still look to me and bear me through our battle with warmth and do not condemn me—

You are the next step . . .

No matter what . . .

G has been left to run his own show so to speak, a terrifying and daunting task for a three year old. The lack of internal regulation and external boundaries had left him exhausted and terrified, more often zooming out, entering a sleep-waking state at all hours and nourishing himself with a limited amount of food. When G tuned in, the world was a disorientating place where he could not relate or match his feelings to what he was experiencing and this sensation expressed through unfocused continuous crying or giggling.

His parents were very afraid of and for their little boy and this fear held them in a certain paralysis leaving them unable to stepping into a parenting role. The fear of hurting him, becoming their own parents, or whether they were doing things correctly very much held them back. Another part of them, had not adopted their parenthood, wanting an easy way out and they continuously gave in. Without realising, the giving in had led them evermore into deeper waters, with G in charge. The deeper waters and his control over his parents in turn was a terrifying prospect for G. This terror left his body rigid and either he would swing from a hyper vigilant state to a sleep state (through the exhaustion of his hyper vigilance). The lack of external regulation reflected through his poor sleep cycles, inability to focus, relate to bodily sensations and stay with his surrounding environment, eating liquid – smooth tasteless foods. The minimal input from himself – almost deemed him in a lifeless state. The lack of boundaries from parents and external/internal regulation threw G into a vicious cycle. There was fear of the position he had put himself in, of wanting to be in control, however the control and lack of containment made him even more fearful, thrown him in a downward spiral that led to him disengaging with the surrounding world into his own.

Working with G was drawing him from his own world almost as if he were suspended at the very bottom of the ocean. However, there was a part of him which chose not to come to the surface, be alive, it was a terrifying prospect for him being charge. Any attempts to reach him he would slip away and return to his abyss. The process of pulling him up from the depths of where his mind had taken him was an exasperating experience. That a child had given up, or found the world around him so terrifying, or of not wanting to engage -enjoy an experience and should boycott the process was a disheartening experience for me. The process of working with him in his depths was flooding and it was heart wrenching that he did not want to follow, that regardless of an however I extended an emotional link and part of myself to him there was no grasp from him or desire to live. Bringing him up from the bottom the ocean and breathing life back into him seemed futile, almost as if I had to let him go and leave him there, perhaps that is what he wanted me to do. I am sure the sensation of giving up on him and passing him by is what the parents must have felt and in part why they chose the easy option approach.

I felt I was at a loss, losing him and hope. Time was moving on and the days, weeks were passing without finding him. He would give me snippets of himself initially enough to feel I had a sense of him. However, there was no development or progression, nothing more than a lifeless body that chose to disengage and that could not stay. G was a ghostly presence. . . there but not there. It seemed that he wanted to remain in his own world suspended in his lifeless existence. My desperation led me to find an inner strength and I found that the only way forward with him was by showing him there was no fear in myself, no going back, no sense of timelessness of his world but sheer conviction of mine. That there was only a body of strength and relentlessness in helping him – making him be with me in the present, complete an activity, eat a food, swim or paddle, whatever or wherever I was I would bring him, drag him mentally with me and not let go, he would be there with me too and experience.

Initially it was a painful process to participate in, feeling his rage, his anger, trying not to react to his bites and enragement. More so, I found that I had to bite-back the upset and not take his actions personally, my jaw would set and my mind hold onto where I wanted to go with him and take him without any inner contemplation. In his most enraged sessions, my face would be calm and my voice even, for G and for the parents, and partly for myself because I felt that if I stepped into those emotions I yielded to an uncontrollable whirlwind, and my own internal ruin. I would finish these sessions shaken and internally distraught, but having masked the sensation externally with calm, consistency and coherence. I was sure that what was at play in myself had not leaked out with him – almost what he provoked internally threw me to work in a more convicted manner externally. Although alone I felt that the dam walls were cracking and some painful part of him or myself were tearing away and screaming to come out and the sand clock was still running would I find him? These moments indicated to me that I needed more time to draw myself together and face him again with psychological armour intact. It also marked that G and I had found each other and made a bond, he was reflecting my inner world and I his. We had engaged and made a link, a link that he potentially and continuously used against me and often it felt as if I could not afford to give way or conceive of emotions whilst with him without him turning them on me. I did not want to become cold and mechanically, it was a test of perseverance and skilfulness to work with him without becoming counterproductive and falling into his trap.

I had to disengage myself emotionally from his state, and almost from myself, by not wanting or wishing for him to follow but making him follow and moving him forward regardless of his choice or my expectation. This continuing, this inner strength that I clung to was an unknown void that he had never been faced with, nor that I usually embraced. It was me, without the me a strange place to place myself. It was, as if I were something heartless, when I was. . .am all heart. At the same time, I had to be sharp and clear what I wanted and how I would proceed. Everything until then had been on his terms and conditions and now they were on mine with determination that even if he would not want to do he would do – no matter what.

The no matter what became my affirmation, and I found that if any part of me felt delight or happiness towards his progress he would regress and sabotage the following action. I had to refrain from feeling, yet also allow the flexibility and adaptability to allow him to try or start, without holding onto any expectation. The process seemed alien – how could someone not want to progress, not want to be in themselves, not want heart and soul, to breath, to live? Almost as if he was so afraid of the world that he chose not to live, the state of fear he was in could not allow him to live, feel or love. The force – determination and sheer pure conviction lacking the feelings was a safer option for him. It provided a robust secure environment. Which I believe he will need for sometime before feeling safe enough to move forward into a world with feelings – a secure scaffolding whilst his internal foundations are reset.

Part of me wished for more time, now I knew how to reach him I was desperate to convey what I knew to the parents. Part of me felt if only I had known that you needed the less human side of me how much could I have achieved, have I failed you?

The void was not reaching out to him and a lack of feeling was a foreign concept. This void allowed him slowly and reluctantly to move towards me. Where was I, he had no sense of me, cautiously I saw how he would regard me and begin to take in the world around him I had shattered the emotional mirror through which he had been able to view the world. He had to see it through his own eyes rather than through other people's emotions.

He would extend his palm out without eye contact, as primates seeking out companionship, friendship. He acknowledged who was in charge as an alpha. In these moments it was clear to me how fearful and how strong headed this little boy was how he nearly led us both into oblivion. It was also at these times that I realised how strong headed I had to become and how I needed to teach the parents to adopt this without becoming cold, that they needed to find their strength, conviction, determination, and lead the way with this new mindset. I hoped that they trusted me, and were courageous enough to take a leap of faith becoming the parents G needed.

The no nonsense policy of making G do things with no room for "poor G", meant that by holding onto he would happily encompass the situation or task. The not wanting to find him or please him (and then watch him slip away), made him in turn try to find me and try to please me. During the first two weeks of treatment every opportunity I had I tried to reach G somehow trying to keep a hold of a sense of him and then I would be disheartened to see how he would slip away once a slightest contact was made. When I finally decided to drag him through activities without any sympathy or empathy, where there was nothing left of me to give I observed that G sought out the lack of contact and sought it out. I had to make him work for it mechanically so it became second nature for him to look for the cues from others.

I realized that G was different to many other cases, and so far immersed lifelessly in own world that there was a risk that if I didn't keep a strong hold on time, focus on goals he would take me to his world where every day slipped into the next. I had to keep a foothold on the belief that I would (not could) find him . . . no matter what.

The siren's song

Trying to find him, her, them – it is like submerging into a bottomless realm, there is no air, no being, no logic – it is being engulfed into a world of emotions where one is at risk of drowning if I stay too long. I am reaching, feeling my way forward – there is nothing to see from the outside, some part of me extends, connects and reaches seeking them out and try to grasp some sense of the senseless world they are in. Some tease and entice me forward, some pull at me with desperation; some remain in the dark depths. Time and time again, I breathe and try to find them – where they are, do they follow, can they follow or will we both drown together? I know their rage, their sadness, the rawness of the inner most self. . . At times I feel as if there is no more air left in my lungs, I must emerge, I must let go. . . I must disconnect before it is too late for me too. I move away, my core is still one; I am still here and no-longer there. In an unfeeling world I am a full feeling being who cannot make sense of my gift. Break the wings of an angel and then ask them to fly –

I feel their panic, their confusion, their pain and fear – they are as sirens with their beautiful eyes, and faces calling me to the depths. When they eternally slip away, I long to swim with them, their song is beautiful, entrancing yet their fate treacherous – the lost ones still call to me through dreams, they beckon me. I anchor myself here now, I master my gift, my curse through my four legged companions, I extend and open to them the channels that seek these souls, I heal my spirit and replenish my dreams with simple connections from the heart to the heart. I do not seek understanding and redemption from others only a sense of space. . . space to breath and find my serenity again. . . Break the wings of an angel and then ask them to fly –

I dance on their specks of dust and spin on the sunbeam pouring through the window, I sway with the trees in the wind feeling their peace and try to bring with me others – so they can understand, see and feel – This is the place where there is no logic, no forwards, backwards, up or down, it is of being and not being too. . . I am as lost as they are that is why I know where to go, where to return to and what to whisper. Yet there are times, the depths are great, the weight on my soul is too much to bear and it is as if I am drowning, falling, it is heart breaking to love them wholeheartedly and let them go – knowing that they are unable to follow, and tempting to stay with these souls too – because to reach them first you must "see" them and love them – they, you, me we are all one. You give some part of yourself to each one, some sense of being and then know it is forever gone, some take it and become whole, some snatch it leaving a void. The void does not close with time, the lost ones are mourned. I need not be parents or family, I just need to be me – that is enough to love and mourn those I could not "save". Remember do not break the wings of an angel and then ask them to fly. . . the cost of falling is too great.

Autism

There is a place called Earth, it's a place I once knew.
I could make sense of it perhaps I was one of the few.
Now I cannot recognise the ever changing set,
Full of people with no feelings or regret.
They tell me I have to stay . . . focus here and now
Not on the light or far away.

How, oh how can you ask me?
It's so painful, are you blind to see?
I am flooded and overwhelmed,
Drowning in your presence and you don't care.
Your eyes are open wide but you don't see but stare.
You ask me to wake up when you're still asleep,
To the misery and senselessness that you keep.
I don't want to fall into your dream
I'm flooded again and just learn to scream.
I am lashing out and don't know how to stop
They say it's stereotyping but it's just my prop
I am trying to cope and act your way
But cannot live, breath and stay!
Can you not connect and be?
Someone real, just like me.

I have a name; I have a place in every population, culture and race.
I have an incidence on the rise; I grow with technology as my guise.
The further you scale in the human mind
The more you'll see of my kind . . .

You claim to be the one who is real,
Yet you're disconnected, you don't feel.
You're further away than I'll ever be.
I haven't sold my principals, I am free.
I live and experience it all, every sense large and small.
To painful to talk or hope that you'll see it my way.
Too painful I know you'll never see what I say.
Perhaps what needs to change is what you rearrange.
A World full of broken communication, lacking direct relation.
I have no bearing on what to hold,
I am continuously beginning to unfold.
The arms that I need and so full of greed,
Full of those expectations and desires
That burn me inside like hells fires.
You saving me, is hypocrisy
Me saving you is all I aim to do.
Can you feel?
Can you see?
The real person called me . . .

REFERENCES

Acquarone, S. (2007). *Signs of Autism in Infants. Recognition and Treatment.* London: Karnac.

Acquarone S. (2009). Variacion en la comprension del trabajo con ninos autistas. In: *Upalala. Ayudando a los que ayudan. Comprender las ansiedades de los profesionales que trabajan con ninos y sus familias.* Argentina–Mexico: Lumen.

Adolphs, R. (2001). The neurobiology of social cognition. *Current Opinion in Neurobiology, 11*(2): 231–239.

Allen, G. (2005). Cerebellum in autism. *Clinical Neuropyschiatry, 2*(6): 321–337.

Alvarez, A. (1992). *Live Company.* London: Routledge.

Alvarez, A. (2012). *The Thinking Heart.* London: Karnac.

Athern, J., & Madill, A. (2002). How do transitional objects work? The clients view. *Psychotherapy Research, 12*: 369–388.

Baranek, G. T. (1999). Autism during infancy: a retrospective video analysis of sensory-motor and social behaviors at 9–12 months of age. *Journal of Autism and Developmental Disorders, 29*: 213–224.

Baranek, G. T., Barnett, C. R., Adams, E. M., Wolcott, N. A., Watson, L. R., & Crais, E. R. (2005). Object play in infants with autism: methodological issues in retrospective video analysis. *American Journal of Occupational Therapy, 59*: 20–30.

Baranek, G. T., Foster, L. G., & Berkson, G. (1997). Tactile defensiveness and stereotyped behaviors. *American Journal of Occupational Therapy, 51:* 91–95.

Baranek, G. T., Wakeford, C. L., & David, F. J. (2008). Understanding, assessing, and treating sensory-motor issues in young children with autism. In: K. Chawarska, A. Klin, & F. Volkmar (Eds.), *Autism Spectrum Disorders in Infancy and Early Childhood: Diagnosis, Assessment and Treatment* (pp. 104–140). New York: Guilford Press.

Bayat, M. (2007). Evidence of resilience in families of children with autism. *Journal of Intellectual Disability Research, 51*(9): 702–714.

Ben-Sasson, A., Hen, L., Fluss, R., Cermak, S. A., Engel-Yeger, B., & Gal, E. (2008). A meta-analysis of sensory modulation symptoms in individuals with autism spectrum disorders. *Journal of Autism and Developmental Disorders, 39*:(1): 1–11.

Bettelheim, B. (1967). *The Empty Fortress: Infantile Autism and the Birth of the Self.* New York: Free Press.

Bick, E. (1968). The experience of the skin in early object-relations. *International Journal of Psychoanalysis, 49*: 484–486.

Bick, E. (1986). Further considerations on the function of the skin in early object relations: Findings from infant observation integrated into child and adult analysis. *British Journal of Psychotherapy, 2:* 292–299.

Bion, W. R. (1950). The imaginary twin. In: *Second Thoughts.* London: Heinemann.

Bion, W. R. (1962). *Learning from Experience.* London: Heinemann.

Blasi, A., Mercure, E., Lloyd-Fox, S., Thomson, A., Brammer, M., Sauter, D., Deeley, Q., Barker, G. J., Renvall, V., Deoni, S., Gasston, D., Williams, S. C. R., Johnson, M. H., Simmons, A., & Murphy, D. G. M. (2011). Early specialization for voice and emotion processing in the infant brain. *Current Biology, 21*: 1220–1224.

Boraston, Z., & Blakemore, S. J. (2007). The application of eye-tracking technology in the study of autism. *Journal of Physiology, 581*(3): 893–898.

Boscolo, L., Cochin, G., Hoffman, L., & Penn, P. (1987). *Milan Systemic Family Therapy: Conversations in Theory and Practice.* New York: Basic Books.

Bowlby, J. (1969). *Attachment and Loss: Volume I: Attachment. The International Psycho-Analytical Library, 79*: 1–401. London: The Hogarth Press.

Bowlby, J. (1988). *A Secure Base: Clinical Applications of Attachment Theory.* London: Routledge.

Brazelton, B., & Nugent, K. (2011). *The Neonatal Behavioural Assessment Scale.* London: MacKeith Press.

Brazelton, T. B., Kozlowski, B., & Main, M. (1974). The origins of reciprocity. In: M. Lewis & L. Rosenblum (Eds.), *The Effect of the Infant on its Caregiver* (pp. 49–79). New York: Elsevier.

Britton, R. (1989). The missing link: parental sexuality in the Oedipus complex. In: J. Steiner (Ed.), *The Oedipus Complex Today* (pp. 83–101). London: Karnac.

Britton, R. (1998). Subjectivity, objectivity and triangular space. In: *Belief and Imagination* (pp. 91–104). London: Routledge.

Bruner, J. S. (1983). *Child's Talk: Learning to Use Language*. New York: Norton.

Bullowa, M. (Ed.) (1979). *Before Speech: The Beginning of Human Communication*. Cambridge: Cambridge University Press.

Burhouse, A. (2001). Now we are two, going on three. *International Journal of Infant Observation, 4*: 51–67.

Carper, R. A., & Courchesne, E. (2005). Localized enlargement of the frontal cortex in early autism. *Biological Psychiatry, 57*(2): 126–133.

Carr, A. (2009). The effectiveness of family therapy and systemic interventions for child- focused problems. *The Journal of Family Therapy, 31*: 3–45.

Carter, R. (1998). *Mapping the Mind*. London: Weidenfeld & Nicolson.

Chiron, C., Jambaque, I., Nabbout, R., Lounes, A., & Dulac, O. (1997). The right brain hemisphere is dominant in human infants. *Brain, 120*: 1057–1065.

Courchesne, E., Campbell, K., & Solso, S. (2011). Brain growth across the life span in autism: age-specific changes in anatomical pathology. *Brain Research, 1380*: 138–145.

Courchesne, E., Pierce, K., Schumann, C. M., Redcay, E., Buckwalter, J. A., Kennedy, D. P., & Morgan, J. (2007). Mapping early brain development in autism. *Neuron, 56*: 399–413.

Danon-Boileau, L. (2007). Early signs related to posture and communication: The child's attitude and the mother's reaction. In: S. Acquarone (Ed.), *Signs of Autism in Infants: Recognition and Treatment*. London: Karnac.

David, F. J., Baranek, G. T., Wiesen, C., Miao, A. F., & Thorpe, D .E. (2012). Coordination of precision grip in 2–6 years-old children with autism spectrum disorders compared to children developing typically and children with developmental disabilities. *Frontiers in Integrative Neuroscience, 6*: 122–128.

Dawson, G., Ashman, S. B., & Carver, L. J. (2000). The role of early experience in shaping behavioral and brain development and its implications for social policy. *Development and Psychopathology, 12*(4): 695–712.

Dawson, G., Webb, S. J., Wijsman, E., Schellenberg, G., Estes, A., Munson, J., & Faja, S. (2005). Understanding the nature of face processing impairment in autism: insights from behavioral and electrophysiological studies. *Developmental Neuropsychology, 27*(3): 403–424.

De Zulueta, F. (1993). *From Pain to Violence: The Traumatic Roots of Destructiveness*. London: Whurr.

Delafield-Butt, J. T., & Trevarthen, C. (2013). Theories of the development of human communication. In: P. Cobley & P. Schultz (Eds.), *Theories and Models of Communication* (pp. 199–222). Berlin/Boston: De Gruyter Mouton.

DeYoung, P. (2003). *Relational Psychotherapy: A Primer*. New York: Brunner-Routledge.

Doidge, N. (2007). *The Brain that Changes Itself*. New York: Viking.

Elsabbagh, M., Volein, A., Csibra, G., Holmboe, K., Garwood, H., Tucker, L., Krljes, S., Baron-Cohen, S., Bolton, P., Charman, T., Baird, G., & Johnson, M. H. (2009). Neural correlates of eye gaze processing in the infant broader autism phenotype. *Biological Psychiatry, 65*: 31–38.

Flanagan, J., Landa, R., Bhat, A., & Bauman, M. (2012). Head lag in infants at risk for autism: a preliminary study. *American Journal of Occupational Therapy, 66*: 577–585.

Fraiberg, S. (1982). Pathological defenses in infancy. *Psychoanalytic Quarterly, 51*: 612–635.

Frazier, T. W., Keshavan, M. S., Minshew, N. J., & Hardan, A. Y. (2012). A two-year longitudinal MRI study of the corpus callosum in autism. *Journal of Autism and Developmental Disorders, 42*(11): 2312–2322.

Freud, S. (1923b). *The Ego and the Id. S. E., 19*: 3–66. London: Hogarth.

Gillberg, C. (2007). *Epilepsy and Comorbidity*. Lecture to Association for Research in Infant and Child Development, May 2007.

Gillberg, C., & Coleman, M. (2000). *The Biology of Autistic Syndromes* (3rd edn). Cambridge: Cambridge University Press.

Glover, V. (2014). Maternal depression, anxiety and stress during pregnancy and child outcome; what needs to be done. *Best Practice & Research Clinical Obstetrics & Gynaecology, 28*(1): 25–35.

Glover, V. (2015). Prenatal stress and its effects on the fetus and the child: possible underlying biological mechanisms. *Advances in Neurobiology, 10*: 269–283.

Glover, V., & O'Connor, T. (2002). Effects of antenatal stress and anxiety. Implications for development and psychiatry. *British Journal of Psychiatry, 180*: 389–391.

Goldberg, W. A., Thorsen, K. L., Osann, K., & Spence, M. A. (2008). Use of home videotapes to confirm parental reports of regression in autism. *Journal of Autism and Developmental Disorders, 38*: 1136–1146.

Griffiths, R. (1954). *The Abilities of Babies. A Study in Mental Measurement.* London: University of London Press.

Griffiths, R. (1970). *The Abilities of Young Children.* London: Child Development Research Centre.

Hartley, S. L., Barker, E. T., Seltzer, M. M., Floyd, F., Greenberg, J., Orsmond, G., & Bolt, D. (2010). The relative risk and timing of divorce in families of children with an autism spectrum disorder. *Journal of Family Psychology, 24*(4): 449–457.

Hobson, R. P. (2002). *The Cradle of Thought.* London: Macmillan.

Houzel, D. (2001). The "nest of babies" fantasy. *Journal of Child Psychotherapy, 27*: 125–138.

Hughes, D. (1997). *Facilitating Developmental Attachment: The Road to Emotional Recovery and Behavioural Change in Foster and Adopted Children.* Englewood Cliffs: NJ: Jason Aronson.

Hughes, D. (1998). *Building the Bonds of Attachment: Awakening Love in Deeply Troubled Children.* Englewood Cliffs, NJ: Jason Aronson.

Hughes, D. (2003). Psychological interventions for the spectrum of attachment disorders and interfamilial trauma. *Attachment and Human Development, 5*: 271–277.

Huntley, M. (1996). *The Griffiths Mental Development Scales from Birth to Two Years.* Association for Research in Infant and Child Development (ARICD). Oxford: Hogrefe.

Jones, W., & Klin, A. (2013). Attention to eyes is present but in decline in 2–6-month-old infants later diagnosed with autism. *Nature, 504*: 427–431.

Kalat, J. W. (1995). *Biological Psychology* (5th edn). Pacific Grove, CA: Cole.

Kanner, L. (1943). Autistic disturbances of affective contact. *The Nervous Child, 2*: 217–250.

Kerstin, U. M. (2011). *The Oxytocin Factor: Tapping the Hormone of Calm, Love and Healing.* London: Pinter and Martin.

Klein, M. (1946). Notes on some schizoid mechanisms. In: *The Writings of Melanie Klein, Vol. 3: Envy and Gratitude and Other Works.* London: Hogarth Press.

Klein, M. (1957). Envy and gratitude. A study of unconscious sources. In: *The Writings of Melanie Klein, Vol. 3: Envy and Gratitude and Other Works.* London: Hogarth Press.

Klein, M. (1961). Narrative of a child analysis. In: *The Writings of Melanie Klein, Vol. 4*. London: Hogarth Press.

Kleinhans, N. M., Richards, T., Weaver, K., Clark Johnson, L., Greenson, J., Dawson, G., & Aylward, E. (2010). Association between amygdala response to emotional faces and social anxiety in autism spectrum disorders. *Neuropsychologia, 48*(12): 3665–3670.

Knapp, M., Romeo, R., & Beecham, J. (2007). *The Economic Consequences of Autism in the UK*. London: Foundation for People with Learning Disabilities.

Lacan, J. (1966). The function and field of speech and language in psychoanalysis. In: *Ecrits*, B. Fink (Trans.) (pp. 237–265). New York/London: Norton.

Lam, K. S. L., Aman, L., & Arnold, E. (2006). Neurochemical correlates of autistic disorder: a review of the literature. *Research in Developmental Disabilities, 27*(3): 254–289.

Landa, R. J., Alden, L., Gross, A. L., Stuart, E. A., & Faherty, A. (2012). Developmental trajectories in children with and without autism spectrum disorders: the first 3 years. *Child Development, 84*(2): 429–442.

Limperopoulos, C. (2008). Positive screening for autism in ex-preterm infants: prevalence and risk factors. *Pediatrics, 121*: 758–765.

Luiz, D., Barnard, A., Knoesen, N., Kotras, N., Horrocks, S., McAlinden, P., Challis, D., & O'Connell, R. (2006). *Griffiths Mental Development Scales – Extended Revised Administration Manual*. Association for Research in Infant and Child Development. Oxford: Hogrefe.

MacFarlane, A. (1977). *Psychology of Childbirth*. Cambridge: Harvard University Press.

Maestro, S., Muratori, F., Cavallaro, M. C., Pecini, C., Cesari, A., Paziente, A., Stern, D., Golse, B., & Palacio-Espasa, F. (2005). How young children treat objects and people: an empirical study of the first year of life in autism. *Child Psychiatry & Human Development, 35*: 383–396.

Mahler, M. (1958). Autism and psychosis: two extreme disturbances of identity. *International Journal of Psychoanalysis, 39*: 77–83.

Maiello, S. (1995). The sound-object. *Journal of Child Psychotherapy, 21*: 23–41.

Maiello, S. (2001). Prenatal trauma and autism. *Journal of Child Psychotherapy, 27*: 107–124.

Mancia, M. (1981). On the beginnings of the mental life in the fetus. *International Journal Psycho-Analysis, 62*: 351–357.

Mandy, W., Charman, T., & Skuse, D. (2012). Testing the construct validity of proposed criteria for DSM-5 autism spectrum disorder. *Journal of the American Academy of Child and Adolescent Psychiatry, 51*(1): 41–50.

Masakowski, Y., & Fifer, W. P. (1994). *The Effects of Maternal Speech on Foetal Behavior*. Paris: International Conference on Infant Studies.

Massie, H., & Rosenthal, J. (1984). *Childhood Psychosis in the First Four Years of Life*. New York: McGraw Hill.

Meltzer, D. W. (1975). The relation of autism to obsessional mechanisms in general. In: D. Meltzer. J. Bremner, S. Hoxter, D. Weddell, & I. Wittenberg (Eds.), *Explorations in Autism: A Psycho-Analytical Study* (pp. 209–222). Strathtay: Clunie Press.

Meltzer, D. W. (1986). *Studies in Extended Metapsychology: Clinical Applications of Bion's Ideas*. London: Karnac.

Miller, L., Rustin, M., Rustin, M., & Shuttleworth, J. (1989). *Closely Observed Infants*. London: Duckworth.

Mills Schumann, C., Carter Barnes, C., Lord, C., & Courchesne, E. (2009). Amygdala enlargement in toddlers with autism related to severity of social and communication impairments. *Biological Psychiatry, 66*(10): 942–949.

Ming, X., Julu, P. O. O., Brimacombe, M., Connor, S., & Daniels, M. L. (2005). Reduced cardiac parasympathetic activity in children with autism. *Brain and Development, 27*(7): 509–516.

Mitrani, J. (2001). *Ordinary People and Extra-Ordinary Protections: A Post-Kleinian Approach to the Treatment of Primitive Mental States*. Philadelphia, PA: Brunner-Routledge.

Munson, J., Dawson, G., Abbott, R., Faja, S., Webb, S. J., Friedman, S. D., Shaw, D., Artru, A., & Dager, S. R. (2006). Amygdalar volume and behavioral development in autism. *Archives of General Psychiatry, 63*(6): 686–693.

Muratori, F., & Maestro, S. (2007). Early signs of autism in the first year of life. In: S. Acquarone (Ed.), *Signs of Autism in Infants: Recognition and Treatment* (pp. 46–62). London: Karnac.

Muratori, F., Narzisi, A., Costanza, C., Umberto, B., & Filippo, M. (2014). Non-pharmacological treatments in autism spectrum disorders: An overview on early interventions for pre-schoolers. *Current Clinical Pharmacology, 9*: 17–26.

Murray, L. & Andrews, L. (2005). *The Social Baby: Understanding Babies' Communication from Birth*. Richmond: CP.

Murray, L., & Trevarthen, C. (1985). Emotional regulation of interactions between two-month-olds and their mothers. In: T. Field &

N. Fox (Eds.), *Social Perception in Infants* (pp. 177–197). Norwood, NJ: Ablex.

Nadel, J., & Butterworth, G. (Eds.) (1999). *Imitation in Infancy*. Cambridge: Cambridge University Press.

Nadel, J., & Decety, J. (2003). *Imiter pour Découvrir l'Humain*. Paris: PUF.

Nadel, J., Guerini, C., Peze, A., & Rivet, C. (1999). The evolving nature of imitation as a transitory means of communication. In: J. Nadel & G. Butterworth (Eds.), *Imitation in Infancy* (pp. 209–234). Cambridge: Cambridge University Press.

Negri, R. (1994). *The Newborn in the Intensive Care Unit. A Neuropsychoanalytic Prevention Model*. London: Karnac.

Noriuchi, M., Kikuchi, Y., Yoshiura, T., Kira, R., Shigeto, H., Hara, T., Tobimatsu, S., & Kamio, Y. (2010). Altered white matter fractional anisotropy and social impairment in children with autism spectrum disorder. *Brain Research, 1362*: 141–149.

O'Connor, T., Ben-Shlomo, Y., Golding, J., Adams, D., & Glover, V. (2005). Prenatal anxiety predicts individual differences in cortisol in pre-adolescent children. *Biological Psychiatry, 58*(3): 211–217.

O'Connor, T. O., Heron, J., Golding, J., & Glover, V. (2003). Maternal antenatal anxiety and behavioural/emotional problems in children: a test of a programming hypothesis. *Journal of Child Psychology & Psychiatry, 44*(7): 1025–1036.

Oberman, L. M., Hubbard, E. M., McCleery, J. P., Altschuler, E. L., Ramachandran, V. S., & Pineda, J. A. (2005). EEG evidence for mirror neuron dysfunction in autism spectrum disorders. *Cognitive Brain Research, 24*(2): 190–198.

Ogden, T. H. (1992). The dialectically constituted/decentred subject of psychoanalysis. II. The contributions of Klein and Winnicott. *International Journal of Psychoanalysis, 73*: 613–626.

Panksepp, J. (1998). *Affective Neuroscience: The Foundations of Human and Animal Emotions*. New York: Oxford University Press.

Panksepp, J. (2001). The long-term psychobiological consequences of infant emotions: prescriptions for the twenty-first century. *Infant Mental Health Journal, 22*(1–2): 132–173.

Parikshak, N. N., Luo, R., Zhang, A., Won, H., Lowe, J. K., Chandran, V., Horvath, S., & Geschwind, D. H. (2013). Integrative functional genomic analyses implicate specific molecular pathways and circuits in autism. *Cell, 155*: 1008–1021.

Paris, R., Spielman, E., & Bolton, R. E. (2009). Mother–infant psychotherapy: examining the therapeutic process of change. *Infant Mental Health Journal, 30*: 301–319.

Paul, L. K., Corsello, C., Kennedy, D. P., & Adolphs, R. (2014). Agenesis of the corpus callosum and autism: a comprehensive comparison. *Brain, 137*(6): 1813–1829.

Perez-Sanchez, M. (1990). *Baby Observations*. Strathtay, Perthshire: Clunie Press.

Pines, M. (1984). Reflections on mirroring. *International Review of Psychoanalysis, 11:* 27–42.

Piontelli, A. (1992). *From Fetus to Child: An Observational and Psychoanalytic Study*. New York: Routledge.

Raphael-Leff, J. (2007). Foreword. In: S. Acquarone (Ed.), *Early Signs of Autism in Babies: Recognition and Treatment* (pp. xvii–xxii). London: Karnac.

Ratey, A. (2001). *User's Guide to the Brain: Perception, Attention, and the Four Theatres of the Brain*. New York: Knopf Doubleday.

Reep, R. L., Finlay, B. L., & Darlington, R. B. (2007). The limbic system in mammalian brain evolution. *Brain, Behaviour and Evolution, 70*: 57–70.

Reid, S. (1999). Autism and trauma. Autistic post traumatic developmental disorder. In: A. Alvarez & S. Reid (Eds.), *Autism and Personality. Findings from the Tavistock Autism Workshop* (pp. 99–109). London: Routledge.

Reissland, N., Francis, B., & Mason, J. (2013). Can healthy fetuses show facial expressions of "pain" or "distress"? *PloS ONE*. DOI: 10.1371/journal.pone.0065530.

Rhode, M. (2005). Mirroring, imitation, identification: the sense of self in relation to the mother's internal world. *Journal of Child Psychotherapy, 31*: 52–71.

Rizzolatti, G., & Fabbri-Destro, M. (2010). Mirror neurons: from discovery to autism. *Experimental Brain Research, 200*: 223–237.

Sartre, J.-P. (1955). *No Exit*, S. Gilbert (Trans.). In: *No Exit and Three Other Plays*. New York: Vintage.

Schore, A. (1994). *Affect Regulation and the Origin of the Self: The Neurobiology of Emotional Development*. Hillsdale, NJ: Lawrence Erlbaum.

Schore, A. (2001a). Effects of a secure attachment relationship on right brain development, affect regulation and infant mental health. *Infant Mental Health Journal, 22*(1): 7–67.

Schore, A. (2001b). The effects of early relational trauma on right brain development, affect regulation, and infant mental health. *Infant Mental Health Journal, 22*: 201–269.

Schore, A. (2013). Regulation theory and the early assessment of attachment and autistic spectrum disorders: a response to Voran's clinical case. *Journal of Infant, Child, and Adolescent Psychotherapy, 12*: 164–189.

Schore, A., & Schore, J. (2008). Modern attachment theory: the central role of affect regulation in development and treatment. *Clinical Social Work Journal, 36*(1): 9–20.

Schultz, R. T. (2005). Developmental deficits in social perception in autism: the role of the amygdala and fusiform face area. *International Journal of Developmental Neuroscience, 23*(2–3): 125–141.

Siegel, D. (1991). *The Developing Mind: Towards a Neurobiology of Interpersonal Experience.* New York: Guilford Press.

Siegel, D., & Hartzell, M. (2004). *Parenting from the Inside Out*. New York: Penguin.

St Clair, C., Danon-Boileau, L., & Trevarthen, C. (2007). Signs of autism in infancy: sensitivity for rhythms of expression in communication. In: S. Acquarone (Ed.), *Signs of Autism in Infants* (pp. 21–45). London: Karnac.

Stern, D. (1983). Implications of infant research for psychoanalytic theory and practice. *Psychiatric Update, 2*: 8–21.

Stern, D. (1985). *The Interpersonal World of the Infant.* New York: Basic Books.

Sunderland, M. (2006). *The Science of Parenting.* London: Dorling Kindersley.

Talge, N. M., Neal, C., Glover, V., & The Early Stress, Translational Research and Prevention Science Network: Fetal and Neonatal Experience on Child and Adolescent Mental Health (2007). Antenatal maternal stress and long-term effects on child neurodevelopment: how and why? *Journal of Child Psychology and Psychiatry and Allied Disciplines, 48*: 245–261.

Teitelbaum, P., Maurer, R. G., & Fryman, J. (1998). Movements analysis in infancy may be useful for early diagnosis of autism. *Proceedings of the National Academy of Sciences of the United States of America, 95*: 23.

Trevarthen, C. (1979). Communication and cooperation in early infancy: a description of primary intersubjectivity. In: M. Bullowa (Ed.), *Before Speech* (pp. 321–347). Cambridge: Cambridge University Press.

Trevarthen, C. (1998a). *Children With Autism: Diagnosis and Interventions to Meet Their Needs*. London: Jessica Kingsley.

Trevarthen, C. (1998b). Passionate observers and imitators: joys and deceptions of companionship with infants. Baby Brain Conference, School of Infant Mental Health at the Tavistock Clinic.

Trevarthen, C. (2001). The neurobiology of early communication: intersubjective regulations in human brain development. In: A. F. Kalverboer & A. Gramsbergen (Eds), *Handbook on Brain and Behavior in Human Development* (pp. 841–882). Dordrecht: Kluwer.

Trevarthen, C. (2004). Brain development. In: R. L. Gregory (Ed.), *Oxford Companion to the Mind* (2nd edn) (pp. 116–127). Oxford: Oxford University Press.

Trevarthen, C. (2011). What is it like to be a person who knows nothing? Defining the active intersubjective mind of a newborn human being. *Infant and Child Development, 20*(1): 119–135 (Special Issue edited by E. Nagy).

Trevarthen, C., & Delafield-Butt, J. T. (2013). Autism as a developmental disorder in intentional movement and affective engagement. *Frontiers in Integrative Neuroscience, 7*(49): 1–16. DOI: 10.3389/fnint.2013.00049.

Trevarthen, C., & Hubley, P. (1978). Secondary intersubjectivity: confidence, confiding and acts of meaning in the first year. In: A. Lock (Ed.), *Action, Gesture, and Symbol* (pp. 183–229). London: Academic Press.

Trevarthen, C., Murray, L., & Hubley, P. A. (1981). Psychology of infants. In: J. Davis & J. Dobbing (Eds.), *Scientific Foundations of Clinical Pediatrics* (2nd edn) (pp. 211–274). London: Heinemann.

Tustin, F. (1972). *Autism and Childhood Psychosis*. London: Hogarth.

Tustin, F. (1990). *The Protective Shell in Children and Adults*. London: Karnac.

Tustin, F. (1994). The perpetuation of an error. *Journal of Child Psychotherapy, 20*: 3–23.

Uddin, L. Q., Supekar, K., Lynch, C. J., Khouzam, A., Phillips, J., Feinstein, C., Ryali, S., & Menon, V. (2013). Salience network-based classification and prediction of symptom severity in children with autism. *Journal of the American Medical Association Psychiatry, 70*(8): 869–879.

Urwin, C. (2002). A psychoanalytic approach to language delay: when autistic isn't necessarily autism. *Journal of Child Psychotherapy, 28*: 73–93.

Van den Bergh, B. R., Mulder, E. J., Mennes, M., & Glover, V. (2005). Antenatal maternal anxiety and stress and the neurobehavioural development of the fetus and child: links and possible mechanisms. A review. *Neuroscience and Biobehavioral Reviews, 29*: 237–58.

Wainstock, T., Lerner-Geva, L., Glasser, S., Shoham-Vardi, I., & Anteby, E. Y. (2013). Prenatal stress and risk of spontaneous abortion. *Psychosomatic Medicine, 75*: 228–235.

Wing, L., & Gould, J. (1979). Severe impairments of social interaction and associated abnormalities in children: epidemiology and classification. *Journal of Autism and Developmental Disorders, 9*(1): 11–29.

Winnicott, D. W. (1949). Mind and its relation to the psyche–soma. In: *Through Pediatrics to Psychoanalysis: Collected Papers* (pp. 243–254). New York: Basic Books.

Winnicott, D. W. (1958). *Through Paediatrics to Psycho-Analysis: Collected Papers*. London: Tavistock.

Winnicott, D. W. (1960). The theory of the parent–infant relationship. In: *The Maturational Process and the Facilitating Environment* (pp. 37–55). London: Karnac (reprinted 2004).

Winnicott, D. W. (1971). *Playing and Reality*. London: Tavistock.

Yirmiya, N., & Ozonoff, S. (2007). The very early autism phenotype. *Journal of Autism and Developmental Disorders, 37*: 1–11.

Zwaigenbaum, L., Bryson, S., Rogers, T., Roberts, W., Brian, J., & Szatmari, P. (2005). Behavioral manifestations of autism in the first year of life. *International Journal of Developmental Neuroscience, 23*: 143–152.

INDEX